Critical theory and social pathology

The Frankfurt School beyond recognition

Neal Harris

MANCHESTER UNIVERSITY PRESS

Copyright © Neal Harris 2022

The right of Neal Harris to be identified as the author of this work has been asserted by them in accordance with the Copyright, Designs and Patents Act 1988.

Published by Manchester University Press
Oxford Road, Manchester M13 9PL

www.manchesteruniversitypress.co.uk

British Library Cataloguing-in-Publication Data

A catalogue record for this book is available from the British Library

ISBN 978 1 5261 5473 6 hardback

First published 2022

The publisher has no responsibility for the persistence or accuracy of URLs for any external or third-party internet websites referred to in this book, and does not guarantee that any content on such websites is, or will remain, accurate or appropriate.

Typeset by
Deanta Global Publishing Services, Chennai, India

For Maïa and Rosa

Contents

Preface	viii
Introduction: on the battle for critical theory	1

Part I: Social pathology and the crisis of critical theory

1	Social pathology: the 'explosive charge' of critical theory	19
2	Distorted by recognition	39
3	Pathologies of recognition	63

Part II: Foundations of pathology diagnosing critique

4	Rousseau and the foundations of pathology diagnosing social criticism	87
5	Hegelian-Marxism: pathologies of reason, pathologies of production	104

Part III: A Fromm-Marcuse synthesis

6	Erich Fromm and pathological normalcy	125
7	The pathological normalcy of what? Towards a Fromm-Marcuse synthesis	145

Conclusion: the Frankfurt School beyond recognition	166
References	173
Index	188

Preface

Neoliberal capitalism is destroying the most basic conditions which enable human survival on earth. This problem is disproportionately caused by the ultra-rich and disproportionately harms the world's poorest. This is not some future horror: this is happening *now*. Clearly, our social world is poorly structured: global warming does not need to be happening! We are fully aware that the capitalocene will likely kill billions and cause untold suffering, and that realisable alternative possibilities exist which could make it entirely avoidable. To my mind, this situation is simply 'bonkers', deeply 'pathological'. I think that seems pretty undeniable. We are persevering with a suicidal approach to societal organisation.

You could be forgiven for forgetting these facts if you focused solely on the media coverage given to various stories over the past few years while I have been writing, and largely trying to distract myself with, this book. Here, in the United Kingdom, rather than focusing on trying to best mitigate the impending mass extinction, we discuss Brexit, 'Partygate', and disgraced princes not sweating while eating pizzas. Meanwhile, in the United States, there has been talk of paedophile satanists operating out of pizza restaurants. The public do not trust politicians; indeed, with Boris Johnson it seems they wilfully elected a man they knew they could not trust, against their material self-interest, to vent their displeasure at perceived self-righteous technocrats. What does this tell us, as critical theorists? Perhaps there is nothing there of note. Perhaps we should learn that news stories get more traction when they involve pizzas? But maybe there is something more: perhaps there remains some vestigial critical consciousness, which is battered and bruised, unsure where to turn? Either way, it is clear that the collective critical consciousness is functioning sub-optimally. If it is alive, it is seriously ill.

Critical theorists combine a challenge to both the social structure and epistemic coherence within the singular framing of 'social pathology'. By drawing on Hegelian-Marxism, Weberian sociology, psychoanalysis, and a host of other ideas and traditions, epistemology becomes political as social rationality and individual critical consciousness are subjected to scrutiny. Or at least, that's the theory. Sadly, along with the structure of the social world and the critical capacities of the populace at large, critical theorists have also recently gone 'bonkers'. Axel Honneth, for many years the director of the Institute for Social Research, was busy saying that we can analyse every social problem through the framing of 'recognition' – no other framework is needed. As better minds than I have already shown, this idea is patently absurd. As a result, critical theory has proved pretty useless of late at analysing the crises of the age. Activists and progressive academics have, understandably, largely disengaged from the Frankfurt School.

In this book, I have tried to rekindle the spark of first-generation critical theory for the present day. I have sought to rebuild the social-theoretical foundations of the research programme, drawing on key insights by Herbert Marcuse and Erich Fromm. For Fromm, a key realisation was that the very 'normalcy' of our current predicament is itself a form of pathology – that seemed an excellent place to start. Marcuse's work enabled me to embellish this insight with specificity that could guide an operationalisable research programme.

This project has occupied nearly six years of my life. Many wonderful people have taught and encouraged me along the way. Three academic guides stand out. I was supported principally by Gerard Delanty – without his kindness and advice, this book would never have been possible. I owe my biggest intellectual debt to him. Darrow Schecter's support and insights have also been crucial in bringing these ideas together. Michael J. Thompson has also been wonderfully warm and supportive, despite my stupid questions and, at times, incessant emails. Before reading *The Domestication of Critical Theory*, I felt something of a lone voice.

As these ideas have grown and this book has developed, it feels like I have lived more than a few chapters of my own life. I have learned an enormous amount and owe a great deal to comrades and friends I met along the way, most notably Tula McFadden (king of pragmatism), Priya Raghavan (a special thank you), Onur Acaroğlu, Denis Chevrier-Bosseau, James Stockman (proof-reading supremo), Ploy-Jai Pintobtang (and her family), Angus Reoch, Estevão Bosco, Javier Zamora García, Malcolm McQueen, Heinz Sünker, Jo Moran Ellis, Ane Englestad, Robin Jervis, Johnbosco Nwogbo, Anna Wimbledon, David Hunziker, and Freddie 'Red' Meade. I was supported over the final hurdle by countless colleagues at Oxford Brookes. Thank you all for making the Gibbs Building feel like home!

Publishing with MUP has been an enjoyable experience, and my editor, Tom Dark, has been brilliant. Thank you, Tom.

Finally, thank you to my family. I am a product of my parent's socialisation and genetics, so they are at least partly to blame for any errors contained in these pages. I dedicate this book to Maïa and Rosa. Maïa selflessly proofread every chapter. I look forward to writing many better books together in the years to come!

Oxford, Spring 2022

It is easier to rob by setting up a bank than by holding up a bank clerk.
Bertolt Brecht

Introduction: on the battle for critical theory

Most of today's nominal 'critical theorists' have abandoned their tradition's Marxian heritage (see Thompson, 2016; Kouvelakis, 2019). Axel Honneth's *Struggle for Recognition* (1992), and his more recent *Freedom's Right* (2014), typify this reverse-entryism. Such a 'domestication of critical theory'[1] is characterised by the embrace of neoliberal norms and institutions, and the betrayal of central Freudo-Marxian insights (see Thompson, 2016: 2–11). While the resulting crisis facing critical theory is political and philosophical in nature, in this book I explain why it is also profoundly *social theoretical*. I argue that to understand the degeneration of critical theory, and to counterpose alternate foundations for a renaissance in normative social research, one must revitalise the tradition's diagnostic core: its understanding of *social pathology*.

While traditional 'liberal' social criticism targets injustices and illegitimate claims to authority, critical theory focuses on the *irrationality* of the social world, drawing upon Hegelian, Marxian, Weberian, and psychoanalytic concepts (Horkheimer, 2002 [1937]; Held, 1980). It is through the framing of 'social pathology' that these diverse traditions are melded into a coherent foundation for social research (Harris, 2021). While a slippery concept to grapple with, 'social pathology diagnosis' is simply 'what critical theorists do'; with 'social pathologies' referring to the social problems which critical theorists disclose and critique. As such, 'social pathology' is the conceptual foundation of critical theory: it is the Frankfurt School's 'master concept', enabling the seamless interrogation of desire, ideology, political economy, society, and, crucially, power and knowledge. Yet, this essential concept has been denatured by contemporary Frankfurt School scholarship, which holds to a 'neo-Idealist' understanding of subjectivity, the result of an ill-conceived retreat from Hegelian-Marxism (Thompson, 2016: 15–38).

The resultant 'defanging' of critical theory (Thompson, 2020: 129) has come at the worst possible moment. We are living through cataclysmic climate change, insurgent neo-fascisms, and spiralling global inequalities. An ascendant technical rationality propels a 'computationality' of thought

(Berry, 2014), while critical study is pilloried by conservatives as 'anti-nationalist' (see Oppenheim, 2018), even seditious (see Dey, 2019), and belittled by neoliberals as 'indulgent' (Bulaitis, 2020). Against this backdrop, I advocate for the urgent renewal of an interdisciplinary Frankfurt School research programme, predicated on the return to a Marxian account of social pathology. I argue that one way this can be achieved is through a nuanced reconstruction of Erich Fromm's and Herbert Marcuse's social theory. Renewing critical theory matters as it offers the vehicle for an explicitly normative critique of the social world, precisely when the subject's capacity for, and inclination towards, critical thought is waning. Yet, as Marcuse wrote in his preface to *One Dimensional Man*, 'the fact that the vast majority of the population accepts, and is made to accept, this society, does not render it less irrational or less reprehensible' (Marcuse, 2007 [1964]: xliv). Indeed, the more subjects are conditioned to blindly accept their social world, the more essential critique becomes.

When done well, social critique can be far more than impotent 'ivory tower' complaint. Through pathology diagnosing social criticism, first-generation Frankfurt School researchers were able to identify the 'historical alternatives which haunt[ed] the established society as subversive tendencies and forces' (Marcuse, 2007 [1964]: xliii). Critique itself was reframed as a crucial form of praxis given its capacity to disclose the potentials for progressive transition, while simultaneously identifying, and through identifying, partially displacing, obstacles impeding social transformation (Horkheimer, 1993 [1931]: 218). Indeed, as Gerard Delanty argued, through pathology diagnosing critique, critical theory gave 'expression to a moral vision of the future possibilities of society ... driven forward by its internal dynamics' (Delanty, 2011: 72) and thus illuminated immanent potentials for transcending societal irrationality. In light of the myriad existential crises of today, critical theory is arguably more important now than ever.

Yet, as I argue in this book, the social-theoretical foundations of Frankfurt School critical theory have collapsed. The Hegelian-Marxian pathology diagnosing imagination, previously a powerful unifying horizon for the research project, has been lost. Once central to the critique of the existing social order, the framing of social pathology is now deployed mainly to identify mere 'second-order disconnect(s)' (Zurn, 2011: 348). In third-generation critical theory this refers to instances where the subject fails to grasp the manifest rationality of existing social institutions, observable through the failure of healthy recognition relationships to develop (Zurn, 2011: 349; Hirvonen, 2015: 209). The study of recognition relationships, and their attendant 'pathologies of recognition', dominates today's Frankfurt School critical theory (Harris, 2019a: 3–9). The 'recognition turn' has comprehensively displaced the critique of capitalist logics and norms as an end in itself (Fraser and Honneth, 2001). Once researched as a force of reification and domination, market institutions are now identified as potential safe harbours, calm normative pools for equitable intersubjective recognition (Thompson, 2016: 10).

Today, arguably *the* leading critical theorist, Axel Honneth, a primary exponent of a 'recognition-monist' perspective (Fraser and Honneth, 2001: 214), identifies norms within the free market which enable healthy recognition relationships. As I argue in Part I of this book, the original Hegelian-Marxian tradition has been lost and must be urgently reclaimed. Throughout *Critical Theory and Social Pathology,* I argue that the intersubjective turn in Frankfurt School scholarship must be urgently reconsidered. Far from promising a route for immanent-transcendence, such theories function as a neoliberal-apologist justification for the socially devastating market order. In direct contrast, I argue that Fromm's understanding of capitalism as a *pathological normalcy* offers a superior foundation for social research.

The central intervention provided by this book is therefore explicitly *social theoretical*. I provide sympathetic reconstructions of displaced social theories, and highlight inconsistencies and philosophical limitations within the dominant theoretical approaches today. This is not a work of empirical sociology, although a few case studies and examples will be provided to help elucidate some of the denser material. The purpose of this book is to make a significant intervention within the *underlying social-theoretical foundations of critical theory*. While social theory can be perceived as dry and uninspiring, such a task is of a vital importance. Poor theory produces poor applied research. I have invested time elsewhere in showcasing the merits of applied pathology diagnosing research; consider my recent edited volume *Pathology Diagnosis and Social Research: New Applications and Explorations* (2021). However, what critical theory desperately requires is an extended consideration of the decay of its pathology diagnosing foundations. That is the task I set myself in this monograph.

Traditional and critical theory

The aim of this book is to provide an urgent course correction for critical theory, specifically the critical theory of the Frankfurt School. Founded in 1923, the Institute for Social Research (*Institut für Sozialforschung*), or Frankfurt School, developed a unique research programme based on a fusion of left-Hegelian philosophy, Freudian psychoanalysis, Marxian philosophy and political economy, aesthetics, legal theory, and Weberian sociology. Max Horkheimer, director of the institute from 1930, is rightly associated with the birth of this radically interdisciplinary project.[2] In his inaugural lecture as director in 1931, Horkheimer launched a blistering attack on the shibboleths of (positivistic) 'Traditional Theory' (Horkheimer, 2018 [1931]: 113–121).[3] For Horkheimer, it was crucial that the political nature of *all research* was acknowledged. In direct contrast to the cherished 'neutrality' of 'Traditional Theory', critical theory was explicit about its political content and its partisan intent. Central to Horkheimer's imagination was a Hegelian-Marxian insight: that the forms of thought (and research) which dominate the social world are closely linked to the historical-material conditions (Horkheimer, 2018 [1931]: 119).[4] All intellectual endeavour retains the 'inherited form' of the 'capitalist system', whereby research projects remain 'moments in the social process of production' (Horkheimer, 2002: 197).

While sensitive to how economic logics shape society, the founding members of the Frankfurt School did not embrace a crude 'Soviet' Marxism. Rather, Horkheimer was critical of purely economistic Marxists, stating explicitly that they 'badly understood Marx' (Horkheimer, 2018 [1931]: 119). What was required instead was an exploration of 'the connection between the economic life (*Leben*) of society, the psychological development of its individuals and the changes within specific areas of culture to which belong not only the intellectual legacy of the sciences, art and religion, but also law, customs, fashion, public opinion, sports, entertainments lifestyles (*Lebensstil*), and so on' (Horkheimer, 2018 [1931]: 119).

This called for a 'rejection of orthodox Marxism and its substitution by a reconstructed understanding of Marx's project' (Held, 1980: 33); an account sensitive to the particular, historically located, relationships between the capitalist subject and contingent social realities. Thus, Horkheimer's critical theory did not merely offer a regurgitated, Marxian-inflected, neo-Hegelianism. His remarkable address presented the urgency of a critical synthesis of Marx and Hegel, but crucially also of Weber and Freud; of psychoanalysis and political economy, sociology and philosophy. Guiding such a heady cocktail was a sociological foundation: critical theory was to provide a form of 'critique' founded upon research of the located social world, seeking to understand, in 'a definite time frame ... in some particular countries, what relations can ... [be] delineate[d] between a particular social group and the role of this group in the economy, the changes in the psychical structure of its members, and the thoughts and institutions created by it which influence it as a whole through the social totality' (Horkheimer, 2018: 119).

Such research was to be located, empirical, and critical, predicated on a form of immanent critique, which sought to identify contradictions within the social world. Such contradictions pointed beyond the existing social order, enabling the critical theorist to identify possible sites for rupture and disclose the forces building towards an objectively superior, 'less-contradictory', society. Original critical theory was thus reconstructive as well as critical, it did not merely target social contradictions to disclose their irrationality; rather, through immanent-transcendence, it offered a form of critique which sought to surpass the existing social order (Strydom, 2011).

Central to 'first-generation' Frankfurt School research was the impact of capitalism upon the social world. While Hegel's philosophy centred the development of *Geist*, reason/consciousness/spirit, as subjects sublate contradictions in their thought processes, Horkheimer was sensitive to Marx's materialist inversion of Hegel's thought. Crucially, the impediments to overcoming contradictory forms of thought were linked to the dominant mode of production. In sum, the market order was understood as impacting the subject's cognitive capacities. The reverberations of market rationality across social domains induced a 'false consciousness' within the subject, impeding social change. As a result, even the subject's alienating and exploitative working and living conditions failed to induce a critical mindset. Or, as Horkheimer wrote,

> the situation of the proletariat is, in this society, no guarantee of correct knowledge. The proletariat may indeed have experience of meaninglessness in the form of continuing and increasing wretchedness and injustice in its own life. Yet this awareness is prevented from becoming a social force by the differentiation of social structure which is still imposed on the proletariat from above and by the opposition between personal class interests which is transcended only at very special moments. Even to the proletariat the world superficially seems quite different than it really is. Even an outlook which could grasp that no opposition really exists between the proletariat's own true interests and those of society as a whole, and would therefore derive its principles of action from the thoughts and feelings of the masses, would fall into slavish dependence on the status quo. (Horkheimer, 2002: 213)

In this regard the work of Erich Fromm and Herbert Marcuse is central to the Frankfurt School project as, in complementary ways, they simultaneously identify both the pathological irrationality of the capitalist system, but also crucially its modes of 'consensual validation' (Fromm, 1963 [1955]: 14, *inter alia*). Critical theory thus acknowledges the political nature of social rationality and the historical nature of the subject's 'natural' thought processes. For critical theorists, the Marxian subject – shaped by their material surroundings – displaces the liberal-Cartesian subject – objective, universal, forever utility-maximising. Rather, the Hegelian-Marxian subject is shaped by their historical and material conditions; victim to manifold social logics and dynamics of domination, which impede their capacity for critical consciousness.

Three generations of critical theory

Frankfurt School research has passed through three distinct generations (see Corradetti, 2021). 'First-generation' critical theory was typified by its explicit Hegelian-Marxian outlook and its commitment to interdisciplinary social research. The work of Max Horkheimer, Walter Benjamin, Theodor Adorno, Otto Kirchheimer, Erich Fromm, Herbert Marcuse, and Friedrich Pollock typifies the breadth and reach of such first-generation scholarship. Uniting left-Hegelian and Western Marxist theories and concepts, the aforementioned theorists provided remarkable analyses of the rise of fascism and of the totalising nature of advanced industrial society. First-generation critical theory is also identified by a penchant for grand narratives and eschatology with accompanying rhetorical flourishes, furthering its disclosing form of social critique (Honneth, 2000). In their co-authored *Dialectic of Enlightenment*, for example, Adorno and Horkheimer provide a starkly negative reading of modernity, tracing the rise of fascism to the 'indefatigable self-destructiveness of enlightenment' thought (Adorno and Horkheimer, 1997 [1944]: xi). With similar romantic grandeur and aesthetic flare, Walter Benjamin's *Theses on the Philosophy of History* takes up 'the history of civilised mankind' (Benjamin, 1968 [1955]: 263). While more measured in aesthetic, Marcuse adopts the same substantive macro-sociology in his opening salvo of *One Dimensional Man*, lambasting the 'comfortable, smooth, reasonable, democratic unfreedom ... of ... advanced industrial civilisation' (Marcuse, 2007 [1964]: 3).

Yet, as the 1960s came to a close, the assertive, and often abrasive, social critique of the first generation receded into an increasingly impotent aesthetics and abstract metaphysics (Jarvis, 1998: 90–123, 124–147). This was brazenly out of step with the political radicalism of the *soixante-huitards*. To his politically radical students, Adorno's *Aesthetic Theory* (1970) and *Negative Dialectics* (1966) seemed both impenetrable and politically quiescent, and his personal politics were increasingly seen to be suspect.[5] This was pithily captured by the student chant, 'If Adorno is left in peace, capitalism will never cease' (Müller-Doohm, 2005: 475).

Risking irrelevance in the eyes of student and activist leaders, Jürgen Habermas sought alternate foundations for the Frankfurt School by returning to a normative sociology. Seeking to reposition critical theory, Habermas became increasingly hostile to both metaphysics (see Habermas, 1990) and the perceived 'productivist bias' (see Jay, 2008: 5) of first-generation scholarship. It is little exaggeration to say that Habermas single-handedly orchestrated a qualitative sea change in critical theory. Today, the name Jürgen Habermas is close to synonymous with 'second-generation' Frankfurt School scholarship (Held, 1980: 249).

Fifteen years proved to be a long time in critical theory, for Habermas's magnum opus, *The Theory of Communicative Action* (1981), could hardly have been more different from Adorno's *Negative Dialectics* 1966). While Adorno's masterpiece was a forbiddingly negative work of philosophy, in which the prospects for progress were slim, Habermas found a repository of untapped normative potential within communicative exchange. Developing this line of scholarship, Habermas instituted an intersubjective-sociological turn within critical theory, with his work bridging Karl Otto-Appel's pragmatism, Weberian sociology, and analytic philosophy (see McCarthy, 1978). In place of the classical Marxist division of 'base' and 'superstructure', Habermas presented a heuristic division between an instrumentally organised 'system' and a communication-oriented 'lifeworld' (see Heath, 2010). For Habermas, the colonisation of the 'lifeworld' by the 'system' was the central social pathology (Habermas, 1987 [1981]: 318); yet there were genuine prospects for resistance. Most notably with his 'discourse theory of democracy', Habermas placed faith in democratic institutions (Olson, 2010), and his wider scholarship precipitated a wave of empirical social research on sites of public-discursive contestation (Murphy, 2016).

While Habermas's impact on Frankfurt School critical theory cannot be understated, it is the work of Axel Honneth, Habermas's *de facto* heir, which is the primary subject of this book. Honneth's work presents a radical extension of Habermas's intersubjective focus, expunging the Marxian legacy of critical theory in favour of a reconstructed 'Jena-period' Hegelianism (Honneth, 1995 [1992]: 1). For Honneth, all social relationships, including those mediated by the market, must be understood primarily as recognition relationships. While Habermas's 'second-generation' critical theory focused on the normative-critical potential of intersubjective communication practices oriented towards mutual understanding, Honneth's 'third-generation' critical theory centres intersubjective recognition (*Annerkunnung*) as the 'originary site' of power relationships. Honneth is unambiguously the 'key thinker in [the] Frankfurt School's third generation' (Fuchs, 2016: 154), and as such I offer an extended critical engagement with his account in this book. In Chapter 2, I offer a detailed reconstruction of Honneth's critical theory of recognition. I argue, drawing closely on, and extending, Fraser, McNay, Coulthard, Thompson, and Fanon, that Honneth's critical theory of recognition has mutilated the Frankfurt School tradition and requires unequivocal rejection on political, philosophical, and, crucially, social-theoretical grounds. As I outline in Chapter 3, it is Honneth's critical theory of recognition which has fundamentally displaced the Hegelian-Marxian framing of social pathology, integral to the potency of critical theory.

Today, one may even hear talk of an emergent 'fourth generation' of critical theory (see Corradetti, 2021), yet such claims remain contested. The most prominent figure associated with this new era is Rainer Forst, whose critical theory of judgement retains many of the central features of Honneth's account, especially his 'neo-Idealism' (Thompson, 2016: 15). While for Habermas the primary entry point to the social world was intersubjective communication, and for Honneth it was intersubjective recognition, for Forst it is practices of intersubjective justification. There are, however, other contenders as the heir to Honneth, for Christian Fuchs, Hartmut Rosa, and Rahel Jaeggi sit as illustrative representatives of fourth-generation critical theory (Fuchs, 2016: 154). Yet, overwhelmingly, it remains Honneth's critical theory of recognition which dominates contemporary critical theory, and, as I shall demonstrate in Chapter 2, Honneth's account has had remarkable reach and traction across disciplinary divides (see O'Neill and Smith, 2012).

'Critical theory' and 'Frankfurt School critical theory'

I am primarily concerned with 'Frankfurt School' critical theory, and it is this tradition which is referred to by the 'generational' typology above. However, the term 'critical theory' has become an increasingly destabilised signifier, no longer referring solely to the Frankfurt School. Razmig Keucheyan's *The Left Hemisphere: Mapping Critical Theory Today* typifies this trend. Keucheyan, helpfully, is explicit that he uses the term 'in a much broader sense', where it 'covers both the queer theory developed by the North American feminist Judith Butler and the metaphysics of the event proposed by Alain Badiou, as well as Fredric Jameson's theory of postmodernism, Homi Bhabha and Gayatri Spivak's postcolonialism, John Holloway's "open Marxism", and Slavoj Žižek's Hegelian neo-Lacanianism' (Keucheyan, 2013: 1). While Keucheyan takes care to distinguish 'Frankfurt School critical theory' from broader critical theory through reserving capitalised 'C' and 'T' for the former, increasingly even this minor differentiation is lost.

This distinction matters as contemporary critical theory risks losing methodological coherence. It would be foolishly conservative to delineate between 'real' and 'impostor' critical theory, reserving the term solely for Frankfurt School approaches. Without innovation no research tradition remains relevant. Yet problems inevitably arise in attempts to unite opposed intellectual traditions within the same theoretical framework. For example, as Amy Allen's *The End of Progress* (2016) demonstrates, Foucault's work can be of substantial utility to critical theory; however, his political commitments and method of critique differ markedly from Frankfurt School approaches. Great care and sensitivity to theoretical and political divergence are required. I have previously written with Gerard Delanty on the need for a gentle course correction in what is considered 'critical theory', not to exclude alternative traditions, but to ensure there remains a social-theoretical 'anchoring' in left-Hegelianism (Delanty and Harris, 2021). Such a caution seems increasingly relevant in light of the trend to incorporate liberal, ideal-theoretical philosophy within the framing of critical theory which has no foundation in social critique. Deconstructionism, post-modernism, post-structuralism, decoloniality, and queer theory are not invested in the framing of pathology diagnosing social criticism, neither do they commit to an immanent-transcendent methodology. This is not to suggest that such alternate approaches are in any way 'inferior'. Rather, these approaches simply adopt different methodological commitments, such as critical discourse analysis, standpoint epistemology, affect theory, and so on. Just as 'chemistry' is not 'geometry', 'post-structuralism' is not 'Frankfurt School critical theory' on the basis of divergent methodological and disciplinary commitments.

Critical theory in crisis

While the unchecked bloating of the signifier 'critical theory' poses problems, it is far from the prime concern for those invested in Frankfurt School research. As Michael J. Thompson (2016) succinctly phrased it, we are witnessing the wholesale 'domestication of critical theory'. Central to Thompson's indictment is the rise of 'neo-Idealism'. Thompson identifies 'neo-Idealism' as a school of thought where 'thinkers proceed from the premise that *there is a self*-sufficiency to the powers of intersubjective reason, discourse, structures of justification, and recognition' (Thompson, 2016: 15).

Neo-Idealists mistakenly invest the cognitive and intersubjective dimension with an ability to evade penetration by the 'potency of social power, rooted in the material organization of social life' (Thompson, 2016: 15). Blind to the impact of 'constitutive power' (Thompson, 2016: 3–5), neo-Idealists fail to acknowledge the denaturing impact of social structures on the subject's cognitive and critical capacities. As such, third- and fourth-generation critical theorists invest 'modern subjects with powers of rationality ... [which they] simply cannot possess' (Thompson, 2016: 5). For neo-Idealists, certain features of subjectivity are immune from social structural power and can be identified as reservoirs of emancipatory potential. As Fraser (2001)[6] and McNay (2008) rightly identify, by making such a transition, contemporary critical theory has embraced a deficient social ontology which submits that social being is predicated upon intersubjective relationships. Rather, a foundational tenet of Hegelian-Marxism is that subjectivation (encompassing all recognition relationships) occurs within a social world strewn with a complexity of power relations impacting the subject. Arguably, the most famous tenet of Marxist philosophy is that 'It is not the consciousness of men that determines their existence, but their social existence that determines their consciousness' (Marx, 2010 [1859]: 92). By 'consciousness', one could substitute the 'capacity to engage in rational intersubjective relationships', one's understanding of vital 'needs', and the manifestations of one's libidinal drives. Intersubjective monist critical theorists[7] such as Honneth fail to acknowledge either the sociologised critique of the later Hegel, or the crucial Marxian inversion of Hegel's idealism. At a high level of abstraction, one could suggest that the 'new conservativism'[8] of contemporary critical theory stems from the failure to appreciate the necessary development of the German idealist tradition, retreating to a neo-Kantianism mislabelled as Jena-period Hegelianism.

Honneth's critical theory of recognition returns to a pure idealism. Intersubjective monisms which appeal to a fictive 'kind of subjectivity that has not been shaped and formed by defective social relations and institutions' fail to understand the complex social nature of power (Thompson, 2016: 6). In short, Frankfurt School critical theory has lost its sophisticated Hegelian-Marxian account of power and has embraced a deficient social ontology. As such, contemporary critical theorists attempt to research the social world with a deficient understanding of the subject. The fundamentally Marxian insight that 'power relations rooted in capitalist forms of economic life structure the deeper socialization processes that shape the cognitive dimension of the personality of subjects' (Thompson, 2016: 64) must be reclaimed.

The 'domestication' of critical theory is not merely philosophical, it is also distinctly *political*. In places, Honneth appears to extol the emancipatory potential of the capitalist order, suggesting aspects of the market should be 'protected from external influences' (see Freyenhagen, 2015: 148). Such an account is particularly prevalent in *Freedom's Right*, accepted by many to be Honneth's *magnum opus* (Schaub, 2015: 108). This is clear in Honneth's normative-reconstructive method, which seeks to 'examine contemporary reality in terms of its potential for fostering practices in which universal values can be realized in a superior, i.e. a more morally comprehensive and suitable fashion' (Honneth, 2014 [2011]: 8).

Such an approach may superficially appear to echo critical theory's immanent-transcendent method, drawing out latent 'higher' forms of reason in the contradictions of the present (Strydom, 2011). However, despite appearances, Honneth's approach is not a form of immanent-transcendence. Rather, *Freedom's Right* is an explicit compromise with the status quo, which views the market order as manifesting, at present, positive norms enabling healthy recognition relationships. The distinction in temporality is crucial here: for the Honneth of *Freedom's Right*, these positive aspects of the capitalist order are not latent within the contradictions of neoliberalism, some obscured subterranean guide towards qualitative social transition, which needs delicate dialectical excavation. Rather, for Honneth, the normative potential for healthy recognition relationships is active within neoliberalism already. *Freedom's Right* seeks to identify the active positives of the market order which are to be extended and supported. For example, at his most explicit, Honneth draws out that in the neoliberal market, 'subjects must recognise each other reciprocally, viewing each other as subjects' (Honneth, 2014 [2011]: 46). Such statements of support for the emancipatory potential of social norms of capitalist society, and explicitly of the norms intrinsic to the market order, would simply be anathema to classical critical theorists, who viewed the market as inducing a pathologically reified form of consciousness. From such a position, the form of petrified subjectivity which the market necessitates recognition of is nothing to build upon: it is a tragedy of epic proportions and an affront to human reason.

The 'domestication' of critical theory's partisan commitments sadly goes far beyond Honneth. Deutscher and Lafont's edited collection, *Critical Theory in Critical Times*, is indicative of such post-Marxian politics (see Thompson, 2017b; Harris, 2018). While Habermas contributed the lead paper to this collection, he was primarily concerned with problems of popular sovereignty in member states of the European Union. His argument derives from an explicitly liberal canon, not the pathology diagnosing tradition anchored in left-Hegelianism. Bizarrely, Habermas's analysis lacked any of the concerns central to canonical critical theory: there was no trace of ideology critique, political economy, left-Hegelianism, Weberian sociology, psychoanalysis, or interdisciplinary social research. To engage in a discussion on the sovereignty implications of joining the European Union without the faintest engagement with political economy or ideology is a surreal undertaking. To do so, in a book titled *Critical Theory in Critical Times*, showcasing arguably the most famous living Frankfurt School theorist, shows the extent to which the critical-theoretical project has transitioned to a dull, neoliberal apologism. A wake-up call is desperately needed: real, impending existential threats exist, which are precipitated by the neoliberal economy.[9]

Primary interventions and structure

Critical Theory and Social Pathology is divided into three parts, each offering a distinct theoretical intervention. Taken in aggregate, the book demonstrates that an alternate account of social pathology to today's 'recognition-cognitive' framing is desperately needed and that a considered Fromm-Marcuse synthesis offers one possible avenue for future development.

In Part I, 'Social pathology and the crisis of critical theory', I connect the broader domestication of critical theory to the deformation of the Frankfurt School's understanding of social pathology. I start with an extended justification for my investment in social pathology, illustrating its role in stabilising the heterogeneous approaches which unite in critical theory. In the theoretical centrifuge of psychoanalysis, political economy, aesthetics, left-Hegelianism, Weberianism, and Marxist social theory, the framing of social pathology diagnosis serves as a stabilising and coalescing horizon, enabling the tradition's normative social research. Yet, contemporary critical theory operates with a radically divergent understanding of social pathology to the Hegelian-Marxian approach which united first-generation Frankfurt School scholarship. Following Axel Honneth's 'recognition' paradigm, contemporary critical theory centres the subject's intersubjective feelings of 'disrespect'[10] as an immanent-entry point to social research. As such, social pathologies are now framed solely as obstacles to intersubjective recognition. I show how this radical intersubjective turn is problematically 'complimented' by a radical cognitivism and a flawed normative-reconstructive methodology. The resultant 'recognition-cognitivist' framing of social pathology is shown to be philosophically unsound, politically quiescent, and in urgent need of revision.

In Part II, 'Foundations of pathology diagnosing critique', I offer a sympathetic reconstruction of the texts which inspired the Frankfurt School's original approach to normative social research. Providing a targeted rereading of Rousseau, Hegel, and Marx, I identify four key features which characterise pathology diagnosing social research. By abstracting the core foundations of pathology diagnosing critical theory, I demonstrate how Frankfurt School research is built upon a simultaneous analysis of the pathological nature of the social world and the exploration of the means of its perpetuation. Both considerations must be addressed by the theoretical apparatus provided. In this regard four key concerns are abstracted, which are required for my proposed future basis for pathology diagnosing social research. These are:

(a) an analysis of the social world's failure to provide for the subject's vital 'needs', and an attendant focus on how the subject's perception of necessity is pathologically recoded,
(b) a pathologically impeded form of consciousness, which prevents the subject achieving self-actualisation and simultaneously represses their capacity for social critique,
(c) the existence of self-perpetuating pathological social logics, or 'vicious circles', and,

(d) the embrace of the impact of constitutive power on the subject, stemming primarily from the compulsions emanating from the system of production; or, put simply, historical materialism.

In Part III, 'A Fromm-Marcuse synthesis', I present a reading of Fromm and Marcuse as harbouring the explanatory-diagnostic characteristics distilled above. I consciously do not present a Fromm-Marcuse synthesis as the only possible route through which pathology diagnosing social research can be rekindled. Rather, I suggest it is one option which succeeds in both carrying the diagnostic potential of the pathology diagnosing perspective, and, with Fromm's framing of 'pathological normalcy', offers an apposite counterpoint to Honneth's normative reconstruction. While Honneth's *Freedom's Right*, and scholarship drawing from it, analyses the social world as rich in normative potential to further recognition relationships as a result of the existing social institutions, Fromm's social theory enables social research which holds the foundational norms of the social world to be deeply pathological. Indeed, the very normalcy of the social conjuncture is held to be a form of pathology which is reinforced by 'consensual validation'.

While Fromm's approach to social pathology is shown to be theoretically fertile, Marcuse is held to offer vital complementary insights. In particular, while Fromm's work is accessible, social-theoretically rich, and deeply invested in the pathology diagnosing tradition, it lacks avenues for easy operationalisation in social research. In contrast, through his work on the technical *a priori* and the social-systemic dynamics of repressive desublimation, Marcuse offers productive entry points for normative, interdisciplinary social research. Taken together, I argue a Fromm-Marcuse synthesis offers the potential for a radical renaissance of Frankfurt School social research. The social-theoretical limitations of recognition theory can be overcome by the powerful tools which are lying dormant within the Frankfurt School's theoretical arsenal. A new era of critical theory beckons because the academy is in desperate need of a powerful form of normative social research. It is evident that the foundational imperatives which steer our carbon-capitalist form of life need to be ruthlessly interrogated, critical theory once had the tools to ask such questions. A return to a Fromm-Marcuse synthesis could enable critical theorists to ask such fundamental questions once again.

Throughout this book I parade my 'love-hate' relationship with Axel Honneth's scholarship. Honneth's *Pathologies of Reason: On the Legacy of Critical Theory* (2009) demonstrates the normative-explanatory capacity of the pathology diagnosing imagination and articulates the distinctive critical-pedagogic potential of disclosing critique. In this regard, Honneth is cited in all parts of this book as an authority on the pathology diagnosing tradition and its significance to Frankfurt School critical theory. Yet, frustratingly, as I will argue throughout, Honneth 'gets it' but does not 'do it' when it comes to his own pathology diagnosing social research. The disconnect which exists between the normative urgency Honneth identifies in first-generation research, as expressed in 'Towards a disclosing critique of society', is entirely absent in the conceptualisation of social pathology advanced in *Freedom's Right*. A central argument in this text is that Honneth's substantive critical theory fails to capture the urgent and valuable insights of first-generation scholarship. As such, Honneth functions as a fulcrum point within critical theory, and within this book, cited as an expert on the distinctive normative import of pathology diagnosis to the Frankfurt School tradition, while, through his own critical theory, serving to fundamentally disfigure and impede the radical critique it enables. Critical theory urgently needs a revitalised framing of social pathology, an understanding of social maladies which can facilitate potent normative social critique. When critical theorists look *beyond recognition*, they will realise that the resources needed for such a critique had been silently lurking in one of the darker, dustier corners of their bookshelves for many decades. It is time to reopen these books.

Notes

1 This is the term popularised by Michael J. Thompson (2016) in *The Domestication of Critical Theory*. I wish to thank an anonymous reviewer who pointed out the gendered nature of this term. While I agree the term 'domestication' has gendered connotations, as this is the term used widely within the literature, and so as to avoid confusion, I continue with it here until an alternate is adopted.
2 Symbolically, Horkheimer wrote the foreword to Martin Jay's classic history of the Frankfurt School, shortly before his passing in July 1973. The foreword is worth reading in full (Horkheimer, 1973: xxv–xxvi).
3 This became the basis for the much-cited essay, 'Traditional and critical theory'.
4 Although he worked within the Marxist tradition, Horkheimer never explicitly embraced the Marxist 'label' for his research (see Aronowitz, 2002: xii).
5 A group of students famously raised a banner reading, 'Berlin's left-wing fascists greet Teddy the classicist'.
6 This is one of Fraser's central arguments in *Redistribution or Recognition? A Political-Philosophical Exchange*.
7 This is Nancy Fraser's term (see Fraser and Honneth, 2001: 214, *inter alia*).
8 To repurpose the title of Habermas's 1990 text.
9 These are not the only crises threatening critical theory; for example, I have written about the need to respond coherently to the decolonial critique of the Frankfurt School. Retaining a critical voice while researching emergent neo-fascisms in post-colonies requires concerted effort, with states such as India being simultaneously post-colony and contemporary coloniser (see Delanty

and Harris, 2021). Critical theory is also increasingly acknowledged to be suffering from a sociological deficit; most recently expressed in Darrow Schecter, *Critical Theory and Sociological Theory* (2019) and in Gerard Delanty's *Critical Theory and Social Transformation* (2020).

10 'Disrespect' being the title of Honneth's 2007 collection, *Disrespect: The Normative Foundations of Critical Theory.*

Part I

Social pathology and the crisis
of critical theory

1

Social pathology: the 'explosive charge' of critical theory

There are already some excellent books which criticise the rapid 'domestication' of critical theory. Chief amongst these are works by Michael J. Thompson (2016) and Stathis Kouvelakis (2019). While I share many of the political and philosophical sympathies of these leading authors, in this book I provide a change of focus from the existing critical literature. My target is the impact Axel Honneth's work has had on the Frankfurt School's *social-theoretical foundations*, and, in particular, the impact the critical theory of recognition has had on the framing of 'social pathology'.

Frankfurt School scholarship can seem imposing to the uninitiated as it elides disciplines, uniting Marxian theory, Freudian psychoanalysis, Hegelian philosophy, political economy, Weber's sociology, and psychology. While this book focuses on a particular debate within contemporary critical theory ('the pathologies of recognition debate'), and will thus be of primary interest to critical theorists, in an effort to make the text more accessible I start this chapter by offering a broad introduction to social pathology scholarship. Even this task, however, has complications, as many of the foundational conceptual tools used by Frankfurt School scholars are now increasingly contested. Because of its centrality to the research programme, the debate which rages over defining 'social pathology' cuts to the heart of the political battle over the future direction of critical theory, and there is increasingly little shared ground between the antagonists.

Having briefly introduced 'social pathology', I track the framing's development and syncretism, before discussing its application in classic works of Frankfurt School research. I acknowledge the breadth and reach of pathology diagnosing critique, then offer an extensive justification of the tradition's philosophical commitments. Before concluding, I explain explicitly why pathology diagnosing critique is important and why its denaturing is an existential threat for critical theory. In sum, through this chapter I argue that the framing of social pathology matters and that it must be a focal point for critical theorists concerned by the broader 'domestication' of their research programme.

Social pathology: an introduction

In the 'Introduction', I offered a shorthand definition of social pathology diagnosis as being simply 'what critical theorists typically do'. This is probably as close as one can get to a framing today which would be agreeable to both enthused 'third-generation' critical theorists and those who criticise the 'domestication' of contemporary critical theory. 'Social pathologies' can be understood as being the 'problems' which critical theorists have traditionally targeted.[1] As such, how one frames such pathologies, how expansively, or how discriminately 'pathology' is defined, matters, as it determines the scope of critical theory itself. As I draw out in later chapters, first-generation critical theorists adhered to a broad understanding of social pathology, sensitive to Freudian and Hegelian-Marxist insights, which enabled remarkable, sweeping critiques of the form of social life. In contrast, contemporary critical theorists stick to a much narrower understanding of social pathology, deriving from their tight focus on the subject's intersubjective and cognitive capabilities (Chapter 3).

But what does the concept of 'social pathology' actually refer to? How does it move beyond other framings of social problems? In orthodox liberal social and political theory, the primary social 'wrongs' which are studied are 'injustices' and 'illegitimacies'. Injustices typically refer to unfair distributions of resources or of opportunities. Illegitimacies typically refer to unfair claims to power or status. These categories remain hegemonic today across most schools of thought, with John Rawls's *A Theory of Justice* (1971) holding canonical status at most universities. Sadly, few undergraduate courses require their students to stop and question whether all 'social wrongs' can actually be meaningfully collapsed into the framings of 'justice' and 'legitimacy'. It is an unchallenged precept of conventional liberal wisdom. Good social worlds are 'just' and/or 'legitimate', and bad social worlds are 'unjust' and/or 'illegitimate'. The most commonly studied social 'wrongs' today, such as racism, unmerited inequality, or human rights violations, can readily slide into the category of 'injustice', so the lack of further inquiry here is understandable. Critical theorists, however, realise things are not quite so simple, and connect the limits of the bourgeois imagination to the deracinating impact of capitalist ideology. While critical theorists do acknowledge that 'injustices' exist, they understand that these are just one subset of social malady: there exists a much broader range of social problems, many of which cannot be subsumed into the liberal conceptual toolkit. Crucially, critical theorists argue that to grapple with the pressing social challenges of the day one must go 'beyond' the liberal register and engage in a thicker and explicitly normative form of social critique.

Because the liberal framework is so hegemonic, it is worth being explicit about the many social problems it fails to capture. A typical unjust society for a liberal theorist would be one in which the distribution of goods and services has no link to merit. Accordingly, a good proportion of liberal ideal theory focuses on concerns of distributional justice. Critical theorists would, of course, agree that a society which had an arbitrary and inequitable distribution of goods would be problematic. However, what matters for critical theorists is not solely the 'end state distribution', but rather the rationality of the 'form of life' which produced the distribution itself (see Jaeggi, 2018). For Frankfurt School scholars, the entire form of social being needs to be open to critique (Honneth, 2000: 121). As such, critical theorists possess the conceptual tools required for a 'thicker' form of critique. Accordingly, in the critical theories of Erich Fromm and Herbert Marcuse, society was not merely 'unjust', 'illegitimate', or 'unfair'; it was critiqued on the basis of its irrationality and for having taken 'a wrong course'. In crude, anti-theoretical language, capitalist society is simply 'bonkers'. Capitalism is based on a bed of contradictions, and the briefest analysis of the market order shows it to be typically self-destructive, inefficient, soul destroying, planet destroying, war-inducing, racism-sustaining, allied to patriarchy, and fundamentally opposed to most shared precepts for a 'good life'. The framing of social pathology diagnosis is the social-theoretical foundation which enables such an expansive indictment to be developed.

As a result of the pathology diagnosing critiques of Marcuse and Fromm, we can understand that a society can suffer from serious problems even when it is formally 'just'. As such, a deeper, more extensive form of critique is required, one capable of looking beyond questions of justice and legitimacy. Consider societies which:

- Create subjects who view the world in a distorted, reductive manner; which induce an impeded phenomenology (as discussed by Herbert Marcuse, see Chapter 7),
- Have structural imperatives which inculcate widespread psychopathologies, such as alienation or clinical anxiety (as discussed by Erich Fromm, see Chapter 6),
- Have self-perpetuating negative dynamics, such as being involved in a cold-war nuclear arms race (see Chapter 6),
- Have socialisation structures which encourage subjects to spend all their time engaging in self-sabotaging activities which impede their capacity to live a happy and meaningful life (see Chapter 7),
- Have social dynamics which lead to subjects desiring self-destructive goods or experiences, which may threaten the very foundations of social life. Consider a society where everyone had equal access to foreign holidays in a world suffering a climate crisis (see Chapter 6).

It is thus clear that societies can, and do, have problems, even existential problems, which do not fit neatly into the liberal conceptual toolkit. Critical theory enables these social pathologies to be explored, and for the causal irrational societal imperatives to be subjected to critique. The development of such pathology diagnosing social theory embraced a plethora of insights. Next, I offer a brief genealogy of pathology diagnosing critique, showing how a remarkably wide range of traditions and disciplines coalesced into the Frankfurt School's distinctive approach.

A remarkable syncretism

Western philosophy is often taught as being a 'series of footnotes to Plato' (Whitehead, 1979: 39). It should perhaps, then, be unsurprising that the first clear engagement with a form of pathology diagnosing social criticism can be traced to *The Republic*. In a key passage, Socrates proposes that the optimal city would be a pastoral idyll, where citizens are happy with a simple diet of 'loaves', 'roast myrtle-berries and acorns' and are content enjoying other simple pleasures. They will 'take care that their families do not exceed their means' and seek to 'bequeath a similar life to their children'. For Socrates's interlocutor, Glaucon, such penury is far from idyllic; he dismisses Socrates's vision as a 'city of pigs' due to its simplicity. In contrast, Glaucon prefers a luxurious city, where the inhabitants can freely enjoy material opulence. In his criticism of Glaucon's polis, Socrates turns repeatedly to medical analogies to present a critique of the problematic dynamics such a city would induce.

Crucially, Socrates argued that a 'fever' may arise with citizens thirsting for ever more luxurious lifestyles. There are two key features to Socrates's response. The first is a simple rival ethical judgement: that a taste for 'unnatural' desires, such as rich fatty foods, is unwholesome, unhealthy, and thus an undesirous trait for a community. This is certainly part of Socrates's criticism, for whom the question of the 'good life' is never far from mind. However, what is striking about Socrates's response to Glaucon is the framing of a *pathological social dynamic* which may emerge, constituting the 'fever' in itself. For Socrates, luxuries are only partly sought for the pleasure they bring in themselves; a substantial allure of a luxurious lifestyle is the ability to demonstrate a relationally higher standing to fellow citizens. This can precipitate an insatiable acquisitive drive throughout the polis ('keeping up with the Joneses'), a dynamic of negative infinity unfolds to which there is no clear end. Such a cycle risks exhausting all social resources for no productive purpose. This is crucially presented as being a 'fever' suffered by the social totality, not just by the polis's subjects.[2] The diagnosis of self-perpetuating negative dynamics remains an integral feature of social pathology scholarship today (Neuhouser, 2012: 631).

Aristotle follows his tutor's lead and repeatedly uses the framing of biological health to determine the 'proportionate blend' of the 'mixed constitution' (Aristotle, *Politics*: 1302b33–1303a3). As such, commentators have argued that Aristotle's political theory can be read as a diagnosis and analysis of 'political pathology' (Tracy, 1969: 304). Crucially, as with Plato, it is the *social body* which can suffer from pathologies. The social metastructure is analysed through recourse to the language of the corporeal body. Due in no small part to Aristotle's influence, scholastic thought turned sporadically to 'bodily sickness' as an analogy for critiquing impaired societal functionality (Nájera, 2017).

Critical theorists broadly agree that Rousseau should be considered the founder of pathology diagnosing social critique (Honneth, 2014). For Honneth, Rousseau's *Discourses* mark the arrival of this distinct form of social criticism, one which represented a rejection 'of an entire form of life' (Honneth, 2014: 7). As such, Rousseau is credited with moving social theorising beyond the mere investigation of 'political-moral legitimacy', or of redistributive justice; rather, the focus became squarely on the analysis of the 'structural limitations … [which society] … imposes on the goal of human self-realization' (Honneth, 2014: 10). Rousseau is thus read as marking the birth of pathology diagnosis as a truly distinct form of social criticism.

Rousseau's analysis stresses the objective impediments the existing social order places on subjects achieving self-realisation, while at the same time articulating the social dynamics which serve to perpetuate the status quo. For Rousseau, the deracinating impact of society on the subject was crucial. 'Vanity and scorn' (Rousseau, 1984 [1762]: 114), rather than being innate to human nature, were reframed as the hallmarks of civil society. The psychopathology of 'inflamed' *amour-propre* was not presented as being inherent to a fixed human nature; rather 'natural man' lived within a joyous 'golden mean' 'between the indolence of the primitive state and the petulant activity of … [his] own pride' (Rousseau, 1984 [1762]: 115). Rousseau is explicit: there is thus nothing natural or static to the pathologies of the social world, rather the contingent historical situation induces self-perpetuating social dynamics which acculturates subjects to context-perpetuating forms of impaired consciousness. For Rousseau,

> The excess of idleness among some and the excess of toil among others, the ease of stimulating and gratifying our appetites and our senses, the overelaborate foods of the rich, which inflame and overwhelm them with indigestion, the bad food of the poor, which they often go without altogether,

so that they over-eat greedily when they have the opportunity; those late nights, excesses of all kinds, immoderate transports of every passion, fatigue, exhaustion of mind, the innumerable sorrows and anxieties that people in all classes suffer, and by which the human soul is constantly tormented: these are the fatal proofs that most of our ills are of our own making, and that we might have avoided nearly all of them if we had adhered to the simple, unchanging and solitary way of life that nature ordained for us. (Rousseau, 1984 [1762]: 84–85)

Rousseau's diagnosis thus presents a critique of macro-social developments which have inhibited, and continue to inhibit, subjects from enjoying the good life. This diagnosis is both sociological and social-psychological; Rousseau presents the objective inferiority of the status quo and the social-psychological reasons for its perpetuation and relative stability. For Neuhouser (2012), it is thus the complexity and depth of Rousseau's critique which makes him the consummate social pathologist.

With Rousseau, distinctive strands of pathology diagnosing social critique coalesced: an ethico-normative claim that the extant society impeded subjects from achieving the good life united with the insight that this can be the result of discernible social dynamics; and that such the social subject is conditioned by such dynamics so that their actions and thought processes serve to perpetuate the suboptimal status quo. The social subject has been fundamentally denatured by pathological developments; while 'born free', 'everywhere … [they are] … in chains' (Rousseau, 1968 [1762]: 49).

Yet, despite his remarkable impact, Rousseau lacked a satisfactory anchor for his normative claim making. Hegel served to provide such foundations for the Frankfurt School with his radicalisation of the critique of reason. While for Kant reason was *noumenal*, Hegel 'sociologised' epistemology, demonstrating that the subject's capacity for thought is connected to the rationality inherent within broader social institutions. The critique of reason became connected to social critique (Held, 2013). The Hegelian framing of 'historically effective reason', and of manifest 'pathologies of reason', is a central constituent of the Frankfurt School imagination. For Horkheimer, the foundational role of critical theory was thus 'to illuminate' the importance of the 'rational organization of human society' (Horkheimer, 1972: 245).

Hegel's critique of reason provides the basis for the Frankfurt School's immanent form of critique; focusing on the forms of thought within the life-world. A pathology of reason is held to exist when society fails to operate at the highest standard of rationality at which it is capable. Such a paradigm leads to the sociological analysis of irrationalities, contradictions, and deficiencies in manners of thought and organisation. Providing such work is sufficiently dialectical, such an approach is able to make a claim to a strong objectivity, for the critique is predicated on the impossibility of a stable contradiction. Such contradictions necessitate resolution in the form of a synthesis, referred to as a 'sublation'.³

Frankfurt School research thus combines Rousseau's analysis of the manifest social conditions impeding the subject's ability to attain the good life with a Hegelian focus on the irrationality of the social conjuncture. Crucially, such irrationality is held to be manifest both in the subject's cognitive capacities, but also within the structuring mechanisms of social institutions. Thus, social dynamics and institutions which evince a deficient form of social rationality, due to harbouring internal contradictions, are held to be objectively pathological. The Hegelian understanding of reason is manifest within the social subject and within social institutions. Frankfurt School critical theory, building upon both Rousseau and Hegel, diagnoses the pathologies manifest in social institutions and the ideological artifice which maintains them through the cognitive impairments induced in the social subject.

Marx's materialist inversion of Hegel's idealistic philosophy is the next essential marker in the development of pathology diagnosing social criticism. Marx 'turned Hegel on his head'⁴ by postulating that historical-material conditions determine the development of consciousness, rather than consciousness determining social-material conditions. This Copernican moment was foundational for pathology diagnosing social criticism; however, it was Marx's *historical materialism* which was his crucial contribution. It is not the evolution of *Geist* which determines social development, but *class conflict*. The class relations of particular societies determine the extant standard of rationality within the social world. Political economy was thus to be central to the critique of pathologies of reason and, in particular, it was central to Marx's understanding of alienation.

The final core ingredient of the pathology diagnosing imagination is psychoanalysis. Sigmund Freud's pioneering work located the origin of neuroses within macro-social processes. Thus, for Freud, patients' anxiety responses were to be understood as precipitants of broader societal pathologies. As Freud wrote, when society 'habituate(s) ... situations and conditions of satisfaction that are not normal', the 'most obvious outcome is nervous illness' (Freud, 1959: 201–202). For Freud, it was evident that the 'systems of civilisation' had become 'neurotic' (Freud, 1930: 143). This insight is crucial for critical theory in two regards. First, it anchors a clear emancipatory interest in the social subject herself. By grounding the epidemic of psychopathologies within malfunctioning societal dynamics, social pathology diagnosis – which may otherwise seem an abstract anti-humanist endeavour – becomes instantly humanised. At its simplest, people do not want to suffer psychopathologies: they wish their anxieties and neuroses to be eased, thus they have an investment in social pathologies being transcended. Second, psychoanalysis provides an entry point to the diagnosis of pathologies of reason: the psychological suffering of social subjects is presented as a manifestation of societal irrationalities.

It is crucial here to stress that critical theorists do not operate within a medicalised, clinical understanding of 'anxiety'; social subjects do not have to be 'ill', for example, diagnosed as per the *DSM*,[5] for social pathologies to be held to exist (Honneth, 2014: 698). Rather, returning to Rousseau, Hegel, and Marx, the submission made by critical theorists such as Fromm and Marcuse is that *alienated* existence, resulting from an irrational form of productive activity, impedes the subject from enjoying an optimally flourishing social life. Fromm repeatedly refers to subject as 'alienated', and as 'suffering from neuroses'. Society is presented as 'insane': not the social subject.[6] Psychoanalysis thus enables critical theorists to 'establish a connection between defective rationality and individual suffering', connecting an otherwise abstract social philosophy with the embodied suffering of the social subject (Honneth, 2007: 38). For Fromm and Marcuse, the normalisation of a society which induces psychopathologies, achieved through the individualised treatment of pathologised social subjects, represents a 'pathology of normalcy' (Fromm 2010 [1991]).

Pathology diagnosing critical theory – the Frankfurt School in action

Adorno and Horkheimer are routinely framed as being consummate social pathologists (Honneth, 2000). In their highly idiosyncratic text, *Dialectic of Enlightenment*, the co-authors presented how the dominant form of reason, instrumental rationality, transforms social behaviour, with devastating effects (see Roberts, 2004). The 'extraordinary sweep' of their diagnosis is remarkable, capturing nearly all human endeavour (Adorno and Horkheimer, 1997 [1944]: 61). A pathologically inflamed instrumental rationality is connected to Enlightenment thought, through which the 'particular' is perceived 'only as one case of the general' (Adorno and Horkheimer, 1997 [1944]: 84–85). This epistemic malady is framed as the crucial antecedent for the 'new kind of barbarism' of capitalist modernity (Adorno and Horkheimer, 1997 [1944]: xi).

Yet, while Adorno and Horkheimer's critique is penetrating, cathartic, and disclosing, few would deny that it lacks sociological specificity. By virtue of its expansive terms of reference, their text does not present as a basis for social research, rather it sits more as a work of disclosing social philosophy and as an epic narrative in its own right. Thus, in this book, I diverge from the dominant focus on Adorno in much contemporary critical theory,[7] and in his stead, turn to the work of Fromm and Marcuse. This is not to suggest any lack of potency or sophistication in Adorno's work; rather, I consider it a less suitable avenue to turn for rekindling pathology diagnosing social research today.

In contrast to Adorno, Fromm and Marcuse provide more sociologically anchored diagnoses of social pathology. The presence of a pathological social dynamics was central to Fromm's work. Chief amongst these was the logic of 'consensual validation' (Fromm, 1963 [1955]: 14): the more people who accept the pathological irrationality of the present, the greater the pressure exerted on other subjects to accede to the dominant norms. Such compulsion to conform mounts proportionately, and accordingly, the inclination towards critique shrinks. Crucially, for Frankfurt School scholars, and explicitly for both Marcuse and Fromm, mass acquiescence is not evidence of coherent rationality. In direct contrast to acceding to the given social conjuncture on the basis of their mass 'democratic uptake', Fromm advanced a 'science of man', capable of determining the objective conditions which enable a flourishing existence. The 'pathological normalcy' of advanced industrial society was thus held to sustain, and to further entrench, an objectively *suboptimal* form of life. In keeping with the Hegelian-Marxism of Adorno and Horkheimer, for Fromm such a pathological society had to be understood as manifest both in terms of its suboptimal alienation-inducing social institutions, but crucially also through the 'social patterned defects' such institutions necessitate and perpetuate (Fromm, 1963 [1955]: 15).

With clear Freudian-Marxian inflection, Fromm declared that the social subject has reneged upon life itself, surrendering a biophilic (see Fromm, 1973) attitude in favour of a desire for 'possession'; humanity has chosen 'to have', rather than 'to be' (Fromm, 1979 [1976]). In a remarkable revisionist-Freudian turn, Fromm argued the libidinal drives of the subject have been recoded due to the deracinating effects of consumptive capitalism on subjectivity. The alienating rhythms of the capitalist mode of production have engendered an all-consuming subject. The desire for possession, rather than for free expression/being, is but one symptom of the 'insane' society. The pathological normalcy identified in Fromm's diagnosis, is profoundly socially located. As Fromm (1944) argued in *Individual and Social Origins of Neurosis*, and, more famously later in *The Sane Society*, it is the particular insane society which produces insane subjects, the inverse of the Latin aphorism '*mens sana in societate sana*' (Fromm, 1963 [1955]: 86).

Likewise, Marcuse (2007 [1964]) presented a Freudian-Marxian synthesis, anchored in a strong Hegelian-Marxism. While Marcuse notably retained a greater fidelity to Freud's belief in universal libidinal drives,[8] his account was heavily influenced by Marxian political economy. One could argue that Marcuse presents the most 'condensed' framing of social pathology, uniting the central insights of Aristotle ('feverish' social dynamics impeding the good life), Rousseau (that such dynamics are social and psychological), Hegel (focusing on the form of reason manifest in both the subject and societal institutions), Marx (anchored in political economy) and Freud (evincing anxiety/neuroses in the subject). In particular, Marcuse's framing of 'repressive desublimation' served to extend this remarkable theoretical latticework, and I return to it in Chapter 7.

For Marcuse, advanced industrial societies evince a tragic 'vicious circle' in which subjects forever defer authentic pleasure, always expecting satisfaction to be delivered by the next hit of consumption. This desire to consume necessitates obeisance to the diktats of capital, encouraging subjects into accepting alienating, exploitative labour conditions. The greater the obeisance to exploitative and alienating labour, the greater the need for the distracting opiate of imminent consumption; yet, the greater the desire for the goods, the greater the necessary obeisance (Marcuse, 2007 [1964]). Tragically, such consumption is never satisfactory; healthy sublimation is not merely deferred, but, by trapping the subject within its vicious cycle, it serves to displace libidinal energies from being directed to objectively emancipatory ends. The promise of a Big Mac and fries temporarily eases the hunger for revolutionary praxis, while never fully sating the subject. Resultantly, advanced industrial society aches with subjects suffering from psychopathologies, who are forever deferring gratification.

While such cursory sketches are painfully reductive, they serve to demonstrate how first-generation Frankfurt School scholarship produced social research built upon remarkable pathology diagnosing foundations. As I argue in Part III of this book, a critical dialogue between Fromm and Marcuse can offer the social-theoretical resources for a renewed account of social pathology.

Off the Frankfurt School's radar

While the depth and breadth of the pathology diagnosing tradition is obvious from the above sketch, it remains remarkable how many alternate uses of the pathology diagnosing analogy exist within wider academia. Most of these alternate accounts remain insulated from the Frankfurt School approach. For example, academics invested in the French tradition may instantly think of the work of Georges Canguilhem when one mentions 'social pathology'. Canguilhem's (1991 [1966]) *The Normal and the Pathological* is a cornerstone of the philosophy of science, and theorists as diverse as Althusser and Foucault[9] acknowledge their debt to this work. However, Canguilhem remains segregated from the Frankfurt School's output. While Canguilhem links epistemology, political economy, and technical development, his work does not sit within the genealogy outlined above. For Canguilhem, what is crucial is the *demarcation* between the 'normal' and the 'pathological': for critical theorists, the term 'pathological' is weaponised to enable a strongly normative critique of the 'normal'. Fromm's 'pathological normalcy' shows the clear disjuncture.

Likewise, Sutherland's (1945) account of 'pathology' remains anathema to Frankfurt School theorists. For Sutherland, 'social pathology' offered a useful entry point to the study of 'criminal' elements within the social body. Again, Sutherland serves to use pathology to enable a demarcation within the social totality, rather than as a means to facilitate critique of the social body *tout court*.

Sitting closer to the central ideas of Frankfurt School tradition is Jiddu Krishnamurti's (2008 [1962]) 'Theosophy'. Originating within Indian philosophy, Krishnamurti's work remains underexplored within the Frankfurt School context, despite sitting remarkably close to Fromm. Krishnamurti turns to the language of 'pathology' to critique the social order, linking individual manifestations of sickness to broader societal maladies, and questions the normative-generative dynamics of the social conjuncture. It remains unclear whether Fromm ever engaged with Krishnamurti's work. It would be curious to see the potential for future syntheses.[10] Further traditions abound with a similar pathology diagnosing lexicon: one might think of Spengler's (1991) *The Decline of the West*, or Cas Mudde's (2010) recent analyses of populism; however, again, neither framing sits within the genealogy outlined above.

One might also think of works of classical and modern literature which serve to disclose the pathological nature of society. Samuel Beckett, F. Scott Fitzgerald, and Richard Yates[11] are obvious candidates. Perhaps the closest literary cousin to pathology diagnosing critique is Allen Ginsberg, who notably engaged with Marcuse's work.[12] Ginsberg's poetry shares the Frankfurt School's syntheses of traditions, referencing Marx, Kabbalah, Freud. One can see in the opening lines of *Howl* the amalgam of psychosocial pathology diagnosis advanced by Fromm and Marcuse: 'I saw the best minds of my generation destroyed by madness, starving hysterical naked' (Ginsberg, 2009 [1956]: 1).

That said, Ginsberg's attack on 'Moloch' sits closer to a Jewish mysticism than Marxian historical materialism, and thus his disclosing prowess comes at the cost of preventing an extended sociological investigation.[13] Yet, this was never his agenda. *Howl* includes repeated intriguing Freudo-Marxian glimpses, linking critique and normalised insanity, such as

> where *you accuse your doctors of insanity* and plot the Hebrew
> socialist revolution against the fascist national Golgotha...
>
> where there are twenty-five-thousand *mad comrades* all together singing
> the final stanzas of the Internationale
>
> (Ginsberg, 2009 [1956]: 11 – my italics)

In Ginsberg's poetry, as in Fromm and Marcuse's critical theory, Marx and Freud, capitalism and 'insanity', are seamlessly connected. Stretching disciplines further, perhaps one should include Lang's 1927 film *Metropolis* within the cannon of pathology diagnosing social criticism. Immediately linked to Ginsberg by Lang's portrayal of 'Moloch', the film depicts a crazed synthesis of technical progress, monstrous deification, and systemic production (see Banaji, 2020). The worker's prostration to the mechanical Moloch of Lang's hellish city has curious echoes of Socrates's discussion with Glaucon, while carrying additional Freudian, Marxian, and Hegelian motifs.

I am keen not to 'police' the parameters of 'social pathology diagnosis' and consider Lang and Ginsberg to offer such critique as much as Adorno, Fromm, or Marcuse. What distinguishes pathology diagnosing social research is not disciplinarity, language, or style; rather, it is a normative-diagnostic disclosing critique of the social totality, drawing upon a latticework of political economy, social philosophy, and psychoanalysis. This leaves enormous scope for creativity and imagination, which is part of what makes reading first-generation critical theory so exhilarating and reading third-generation critical theory so depressing. *Minima Moralia*, *The Sane Society*, *One Dimensional Man*, and *Dialectic of Enlightenment* are not 'ordinary' texts of orthodox argumentation. Their mode of presentation is self-consciously unorthodox, deliberately 'disclosing', rather than conventionally didactic.

The sophisticated latticework of ideas which melt into the Frankfurt School's foundations are both blessing and curse. An undergraduate encountering the term afresh will be understandably unsure whether 'social pathology' applies *exclusively* to 'cognitive disconnects' in a recognition-cognitivist, normative-reconstructive imaginary (Honneth), or whether it refers to a foundational deficiency at the heart of Enlightenment thought (Adorno); whether it refers to patterns of consensual validation (Fromm), or deformed modes of engaging with the world (Marcuse). Or, even whether it has no clear meaning whatsoever![14] In contrast, I persist in the belief that social pathology is best understood as referring to the distinct social-theoretical core of critical theory. While such foundations have suffered subsidence, they can and must be rebuilt.

A justifiable foundation for social research

My central claim in *Critical Theory and Social Pathology* is that pathology diagnosing social research requires an urgent renewal. However, if fundamental objections can be raised to the efficacy of any form of pathology diagnosing research, then my project would obviously be futile. Therefore, I now sympathetically present, and offer rebuttals to, the central criticisms which are targeted at the pathology diagnosing imagination. There are, of course, multiple criticisms which can be levelled at any approach to social research, and while this is therefore not an exhaustive list, it is indicative of the broader critical literature.

Perhaps the most obvious criticism of pursuing research through the framing of social pathology is that society is simply not an organic body *qua* a biological living organism. Such an argument submits that societies do not suffer 'ill' health as they do not 'live' in a strict biological sense. Even if one accepts the premise of there being such a thing as 'social life', or of societies having 'life cycles', existing and ending over time, such a 'life' is qualitatively distinct from the life of organic, biological bodies. Thus, while I can meaningfully state that 'my grandmother is ill', I cannot state that 'my society is ill' without providing substantial and complicated philosophical justification. This may seem a serious challenge for pathology diagnosing social critique, for, as established above, Aristotle, Rousseau, Freud, and Fromm explicitly describe the social body itself as 'fevered', 'ill', 'insane'. It might be submitted that embracing such a framing requires acceding to what MacLay has described as the 'social organism' tradition (MacLay, 1990). A convincing anti-theoretical argument against such 'organismic' approaches is that they require too many leaps of the imagination. In more academic prose, one could say that they require extensive ontological support which does not appear immediately available. In short, because society sits so far from being a biological organism, serious – and potentially irredeemable – complications appear to emerge.[15]

I contend that two satisfactory rejoinders can be rallied. First, a distinction can be drawn between the embrace of a strong naturalist social ontology and the utilisation of the framing of 'pathology' as a useful signifier to identify impaired functionality. There is a clear difference between arguing that society is alive in a meaningful, biologically comparable form, and is suffering from an actual illness, and merely using the word 'pathology' as synonymous with 'malfunctioning' (Ratner, 2017). Similarly, we can helpfully use the signifier 'virus' to describe malware impeding the functioning of a computer without being accused of thinking a MacBook Pro is a sentient organism. While this rebuttal still raises the debate of the desired 'function' of the society, the question of an unjustifiable organistic social ontology is displaced. Such a rejoinder simply disconnects the word 'pathology' from questions of social organicism. The second possible rejoinder is the path usually trodden by critical theorists, and submits that the embrace of a 'weak naturalism' does not necessitate a strong 'social organicism' (Strydom, 2011: 10). Piet Strydom is most explicit on this point, writing that the belief that 'there is a continuity between nature and socio-cultural form of life ... is not to be ... interpreted in a strong determinate sense which could lead to an epistemological reduction of society to nature' (Strydom, 2011: 10). Simply put, the idea that we can talk of there being similarities between nature and socio-cultural life does not mean that critical theorists are committed to viewing society as being a living being. While the first argument served to negate the biological content of the term 'pathology', the second embraces the medicalised language, while providing significant distance between a 'weak naturalism' and a 'strong organicism'. One can talk of 'social life' without seeing society as being a living creature in a meaningful sense.

A second oft-repeated criticism of pathology diagnosing social research targets the framing of 'pathology', distinct from its organicism. The ideas of 'sickness' and of 'health' are presented as being politically and philosophically problematic in themselves. Such an argument also has intuitive appeal. Discourses of 'degenerate' or 'sick' peoples and 'ill societies' have an extremely sinister, well-mapped history, encompassing extreme elements of the political right. Such discourses bring social research dangerously close to the semantic fields of eugenics, fascism, and ethnic cleansing. Michael Biddiss (1997: 342), for example, noted that Hitler viewed 'society not merely as resembling, but rather as effectively constituting a biological organism' with 'healthier elements ... constantly struggling against others' threatening the 'degeneration' of the state. Hitler thus explicitly 'liked to link his own political endeavours' with 'the scientific achievements of Pasteur and Koch' (Biddiss, 1997: 342). Biddiss is clear that, for the Nazi Party, the turn to a medicalised discourse served to rhetorically legitimate a 'biocratic' 'racial state'.[16]

A related criticism springs from the work of Foucault, who argued that there is no such thing as 'objective' biological illness. In *The Birth of the Clinic* (1963), Foucault demonstrated how 'health' and 'illness' are discursively created and perpetuated; they are, in short, social constructs. There is no unmediated relationship between the idea of 'health' and of biological functionality. For Foucault, the discourses surrounding health and illness are utilised to 'discipline' subjects rather than merely to enable their efficient return to an objective 'health' (Dreyfus and Rabinow, 1982: 173). For Foucauldians, the terms 'deviance', 'insanity', and 'pathology' are utilised to legitimate governmentality, not to 'heal' and emancipate. The idea of 'health' as an objective referent is collapsed. Conducting social research predicated on an analogy to 'healthy' and 'unhealthy' bodies would thus be limited analytically and problematic politically.

Again, satisfactory rejoinders can be rallied. Critical theorists can simply surrender the vocabulary of 'pathology' and transition to a non-medicalised semantic field with near-identical analytical purchase. In this regard, perhaps the language of 'pathology' *should* be dispensed with, as it would be of little loss, beyond being a minor inconvenience to adopt a new signifier. Moving to the language of 'dysfunctionality' may be preferable, and it sits closer to the crux of the framework: that the existing social conditions do not optimally enable social subjects to attain the good life. True, the idea that individual suffering is connected to social irrationality is neatly captured by the idea of 'social pathologies' as well as 'individual pathologies'; however, this idea would still remain, just with different signifiers. Yet, to the committed post-structuralist, any alternate term, however distant from the biological, may still have trace echoes of 'pathology'. Further, attempts at a 'rebranding' might be identified as a dangerous 'newspeak', disguising the identical, problematic 'disciplinary' intent. As a result, as the language of 'pathology' is ultimately incidental to the critique advanced, it is perhaps simplest to retain the term as it carries analytical and popular purchase, clearly demonstrating the desire for a 'thicker' form of social criticism. There is a popular resonance with the idea that 'society is sick', especially in light of the COVID-19 pandemic.

A further argument supporting retaining the term 'pathology' would be to stress that Foucault's analysis demonstrated how *subjects* are governed through the language of 'pathology'. Such a criticism would be misplaced with pathology diagnosing social criticism, as the target of critique is never individual social subjects, or even social groups, but rather *society* itself. Indeed, the central objective of pathology diagnosing social critique is to show how the pathologies manifest within subjects have social, rather than individual, origins. Pathology diagnosing social critique therefore ultimately sits closer to Foucault's own politics than one might initially realise.

Yet, the Foucauldian argument that 'illnesses' and 'pathologies' are social constructs requires further consideration. If 'illnesses' are a social construct and do not have a purely scientific and objective referent, does that impact the diagnosis of 'social pathologies' too? How are we, as critical theorists, able to determine when something is 'well' or 'unwell'? This challenges the normative foundations of social research (see Honneth, 2000). How can social researchers claim anything is 'good' or 'bad', 'healthy' or 'sick', 'functional' or 'non-functional'? Reflecting the broader normative crisis induced by post-modernism and post-structuralism, academics of varying stripes are increasingly suspicious of any claims being presented as objective fact: especially claims which suggest 'social structure X is better than social structure Y' (see Rorty, 1990, *inter alia*). There are a variety of good reasons for a certain degree of suspicion towards such grandiose claims (Honneth, 2000: 118–119). However, the result of the fashion for hyper-social constructionism has been the ascendancy of what Francis Wheen wryly called 'the demolition merchants of reality' (Wheen, 2004: 78). A disjointed amalgam of broadly post-structuralist inflected thought has attained dominance, which, *in extremis*, serves to preclude the possibility of making even vague claims towards 'the good life'. Like Wheen, Carl Ratner is also explicitly hostile to such an anti-normative turn, echoing Fromm in claiming that there are *obviously* objective conditions which are more conducive to human beings living a happy, meaningful existence than others. For instance, most people would agree it is best not to be freezing to death or on fire. This may sound glib; however, the obvious nature of these extremes demonstrates the insanity of hyper-relativism. As a result, while Foucauldians may be correct in stating that 'health' and 'illness' are social constructs, this need not detain critical theorists for too long: contradictions exist, dialectical theory remains valid. Whatever post-structuralist theorists assert about the power-mediated relationship between the signifiers 'poison' and 'health', or the discursive construction of our notion of 'mortality', if critical theorists and post-structuralists both take multiple cyanide pills, both will be equally dead. Wheen's 'demolition merchants' did not finish the job.

That said, the normative challenge to critical theory is multifaceted – extending beyond appreciating the political and adapting nature of thought and language. Ultimately, critical theory is explicitly normative. But, expressed reductively, any claim that 'X represents an objective social problem' is seen to be increasingly unsustainable in conditions of normative crisis: not merely a result of the destabilising effects of post-modern and post-structural thought. Cultural pluralism and post-metaphysical thinking both challenge theorists' abilities to declare 'X' superior to 'Y'. Further, any claim which suggests that we can view 'X representing an objective social problem because it impedes social subjects' capacity to attain the good life' serves to fall into all three of these challenges: post-structural, cultural pluralist, post-metaphysical. As such, pathology diagnosing critical theory needs to be able to present a convincing justification for its normatively weighty analysis of the social world; such 'strong', or 'thick' social criticism needs to be seen as more than just 'transcendent metaphysics' or a 'partisan' ethics. I believe three clear rejoinders can be offered to this broader challenge, demonstrating how normatively undergirded social research remains philosophically and politically justifiable today.

One response is that offered by Axel Honneth: present a 'weak formal anthropology' as a foundation for social research (Honneth, 2007: 42). Honneth's position can be seen as something of a delicate compromise with ethico-cultural relativism, acceding to the claim that the particulars of the good life are no longer the justifiable domain of specialised, academic knowledge. Rather, with the widespread embrace of ethico-cultural meta-pluralism, social research has to respond accordingly. As such, Honneth is cautious of making proscriptive ethical statements which are 'thick': which are overly explicit in deeming certain lifestyle choice 'right' or 'wrong'. Rather, in place of making such claims, Honneth proposes that mutual agreement might be reached on the foundational formal anthropological requirements for people to live a good life however they, themselves, see fit. Thus, the normative challenge is both embraced and rebuffed; with sufficient abstraction from an explicit ethics, Honneth claims that agreement can be reached on the basis of the conditions all subjects require for their own ethical judgements to be realised. On the basis that such a foundation is 'sufficiently abstract' (Honneth, 1995: 174) and based solely on a 'formal anthropology', Honneth's response seems an acceptable rebuttal. As such, a social world where subjects are unable to realise any conceptions of the good life, due to a lack of water, food, shelter, and so on, can be deemed justifiably normatively inferior to a social formation where such foundational formal requirements are met. Despite the many flaws in Honneth's critical theory, in this important regard Honneth's work contains a clear, explicitly stated normative basis for conducting critical theory within today's 'normative crisis'.

If Honneth's 'weak formal anthropology' is presented as a nuanced compromise between critical theory's desire for a strong normative foundation and the post-structuralist suspicion of the invalidity of any strong normative foundations, Frederick Neuhouser's response offers no such subtlety and is attractive precisely because of his brazenness. For Neuhouser, pathology diagnosing social research is normative: deal with it! All approaches to social research have various strengths and weaknesses. A central feature of a thick form of social criticism, which is crucial to our capacity to explore the social totality at a foundational level, is a normative anchoring. As Neuhouser (2012: 630, translated from German) wrote,

> A social theory that takes the idea of social pathology theory (seriously) rests implicitly on a vision of social reality according to which the social, as distinct from the merely political, cannot be adequately grasped or evaluated without attributing ends to social practices and institutions that are in a broad sense ethical (in the sense of being bound up with ideas of the good life or human flourishing).

Clearly for Neuhouser, there is no point pretending this is not the case, and there is no point spilling gallons of ink trying to justify it. What Neuhouser deems 'thick' social criticism is simply normative: a brazen response, that critical theory 'just does this: deal with it', has a certain candour and ease to it. However, without a sophisticated appreciation of the manner through which critical theory offers such a normative critique, such a riposte may seem hollow.

Fortunately, for Frankfurt School theorists, as Strydom elaborates in *Contemporary Critical Theory and Methodology*, a sophisticated immanent-transcendent approach is central to their social criticism. As explored above, Frankfurt School critical theory explores contradictions within the immanent social domain. In this regard, critical theorists remain, formally at least, dialectical. While their substantive research may extend in different directions, the analysis of contradictions remains a central thread of their analyses. As such, critical theory remains philosophically justifiable, contingent on its immanent anchor to the social world and to its methodologies being sufficiently dialectical.

A final consideration is worth stressing here. Extending Neuhouser's riposte above with a particular critical theoretical twist, recall that Frankfurt School scholars believe that an 'objective' and 'positivist' social science is impossible. As per my discussion of Horkheimer's *Traditional and Critical Theory* in the 'Introduction', 'value-free' research is never the goal for critical theorists; it is held to be *both* impossible and undesirable. Thus, the charge that pathology diagnosing social criticism is unduly normative can be embraced as a positive. By admitting to its explicit normativity, and reflecting upon it, critical theory remains one step ahead of other approaches, which, in their attempted objectivity, may fail to recognise their susceptibility to structural power.

The 'explosive charge' of critical theory[17]

I end this chapter by presenting three distinctive strengths which are unique to pathology diagnosing research. I do this to justify my investment in rejuvenating research predicated on exploring social pathologies.

First, through the diagnosis of social pathologies, critical theorists possess the tools to provide a critique of our current form of life. Such a critique transcends the liberal framings of 'justice' and 'legitimacy' and is able to question the fundamental drives and goals towards which societies strive. As such, critical theory is able to engage in social critique which possesses an ethico-normative character, seeking to explore the aspects of social reality which violate the 'conditions which constitute a necessary presupposition for a good life among us' (Honneth, 2004: 338). Pathology diagnosing research is structured and developed to provide such a 'thicker' form of social criticism. The problems which the social world faces today go far beyond injustices and illegitimacies of rule. We are facing impending climatic catastrophe. What is required is a theoretical apparatus capable of engaging with the fundamental ends to which our society is oriented.

Second, through its conceptual sophistication, and its syncretic amalgam of insights from a range of traditions, pathology diagnosing critical theory enables a research programme which connects the desires of subjects, dynamics of political economy, and the forms of reason which dominate. Through an analysis of the logics of consensual validation and repressive desublimation, critical theory possesses the tools to provide an interdisciplinary macro-sociological analysis exactly when it is most needed. Global warming is not merely an economic problem, neither can it be understood solely through psychoanalysis, political theory, psychology, or empirical sociology. What is required is a research project capable of uniting insights from these disciplines in a coherent manner, while sensitive to disciplinary variation. The meta-methodological foundation of 'immanent-transcendence' enables such an amalgam. Pathology diagnosing research is uniquely powerful as it is able to provide coherent interdisciplinary normative-explanatory social critique, such as repressive desublimation, on the basis of its shared Hegelian-Marxism.

Thirdly, pathology diagnosing critique seeks to simultaneously diagnose the contradictions of the social totality and the obstacles inhibiting their transcendence within the same analysis. As I discuss at length in Chapter 6, Erich Fromm's account of 'pathological normalcy' typifies this conceptual purchase. When done well, pathology diagnosing critique is able to disclose both the pathological nature of our normal social world, but equally the means through which such a pathological world comes to be normalised. Critical theorists thus work to expose both the pathological nature of the everyday functioning of the social whole, and the pathological manner in which such a contradictory society manifests as normal and natural.

When taken together, I consider these to be remarkable strengths. Pathology diagnosing social research enables a vital critique of the social world. With the ever-pressing threat of climate change and with rapidly accelerating global economic inequities, the necessity for such potent critique is immediately apparent. We live in a complicated and precarious moment, as such social researchers seeking to get to grips with the nature of our social problems require a multifaceted theoretical infrastructure. Social pathology diagnosis offers the only social-theoretical foundation capable of simultaneously diagnosing the objective problems of our way of life and the obstacles to progressive transformation within a singular conceptual apparatus. Critical theorists cannot permit these vital foundations to become 'domesticated' at a time when normative-diagnostic and disclosing social research is needed more than ever.

Notes

1. As will be discussed in Chapter 3, even this is no longer so clear-cut, with Axel Honneth's *Freedom's Right* offering a radical demarcation of 'social pathology' and introducing an entirely new conceptual framing of 'misdevelopments'.
2. In keeping with Whitehead's famous claim, Frederick Neuhouser (2012) has connected the discussion of the 'fevered' city in the *Republic* to Rousseau's diagnosis of society suffering from a pathologically 'inflamed' *'amour-propre'* two millennia later.
3. For an excellent introduction to Hegel's method and its influence on Marx, see Marcuse's *Reason and Revolution: Hegel and the Rise of Social Theory* (1969).
4. As per the afterword to the second German edition of *Capital*, Vol. 1. The full quote is, 'The mystification which dialectic suffers in Hegel's hands, by no means prevents him from being the first to present its general form of working in a comprehensive and conscious manner. With him it is standing on its head. It must be turned right side up again, if you would discover the rational kernel within the mystical shell.'
5. The *DSM* is the *Diagnostic and Statistical Manual of Mental Disorders*. It is the 'bible' for clinical psychiatrists, offering a widely accepted taxonomy of psychopathologies.
6. This reading of Freud, profoundly influential to Fromm and subsequent critical theorists, can be traced to Georg Groddeck (1929).
7. For an excellent indicative study, see Freyenhagen's *Adorno's Practical Philosophy: Living Less Wrongly* (2013).
8. This formed the basis of the so-called *Dissent* dispute, discussed further in Chapter 7.
9. Foucault wrote the introduction to the 1991 edition cited above.
10. Allen Ginsberg may perhaps be the most plausible connecting thread between Frankfurt School inflected pathology diagnosing research and Krishnamurti, having presented an iconoclastic recital of *Howl* during his visit to Banaras Hindu University.
11. I am thinking here of *Revolutionary Road* (1961) in particular.
12. For instance, both attended the 'Congress on the Dialectics of Liberation' in 1967 at the Roundhouse Theatre in London (see Cooper, 2015).
13. Yet the 'disclosing nature' of Ginsberg's verse is not in question. M. L. Rosenthal observes that Ginsberg 'brought a terrible psychological reality to the surface' (Parini and Miller, 1994).
14. Holton has argued that framings such as social pathology have become 'pervasive' in social theory; they have 'become devalued and confused' (see Holton, 1987: 502).
15. For an extended analysis of the Marxist rejection of organicism, see Jay, 1984: 27. For an analysis of the liberal rejection of organicism, see Casillo (1992).
16. Referring to Michael Burleigh and Wolfgang Wippermann (1991).
17. The 'explosive charge' of critical theory is how Honneth (2004: 338) memorably framed 'social pathology'.

2

Distorted by recognition

Axel Honneth's work has been at the forefront of critical theory for over three decades (see Petherbridge, 2013; van den Brink and Owen, 2007; Deranty, 2009; Zurn, 2011, 2015). Martin Jay, renowned historian of the Frankfurt School, wrote that Honneth's critical theory is 'ingenious and provocative' (Jay, 2008: 3). Judith Butler considered it 'an honour' to engage with his work and has written that she can 'hardly do justice to the complexity of the theory' he has produced (2008: 97). Developing Jürgen Habermas's 'intersubjective turn', Honneth provided the foundations for a new critical theory of society, centred upon the subject's experiences of 'misrecognition' (Honneth, 1995 [1992]). For Honneth, recognition relationships provide the optimal entry point for social research (see also McNay, 2008: 47). The subject's experience of denied recognition, of intersubjective 'disrespect', is held to possess remarkable insight, signalling a disconnect between society's 'moral grammar' and the contingent norms of its practices and institutions (Honneth, 1995 [1992]: xviii, 166). Honneth's critical theory of recognition is clearly distinguished by its investment in a politics and scholarship focused exclusively on *recognition*.

Despite its remarkable (and at times, toe-curling) reception, I argue that Honneth's work fails on its own terms and represents a betrayal of the original aims of critical theory. By drawing upon the work of Michael J. Thompson, Nancy Fraser, and Lois McNay, I argue that Honneth's critical theory actually serves to retrench existing privileges and fails to provide an immanent critique of society. Further, I contend that Honneth's account is not merely philosophically and social-theoretically flawed, but politically problematic: implicitly supporting vested interests, and reneging on the transformative aspirations of a critical theory of society. While these may seem highly charged provocations, I am far from the first to identify reactionary inflections within Honneth's critical theory. Michael J. Thompson (2016) has argued that Honneth's work continues a broader 'domestication' of critical theory initiated by Habermas, while Stathis Kouvelakis (2019) holds Honneth's account to be central to a wider 'defeat' of social critique.

While Chapter 1 drew out the distinctive normative power of pathology diagnosing social research, here in Chapter 2 I unite and extend existing critical voices to demonstrate the etiolated condition of contemporary critical theory. In Chapter 3, I come to the crux of my own distinctive contribution to this debate, demonstrating how Honneth's approach has percolated through to the social-theoretical foundations of critical theory, eroding the pathology diagnosing bedrock of Frankfurt School research. Part I of *Critical Theory and Social Pathology* thus demonstrates the necessity of renewing pathology diagnosing social research and the urgency of displacing Honneth's recognition approach.

What is 'recognition'?

Defining 'recognition' is extremely challenging. Paul Ricoeur (2005: 5–16) has identified as many as twenty-three distinct understandings within the scholarly literature, demonstrating the scale of the task. While the commonplace verb 'to recognise' typically means 'to identify' (as in 'I recognise that bird as a puffin'), 'recognition' carries a secondary meaning closer to 'I acknowledge' (as in 'I recognise your right to your own views'). One thus speaks more formally of 'recognition' of statehood, or of human rights. The German, *Anerkennung*, also carries multiple meanings; however, it centres this process of *acknowledgement* bearing *status attribution*. It is this productive intersubjective praxis which is crucial to recognition theory.

Of the many attempts to define 'recognition', Onni Hirvonen's framing is perhaps the most accessible. For Hirvonen, 'recognition' is a 'positive status attribution that happens *between persons* and which also *constitutes* those persons' (Hirvonen, 2015: 210 – original italics). A distinctive feature of intersubjective recognition is that it is 'subjectifying'; simultaneously both 'responsive to personhood' and crucially also constitutive of it (Hirvonen, 2015: 210). To be 'recognised' is thus to have 'subject' status conferred and acknowledged. As Heikki Ikäheimo has detailed, it is this mutually constitutive feature of the recognition relationship which informs the ontological commitments of the critical theory of recognition (Ikäheimo, 2007: 227).

The orthodox account traces the birth of recognition theory to the post-Kantian philosophies of Fichte and Hegel (Laitinen, Särkelä, and Ikäheimo, 2015: 3). While the Kantian subject was independently conjured into the social ether, for Fichte and Hegel, subjectivation, and especially self-consciousness, necessitated a social component. As Laitinen et al. draw out, Fichte and Hegel came to hold that it was only 'through recognition of others ... [that] ... individuals begin to relate to themselves and their environment' (Laitinen, Särkelä, and Ikäheimo, 2015: 3). The idea of a 'recognition moment' is thus central to the development of Western philosophy, marking the 'sociologising' of Kantian thought (Kok and Van Houdt, 2014).

Central to this post-Kantian turn is the much discussed tale of 'lordship and bondage' (*Herrschaft und Knechtschaft*), or 'master and slave', in Chapter 4 of Hegel's *Phenomenology of Spirit* (Hegel, 1977 [1807]: Chapter 4). The famous 'struggle for recognition' (*Kampf um Annerkunnung*) centres the themes of dependency and dominance within the recognition dyad (Kelly, 1966). The unifying narrative in the *Phenomenology* is the development of 'self-consciousness', and the recognition struggle proves a central point in this progression. Hegel's prose is inaccessible and open to competing interpretations; however, the central facts of the parable can be summarily distilled. An abstract self-consciousness, until now finding the world entirely constituted of 'objects', encounters another 'independent existence' (Hegel, 1977: paragraph 182; 112). Such an encounter is horrific, psychologically scarring, and sparks an existential struggle. Both beings understand that they will only retain their dominance through the other acknowledging their unique 'subject' status. A conflictual dance ensues in which both try to outflank the other, to establish supremacy as the sole self-conscious being. The fear of being reduced to 'object' status relative to a self-conscious Other is overwhelming. This encounter descends into a struggle to the death, for total domination of the Other. Yet this desire for destruction of the Other is quickly acknowledged to also be inadequate, offering merely an abstract negation; it will not serve to re-legitimate the subject's sense of unique self-consciousness. Death is feared and undesirable. Eventually, an inequitable truce emerges, with the existential struggle placed on hold through the acceptance of one party to bondage, to slave status. The temporary cessation of hostilities is shown to enable an unsatisfactory acknowledgement of both parties' status as self-conscious beings. The master requires the slave to acknowledge the master's consciousness, while the slave's enfeebled self-certainty persists through the knowledge that, despite his lowly status, his recognition remains essential to the master's self-consciousness. Yet, such an equation remains inadequate for true self-consciousness to flourish, the slave grants the master recognition only due to his fear of death. There is a twist in the tale, though, with redemption for the slave: as the slave toils, he comes to recognise his subject status through the products of his labour. Through his sweat and hardship, the slave realises that he shapes the world around him, and this realisation induces a form of renewed self-consciousness. In contrast, the master becomes ever more dependent on the products of the slave's labour, leading to the ironic enslavement of the master to the toil of his own slave. Such a reversal has been extensively analysed by Marxist scholars,[1] although Marx's own analysis on the slave's change in fortunes is ambiguous.[2]

While this tale has been interpreted in countless ways, from Kojève (1980 [1947]) to Brandom (2019), the primary lesson Hegel offers is that the development of self-consciousness is *social*. Intersubjective and symmetrical recognition is the optimal outcome of social interaction, and Hegel's subsequent *Philosophy of Right* outlined how a society might be structured to enable the mutual recognition of all subjects in a rationally organised society.

Recognition theorists all owe an outstanding *philosophical* debt to Hegel. Yet, as a distinctly sociological-political agenda, 'recognition' matured with the accessible prose of Charles Taylor (1992). While Axel Honneth remains the figure most intimately associated with 'recognition' today,[3] it was Charles Taylor's *Multiculturalism and the Politics of Recognition* which brought recognition to the forefront of the activist-academic imagination (Heywood, 2007: 316; Martineau, Meer, and Thompson, 2012: 2). Taylor introduced recognition as a useful perspective through which to comprehend the demands of the 'new social movements' of the late 1980s and early 1990s. For Taylor, recognition is the ideal framing through which to understand 'identity' and its associated politics. As Taylor worded it, identity, recognition, and social being are closely connected; living in a social world without due recognition can 'inflict harm, can be a form of oppression, imprisoning someone in a false, distorted, and reduced mode of being' (Taylor, 1992: 25).[4]

The intersubjective turn in critical theory

While Taylor drew on Hegel on Fichte, his work remained outside the ambit of Frankfurt School critical theory. Taylor was not primarily invested in Freudo-Marxian insights, and his contribution is chiefly located within communitarianism and political philosophy. As such, the 'recognition turn' came to critical theory more as a development of the pre-existing 'intersubjective turn', based upon the work of Jürgen Habermas.

Habermas sought to overcome the perceived 'productivist bias' of first-generation critical theory and to dispense with its metaphysical assumptions. Instead of according primacy to Hegel and Marx, Habermas invested in alternative traditions, bridging continental and analytic philosophy, American pragmatics, systems theory, developmental psychology, and a plurality of other social theoretical approaches (Fultner, 2011: 4). In *The Theory of Communicative Action*, Habermas's (1984, 1987 [1981]) aim was to reconstruct 'reason', not as some transcendent ontological substrate, but as an empirically verifiable form of intersubjective praxis.

Communication was not just presented as an opportune entry point for researching the social world. Rather, like recognition theorists to come, Habermas identified within the intersubjective moment the possibility for radical emancipatory praxis. Habermas developed an understanding of 'communicative action' – expanded upon at length in Volume Two of *The Theory of Communicative Action* – which was associated with the transmission of cultural knowledge and oriented towards achieving productive mutual understanding. 'Communicative action' was to become the core of much of Habermas's subsequent scholarship, with integrative exchange being traced within the various corners of the lifeworld, such as democratic institutions and legal systems. Habermas's mature critical theory centred upon tracking the threat posed by the colonising logics of the (economic) 'system' to the 'lifeworlds' spaces of communicative exchange. In stark contrast to the flare of first-generation Hegelian-Marxian eschatology, Habermas's idealised social world was a more prosaic 'ideal speech situation': where subjects have equal opportunity to engage in public-sphere communication.[5] While the specifics of Habermas's critical theory are not the focus of this book, one can surmise that Habermas's work reoriented critical theory towards processes of intersubjective exchange through his investment in communicative action.

Honneth's critical theory of recognition

The 'recognition turn' in critical theory clearly had two principal antecedents. Habermas had brought forth an intersubjective turn in Frankfurt School research, while simultaneously 'recognition' had developed a broad socio-political traction, primarily through the work of Charles Taylor. Axel Honneth's critical theory of recognition served to thread together these twin developments, bringing recognition to the foreground of Frankfurt School research. Today, Honneth's *The Struggle for Recognition* is 'generally acknowledged' as 'presenting the most ambitious agenda ... utilizing the idea of recognition' in contemporary social theory (Laitinen, Särkelä, and Ikäheimo, 2015: 6). As such 'recognition' is now primarily associated with Axel Honneth and critical theory.

Previous theorists invested in the notion of recognition, from Rousseau to Hegel to Taylor, saw some variation of a primary intersubjective dyad as essential to self-consciousness, or to the rise of '*amour-propre*', or to the acknowledgement of difference within multicultural society. In contrast, Honneth's approach is distinct in its claim to capture the social totality through recognition theory alone. As Varga and Gallagher (2012) see it, Honneth's theory opened the door to a species of social critique which claims to analyse society *in toto* on the basis of the forms of 'primary intersubjective' recognition relations. Honneth's claim is thus spectacular in the comparative breadth of his engagement with recognition. His critical theory has been referred to repeatedly as recognition 'monist', as he claims the ability to explain the entirety of social action through a unitary recognition perspective (Fraser and Honneth, 2001: 214). Honneth's critical theory is thus remarkable, if nothing else, through the largesse of its purported explanatory and critical capacity. For Alexander and Lara, this is what distinguishes Honneth's recognition theory: the claim to have constructed an entire critical theory of society derived solely from the central tenets of recognition (Alexander and Lara, 1995). Martineau, Meer, and Thompson are thus among the many scholars to comment on *The Struggle for Recognition* as presenting a truly radical expansion of recognition theorising (Martineau, Meer, and Thompson, 2012: 3).

Extending ideas first expressed in his *Kritik der Macht*, Honneth sought to develop a new critical theory, free 'from ... [the] ... exclusive focus on the domain of material production' (Anderson, 1995: xi). In short, Honneth wanted critical theory to move beyond a perceived restrictive focus on labour and on capitalism, and to analyse the social world through a broader aperture. In contrast to the perceived past productivism, Honneth posited a 'primal dyad' which 'lies at the heart of social relations' (McNay, 2008: 47). Anchoring himself in Hegel's classic parable, Honneth saw the recognition of subject A by subject B, and vice versa, as the optimal entry point to social reality as it marked the genesis of social being. As McNay words it, central to Honneth's account is the belief that society is best comprehended, not as a locus of intersecting productive or reproductive logics, but fundamentally as 'extrapolations of psychic dynamics' (McNay, 2008: 138). As presaged above, Honneth's critical theory of recognition presents all social encounters, including the economic, as intersubjective processes. In the words of Honneth's long-term translator, Joel Anderson, *The Struggle for Recognition* truly sought to provide an 'alternative account' to preceding critical theories (Anderson, 1995: xi).

Displacing the perceived 'economistic' historical materialism of his predecessors, Honneth's (1992) *Kampf um Annerkunnung* centres 'struggles for recognition' within Frankfurt School research. To achieve this, Honneth radically extended a previously neglected line of Hegel's scholarship, dating to the philosopher's time in Jena. As Anderson framed it, 'Honneth takes from Hegel the idea that full human flourishing is dependent on the existence of well-established, "ethical" relations – in particular, relations of love, law, and "ethical life" (*Sittlichkeit*), which can only be established through a conflict-ridden developmental process, specifically, through a struggle for recognition' (Anderson, 1995: xi).

Honneth's project brought Hegel's Jena-period insights into dialogue with Mead and Winnicott, uniting sociology, psychoanalysis, and empirical psychology to advance the merits of viewing the social whole as a latticework of recognition relations. Anchored in a purportedly empirically verifiable formal anthropology, Honneth presented law, the market, and systems of familial and erotic love as sites for the provision of essential forms of recognition. As a result, Honneth united otherwise disparately theorised struggles within a singular rubric, arguing that all feelings of 'disrespect' and 'injustice' are commonly structured 'relational disorders' that should optimally be 'assessed within the categories of mutual recognition' (Honneth, 1995 [1992]: 106).

Honneth's primary categorisation is threefold, viewing recognition claims as relating principally to the desires for (i) love, (ii) respect, and (iii) esteem, relating accordingly to the family, the marketplace, and the legal system. Crucially, the market is framed as a manifestation of intersubjective relations, rather than as driven by a distinct, pathological rationality, or by a finite series of impersonal economic laws or dynamics. For Honneth, one must thus 'speak of capitalist society as an institutionalised recognition order' (Fraser and Honneth, 2001: 137). Demands for alternate distributions of risks and rewards within the social world, be it an extension of housing benefit, or a desire to avoid redundancy as a result of a corporate merger, need to be framed as struggles for recognition. From such a position, the market is not driven primarily by a capitalist logic of accumulation; rather, crucially, recognition provides an entry point to *all* social realms. Demands for redistribution are not seen as being qualitatively distinct, rather, they are just a 'specific kind of struggle for recognition in which the appropriate evaluation of the social contributions of individuals or groups is contested' (Fraser and Honneth, 2001: 171). As stressed above, for Honneth, the entirety of conflict within the social world truly can be grasped as 'the expression of struggles for recognition' (Fraser and Honneth, 2001: 137).

Honneth's account was supremely attractive to a generation of critical theorists at a particular historical moment – in the wake of the fall of the Berlin Wall and a widespread dismissal of Marxism(s). Honneth's framing purported to offer a unified framework through which the social totality can be researched which no longer afforded a perceived undue primacy to productive forces within society. His theory of recognition appeared as a way of keeping critical theory alive in the new socio-political landscape. Better still, Honneth's account was presented not as a retreat to the 'ivory tower', but was seen to be providing an accessible and immanent entry point to social research. By simply asking subjects about their experiences of disrespect and misrecognition the researcher could purportedly explore the normative grammar of the social world and its contingent limitations.

Philosophically, Honneth's account appeared to present a further boon, seemingly resolving the normative challenge hampering broader social philosophy and social research in a manner sensitive to cultural variation. Recognition thus features in Honneth's account as more than merely an accessible entry point for social critique. Rather, for Honneth, recognition provides a normative anchor, presenting the objective, formal conditions for a conception of ethical life, enabling comparative ethico-normative judgements to be passed (Honneth, 1995 [1992]: 171). For Honneth (1995 [1992]), there are clear, essential intersubjective conditions necessary for subjects to enjoy personal integrity. The denial of these basic intersubjective conditions is held to be a breach of a fundamental normative grammar which must be respected. Honneth's framing is attractive to many because it presents a necessary set of preconditions for a flourishing existence in the associated forms of recognition (love, respect, esteem); however, the manner through which these are attained is open to cultural difference. As Honneth (1995 [1992]: 175) words it, from such a theory, 'what can count as an intersubjective prerequisite for a successful life becomes historically variable'.

The attractions of Honneth's approach are obvious; in place of a perceived productivist bias and outmoded Marxism, a new critical theory was presented, capable of comprehending the totality of social struggles through a new, normatively undergirded foundation. The critical theory of recognition was presented as enabling an easy entry point for immanent social criticism, offering an approach which is formally normative while sensitive to substantive socio-cultural variation. Through a singular theoretical perspective and accessible vocabulary, which had a pre-existing activist and scholarly popularity, Honneth's approach seemed ideal for a new generation of critical theorists. Reeling from bearing witness to the proclaimed 'end of history', threatened by the increasing hegemony of Rawlsian ideal theory, and increasingly lacking a revolutionary subject, many Frankfurt School researchers embraced Honneth's project as nothing short of an intellectual salvation.

False promises of recognition

Yet, upon publication, Honneth's critical theory proved highly contested. More than two decades later, the academy remains deeply divided as to the merits of Honneth's recognition framework, which, as the next chapter demonstrates, continues to dominate critical theory today. It is worth reemphasising that almost all academics identify some utility in a recognition heurism. Indeed, some of Honneth's most vocal critics explicitly champion recognition as a vital component in their own social research.⁶ What is crucial, and central to most criticisms, is the distinctively *monistic* nature of Honneth's account – his central claim being that recognition theory, without need of any accompanying philosophical, sociological, or politico-economic support, offers a means of understanding the social world in its entirety. It is this claim to have found a singular framework through which to advance a critique of all societal domains, a proclaimed optimal 'perspectival monism', which is particularly divisive.

As I argue below, drawing on Thompson, Fraser, and McNay, and various decolonial theorists, Honneth's perspectival monism is fundamentally flawed and precipitates political, philosophical, and social-theoretical complications. To many scholars, it is highly contentious whether we shall ever see a singular critical perspective which can capture all social struggles. Honneth's critical theory of recognition certainly does not succeed in this ambition.

The social world is not a recognition order

At the core of Honneth's approach is the belief that 'recognition must represent the unified framework' for contemporary critical theory (Fraser and Honneth, 2001: 113). Thus, a fatal flaw in Honneth's account is the obvious counter-claim there are many crucial facets of society which have 'little to do with recognition' (Fraser and Honneth, 2001: 35). This is immediately obvious when one considers the capitalist marketplace. For Honneth, 'distributional injustices must be understood as the institutional expression of social disrespect – or, better said, of unjustified relations of recognition' (Fraser and Honneth, 2001: 114). As Fraser, Thompson, and McNay have demonstrated, this is patently absurd. Honneth's social theory demands the researcher views recognition as the 'fundamental overarching' social category, with all other dynamics merely 'derivative' (Fraser and Honneth, 2001: 2–3). Such an account serves 'to subsume the problematic of redistribution (*inter alia*) within' the recognition theoretical optic (Fraser and Honneth, 2001: 3). This is unviable. One cannot view the market as merely epiphenomenal to relations of recognition. As Fraser beautifully articulates,

> the economic logic of the market interacts in complex ways with the cultural logic of recognition, sometimes instrumentalising existing status distinctions, sometimes dissolving or circumventing them, and sometimes creating new ones. As a result, market mechanisms give rise to economic class relations that are not mere reflections of status hierarchies.
>
> Neither those relations nor the mechanisms that generate them can be understood by recognition monism. An adequate approach must theorize

both the distinctive dynamics of the capitalist economy and its interaction with the status order. (Fraser and Honneth, 2001: 214)

Fraser's account is altogether more convincing: quite simply, 'not all maldistribution is a by-product of misrecognition' (Fraser and Honneth, 2001: 35). As Fraser suggests, the 'distinguishing feature' of capitalist modernity is the 'creation of a quasi-autonomous, impersonal market order that follows a logic of its own': a logic which is not merely epiphenomenal to the given society's recognition order (Fraser and Honneth, 2001: 24). Rather, one must consider

> the supply and demand for different types of labor; the balance of power between labor and capital; the stringency of social regulations, including the minimum wage; the availability and cost of productivity enhancing technologies; the ease with which firms can shift their operations to locations where wage rates are lower; the cost of credit; the terms of trade; and international currency exchange rates. (Fraser and Honneth, 2001: 215)

Such processes, central to contemporary society, are not primarily intersubjective. *Pace* Honneth, they cannot be productively theorised as such. The generative mechanisms of social status and the generative mechanisms of wealth are distinct, yet interconnected. Neither can be adequately theorised in isolation, and neither over-determines the other. Such a claim is not to unduly privilege an analysis of production within society at the expense of recognition and identity claims. Rather, it seems obvious that one must analyse both the status-order of society and its distributive mechanisms. The market cannot be adequately theorised without an analysis of recognition relations; yet, neither can the study of recognition relationships alone provide an adequate study of the market. Fraser illustrates this by way of a powerful example, asking her reader to consider a skilled, privileged, white male worker, who is loved, respected, esteemed, and rewarded in all aspects of his life. Yet, as a result of a speculative corporate merger, the man is made redundant. His competency, status, wit, affection, and standing are not central to his dismissal. His redundancy is not a result of a loss of interpersonal recognition. Rather, the market is a manifestation of quasi-autonomous dynamics, which are *not* epiphenomenal to the status order. By comprehending all institutional logics as derivative of (a) foundational intersubjective dyad(s), Honneth's critical theory of recognition fails to provide purchase for a meaningful analysis of crucial features of the social world.

Neo-Idealism: power precedes recognition

In addition to the social-theoretical limitations of recognition theory, outlined above, Michael J. Thompson and Lois McNay have both targeted the 'reductive understanding of power' manifest in Honneth's account (McNay, 2008: 2). Honneth presents the recognition dyad as the genesis of social power relations. For McNay (2008: 138), there is a 'unidirectional causal dynamic' to Honneth's 'ontology of recognition', with society being held to be nothing more than 'extrapolations of psychic dynamics'. The recognitive encounter between subjects A and B is held to be the foundational core of all social integration, of social power, and of social being. Both Thompson and McNay carefully deconstruct the limitations of this account, demonstrating how Honneth's critical theory is predicated on a deficient understanding of power. In summary, for Honneth, the social world starts with intersubjective recognition: recognition comes first. Intersubjective relations are held to be the necessary point of departure for any analysis of the social world. Yet, such a framing is blind to the complexity of factors which shape the subject's consciousness, impacting the subject's capacity, or inclination, to recognise other subjects. In contrast, Honneth's theory presupposes an impenetrable subject, untarnished by power relations or ideology, capable of entering intersubjective relations, absent any influence from society more broadly.

In contrast, Michael J. Thompson reminds us that a central insight of Frankfurt School critical theory is that 'power relations rooted in capitalist forms of economic life structure the deeper socialization processes that shape the cognitive dimension of the personality of subjects' (Thompson, 2016: 64). Honneth's approach is held to suffer from a problematic 'neo-Idealism', blind to the social dynamics and structures shaping subjectivity that 'pulse beneath the surface of everyday life' (Thompson, 2016: 7). For Thompson, critical theorists must pay attention to the 'potency of social power, rooted in the material organization of social life' (Thompson, 2016: 15). Thompson (2016: 15) defines neo-Idealism as '[a school of thought where] … thinkers proceed from the premise that *there is a self-sufficiency* to the powers of intersubjective reason, discourse, structures of justification, and recognition' (my italics).

Honneth's account is unsalvageable as the primacy he affords to recognition necessitates investing 'modern subjects with powers of rationality … [which they] … simply cannot possess' (Thompson, 2016: 5). In direct opposition to the founding insight of Frankfurt School research, Honneth's theory 'detaches itself from a theory of socialization that is actually fused to the concrete structures of social power and its capacity to shape consciousness and cognition' (Thompson, 2016: 3).

Honneth clearly overinvests in recognition. Social subjects are impacted by the constitutive power of the social world, which shapes ideas, values, and cognitive capacities. The subject does not have a pure, unmediated ability to enter into intersubjective relationships (through any form of dyadic praxis: recognition, judgement, communication). Rather, social power pervades subjectivation and shapes consciousness. As McNay (2008: 47–48) framed it, Honneth's 'ontology of recognition understands the sources of inequality as generated through an interpersonal dynamic of struggle, but this face to face dynamic is disconnected from a socio-structural account of power'.

Critical theorists must not forget that power relations are not merely a 'post-hoc effect' of intersubjective praxis (McNay, 2008: 47). Rather, power shapes the foundational epistemic capacities and desires of social subjects. In direct contrast to Honneth's account, and supporting Thompson and McNay, I claim that social power exists prior to intersubjective relationships. Honneth's account must be dismissed as irredeemably neo-Idealist, blind to the impact of socio-structural constitutive power on the subject. Honneth's account is causally inaccurate and blind to how power operates: recognition relationships must be understood as a manifestation of antecedent constitutive powers impacting the subject, the result of interconnected social-structural dynamics. Power does not start with recognition; rather, the subject's predilection for, and ability to enter into, intersubjective relationships is a result of antecedent socialisation processes, which prefigure the recognition moment. One thus cannot commence upon social research through a recognition monist framework.

A false universalism

A further appeal of Honneth's recognition theory is the purported universality of the intersubjective dyad. Recall that for Honneth, all subjects are held to require set forms of recognition. McNay, Fraser, and Fanon help disclose the problematic nature of this claim; reminding us that, *pace* Honneth, socio-cultural variation throws up a range of atypical relationships and that the reality of many non-Western subjects simply does not fit within Honneth's template. For example, in light of the experiences of children, and those with learning difficulties, it is instantly apparent that there is no homogeneity to the forms of intersubjective praxis required to live a happy and meaningful life. To speak of demands for 'love', 'respect', and 'esteem' would be absurd in the case of many subjects with serious cognitive impairments. However, crucially, such subjects demonstrate a tremendous sensitivity to their intersubjective exchanges, benefiting from a plurality of forms of dyadic praxis. Children with advanced special educational needs may benefit from the mutual experience of sensory exploration, for example. This can be crucial to their intersubjective life and to the development of a sophisticated sense of self-worth. Such subjects may lack the cognitive capacities to enter into Honneth's typical recognition relationships; however, their subject status must be stoutly defended, both political and philosophically. In short, one can identify groups of subjects who do not fit within Honneth's account, whose personhood and social consciousness must be robustly defended. This matters, as it is crucial that critical theorists do not present approaches to social research as working universally, only to exclude some of the most vulnerable people within society. In the example above, it is clear that many subjects who benefit from nuanced forms of intersubjective praxis do not engage in the form of status-attributional recognition relationship described by Honneth.

While one may present young children and adults with learning difficulties as 'exceptional cases' to Honneth's universal dyad, a further structural challenge comes in the form of the struggles of the colonial subject. When the critical theorist reflects on coloniality, the 'ahistorical' and 'reductive' nature of Honneth's approach becomes even more apparent (McNay, 2008: 24). Fanon's *Black Skin, White Masks* helps to illustrate the problems of entrenching the 'primacy of recognition anthropologically, below the level of historical contingency' (Fraser and Honneth, 2001: 206). As Fanon (1967 [1952]): 60) words it, the 'crushing object-hood' of 'blackness' locks the colonial subject into oppressive psychic dynamics. *Pace* Honneth, there is no potential for transcendence or emancipation through intersubjective praxis for the colonial subject. The fundamental emancipatory dyadic relationship is unattainable in the contingent lifeworld of the colonial subject. Fanon teaches us that the colonial subject is never acknowledged as a self-conscious being; they are locked into a state of permanent, crushing immanence. The slave's struggle is not a personal desire for recognition; such a framing is meaningless. The struggle is 'not personal but social' (cf. Fraser and Honneth, 2001: 55). Crucially, the absence of the conditions of possibility for recognition does not preclude the possibility of radical, agentival subjectivities, capable of myriad political acts of resistance.

Normative chaos

By anchoring his critical theory in a formal anthropology, Honneth contends that recognition offers a normative grounding for social research. By focusing upon the subject's feelings of disrespect, critical theorists can ostensibly track the 'normative objectives of emancipatory movements' while retaining an 'objective' distance. The key components enabling such 'objectivity' to Honneth's approach are thus the normative grammar of recognition, built upon his formal anthropology (Fraser and Honneth, 2001: 113). Intersubjective practices of recognition which fail to enable the subject to experience 'love', 'respect', or 'esteem' can then be held to be objectively 'wrong'. However, Honneth's claim can be instantly challenged as it is immediately obvious that there are both 'justified and unjustified claims for recognition' (Fraser and Honneth, 2001: 27). A further complication is that rival claims to recognition often exist which may be mutually incompatible. For Honneth, a clear 'moral injustice is at hand whenever, contra to their expectations, human subjects are denied the recognition they feel they deserve' (Honneth, 2007: 71). But how does the researcher productively operationalise this in the messiness of social reality? How does the researcher weigh competing claims for recognition?

By way of an example, consider a male blue-collar worker who is in an abusive relationship with his partner who is not employed in the formal labour market. Upon returning home from a day's paid work, the husband may misogynistically demand recognition, framed as 'love', for his paid labour by receiving a hot meal, sexual satisfaction, general propitiations, and obedience in a patriarchal and reactionary manner. In contrast, the housewife may demand 'esteem' for her many hours of domestic labour, which may be even more laborious, viewing her own contributions as greater, or merely 'equal but different'. The conflict in terms of unequal valuations of labour manifests in competing claims to recognition. How does the recognition theorist determine which account is correct through a recognition lens? How, using the terms of recognition alone, can the claim to 'esteem' from the misogynist be denied, while the claim for the recognition of care labour as labour be acknowledged? Such judgement fundamentally requires a further normative infrastructure. Put simply: the purported anthropological need for recognition is not enough to arbitrate between rival claims for recognition.

More problematically still, how does the recognition theorist respond to the case above where the abused partner has been socialised to acquire her intersubjective recognition through a limiting, extractive, sexually abusive relationship? Feminists have often spoken of the challenges of victims who do not comprehend their abuse: their partner hits them 'because they love them'. While the radicalised partner may be aware of their oppression and may struggle for due recognition, how does the recognition theorist engage with the reality that multiply marginalised subjects are socialised to find satisfaction and recognition within inequitable and often abusive power relationships? The abused wife who accepts sexual violence as a form of 'love' from her partner, who feels a sense of love through her quiet endurance of coerced acts, does not register on the radar of recognition theory. She feels recognised; it is merely that the acts which provide her with recognition are themselves problematic.

Through the example of the abused wife who derives recognition from coerced sexual acts, the broader social-structural realities of power shine through. One's feeling of 'recognition' is not evidence of a justifiable normative grammar. As Berlant and McNay write, respectively, there is no 'prelapsarian knowledge', no 'pure', 'true', 'definite' entry point to studying oppression through some insight provided by recognition theory (Berlant, 2000: 43, cf. McNay, 2008: 141). The social world remains messy and complicated, competing claims for recognition require a further criterion for normative judgement, while many subjects accede to their circumstances without struggling for, what might seem to many to be, more equitable recognition relationships. Critical theorists should find none of this surprising. Once upon a time, critical theorists were aware that ideology existed! Subjects are conditioned by their circumstances. Honneth's neo-Idealism collapses in the normative chaos of social reality. The subject has no innate capacity to determine 'right' from 'wrong'; there is no universal normative grammar which can be accessed through analysing intersubjective recognition relationships. This is because, as Marx declared 150 years ago, 'It is not the consciousness of men that determines their existence, but their social existence that determines their consciousness' (Marx, 2010 [1859]: 92). Honneth's critical theory of recognition has forgotten this foundational lesson. The subject achieves consciousness within an ideological social world, where notions of 'right', 'norm', and 'natural' are social constructs, rather than offering an innate guide to some transcendent truth. Honneth's claims to having solved the theory immanent problem, and having located a normative anchor for social research within recognition, are unfounded. In contrast, Honneth's recognition monism 'serves more' to legitimate a 'metaphorical hall of mirrors for the self', where 'selves that are pathologically shaped by/through culture' are deemed aspirational, legitimate, and guides for normatively weighty critique (Thompson, 2016: 65).

Political chaos

Critical theory is, by definition, political, seeking the progressive transformation of the social world (Horkheimer, 2002). Honneth's account is presented as offering a way for critical theorists to achieve this objective by focusing social research on immanent social movements, supporting and analysing grassroots struggles (for recognition) (Fraser and Honneth, 2001: 113). The recognition approach should, therefore, enable a closer relationship between political campaigns and critical scholarship, advancing the socialist vision of a more equitable and more rational society. However, as Nancy Fraser draws out, the recognition turn has been catastrophic in terms of progressive political strategy and has demonstrably impeded anti-capitalist transition (Fraser, 1995).

Fraser notes that struggles for recognition increasingly seek favourable terms of *inclusion* for a group of subjects within the (capitalist, racist, patriarchal) social order. For instance, discriminated groups have typically sought recognition in the form of being granted legal personhood within capitalism, such as being granted the right to own property, to vote, or to equal marriage (Fraser, 1997: 126). For Fraser, recognition-oriented protests can serve to strengthen the hold of the economic structure: emboldening capitalist and anthropocentric logics by their co-option of the broader campaign and attendant erasure of redistributive demands. Fraser refers to a precipitant 'eclipse of … [the] … socialist imaginary centred on terms such as "interest", "exploitation", and "redistribution"' (Fraser, 2008: 12). For Fraser, one can draw a crude binary between 'transformative' movements which primarily seek a more rational *distribution* (of goods, resources etc.) within society, and groups which seek better social 'inclusion' on the basis of a perceived misrecognition (Fraser, 1995; see also: Fraser, 1997: 126). Obviously what socialist transition demands is *both* a more rational distribution *and* a more rational recognition order, or 'cultural recognition' and 'social equality' (Fraser, 2008: 69). However, Fraser teaches us that capitalism is very good at co-opting recognition movements in a manner which retrenches, rather than ameliorates, capitalist irrationality, 'displacing' campaigns for redistribution (Fraser, 2000: 107).

As such, a crucial challenge for progressive campaigns today is to avoid co-optation by neoliberal imperatives. There is a strong allure: movements for recognition which accede to the neoliberal consensus routinely achieve their goals, at the cost of inadvertently buttressing extractivist economic logics. For example, Gay Pride, while originally aligned with mining unions and demands for equitable distribution of wealth and a rational economy (Lemmey, 2020), has now become a 'parade', sponsored by Gilead (see Abad-Santos, 2018) and American Express (see Gutman, 2012). Support for Pride, once a frontline organisation challenging capitalist exploitation, has now become an advertising mainstay for many transnational corporations. Pride demonstrates the fate of a cultural politics of recognition, and justifies Fraser's critique of unidimensional recognition campaigns.

Interestingly, in contrast, Black Lives Matter (BLM) has refused to focus solely on recognition demands and retains an incendiary hostility to the carceral-capitalist system in the United States (Woodward, 2020). As such, BLM holds its revolutionary 'transformative' potential, seeking not just increased legal recognition ('inclusion'), but also proudly demanding redistribution in the form of an end of the indentured labour of the US prison system ('transformation') (see Lawrence, 2015). Perhaps the epitome of such redistributive demands is the call for reparations for centuries of slavery. But thirty pieces of silver are glittering; hawkish neoliberal organisations abound, seeking to co-opt the dynamism of BLM, hoping to displace its redistributive edge (Arnade, 2020). More broadly, the campaign for racial equality is being stripped of its redistributive dimension as it enters the political mainstream (Maqbool, 2020). For instance, the Football Association in the United Kingdom allows a focus on 'rights' and 'taking a knee', while distancing itself from BLM and from the movement's central redistributive calls (e.g. reparations, defunding the police) (see McInnes, 2021).

One sees a similar logic of co-optation and depoliticisation with attempts to 'decolonise' institutions. Decolonisation refers to campaigns to challenge 'racial' and epistemic hierarchies, and to draw attention to ongoing neo-colonial policies (Bhambra, Gebrial, Nişancıoğlu, 2018). While attempts to 'decolonise' curricula are increasingly mainstreamed, as it is readily commensurable with the liberal acknowledgement of difference, campaigns for material redistribution are quickly silenced (Saini, 2020). Through the case study of 'decolonisation' demands, one can witness the crude transformative-inclusive binary in action: demands for recognition of alternate 'perspectives' and 'epistemes' are increasingly acceded to. Indeed, a decolonial sensitivity can be packaged as a selling point. In contrast, campaigns to prevent the outsourcing of cleaning or security staff (overwhelmingly members of the racialised precariat), or demands for compensation for historical colonial oppression in the form of reparations, are quickly dismissed, and provoke extended and bitter struggles if pursued (Schwartz, 2017). The challenge for recognition theorists is that struggles which involve *both* demands for recognition and redistribution can be co-opted through an enthusiastic embrace of recognition demands – enabling certain subjects, epistemes, or subaltern histories – on the condition that demands for structural changes to distributional logics are displaced. Critical theorists risk backing a liberal politics of inclusion, typified by equality, diversity, and inclusion (EDI) initiatives, which can serve to further marginalise progressive actors seeking qualitative transformation of the mechanisms of wealth creation and distribution.

Fraser identifies a further political-strategic challenge arising, with critical theorists allying themselves to a politics according primacy to recognition claims. If the primary desire of a critical theory of society remains the creation of a more rational and less extractive society, activists will inevitably find themselves in contradictory alliances if they embrace a recognition-centric politics. A critical theorist invested in recognition campaigns for equal marriage, for example, might march with Pride on Saturday, an event sponsored by high finance, seeking fairer inclusion for gay people within capitalism. On Sunday, seeking 'recognition' of workers impossible within capitalism, and seeking socialist transition, they may march for an abolition of the class system – fundamentally incompatible with their demands for recognition *within* the system. In sum, a politics of recognition is open to co-optation, rife with contradiction, and open to 'domestication'. For Fraser, EDI-style initiatives which 'alter end state patterns of distribution and recognition without disturbing the underlying framework[s]' should be rejected in favour of truly 'transformative' approaches; campaigns seeking to overhaul the foundational social structures which determine distribution and esteem (Fraser, 1997: 128). The work of Young (and Honneth) should thus be rejected as little more than 'a brief for affirmative recognition', which actively impedes 'transformative redistribution' (Fraser, 1997: 128).

Political complicity

For Nancy Fraser, activist mobilisations around campaigns for recognition is just poor politics. Recognition claims are easily open to co-optation, and are forever at risk of collapsing into a strategic impasse. However, she raises a deeper concern: recognition theory is not simply poor at critiquing neoliberalism, rather, it actively 'represses the critique of political economy' and reproduces the prevailing 'neoliberal amnesia' (Fraser and Honneth, 2001: 198). Pushing the criticisms of Honneth's critical theory further, one can argue that 'recognition' theory is not merely poor at criticising capitalism, but that it actively seeks a compromise with market logics. For Honneth, the market can produce healthy recognition relationships, enabling subjects to feel esteemed (Honneth, 2014 [2011]: 208). Michael J. Thompson (2016: 1) is thus entirely justified to question whether recognition theory does more to 'inculcate conformity to the prevailing reality', than to advance radical political praxis. In short, the criticism of the politics of recognition needs to be expanded – it is more problematic than simply offering poor strategic foundations for advancing socialist transition. The more pressing concern is whether contemporary critical theorists invested in recognition truly desire such structural economic transformation to start with.

As Thompson (2016: 10) reminds us, the function of critical theory is to 'explode the reified forms of thought' inculcated by capitalist rationality. As such, the critical theorist must focus on the 'organised forms of power that reproduce social pathologies', paying close attention to capitalist dynamics and their constitutive impact on subjectivity (Thompson, 2016: 3). The focus is on capitalism as an unambiguously irrational and pathological social system. Lukács articulates this rousingly in *History and Class Consciousness*:

> Our intention here is to base ourselves on Marx's economic analyses and to proceed from there to a discussion of the problems growing out of the fetish character of commodities, both as an objective form and also as a subjective

stance corresponding to it. Only by understanding this can we obtain a clear insight into the ideological problems of capitalism and ... [possibilities for] ... its downfall. (Lukács, 1972 [1923]: 84)

A pure hostility to capitalism is explicit in this excerpt. The 'confrontation with the forms of organized power that reproduce social pathologies', as expressed by Thompson, is instantly visible (Thompson, 2016: 3). Reading Honneth, and contemporary recognition theorists, one questions whether socialist transition is still desired.[7] Capitalism is presented as offering forms of recognition which are themselves sufficient for subjects to live a good, happy life, experiencing 'love', 'respect', and 'esteem'. This appears to me to be absurd. To my mind, the increasingly exploitative nature of neoliberal capitalism, with its thriving gig economies and expanding detention centres, requires radical, excoriating criticism. The political complicity and relative comfort with which Honneth theorises neoliberalism is a theme which I return to, as this political 'domestication' is entirely reflected in the denaturing of contemporary critical theory's understanding of social pathology.

The allure of recognition theory

Considering the evident political, philosophical, and social-theoretical weaknesses of the dominant recognition perspective, the continuing allure of Honneth's critical theory today is worth investigating. As alluded to above, the move to centre Frankfurt School research around 'recognition', and to displace foundational Marxian insights, occurred within a poignant historical moment for progressive scholarship. The fall of the Berlin Wall, the world-historical failure of 'actually existing communism', and the relative period of stability within the capitalist economy, all served to add to the appeal of Honneth's non-Marxian perspective. Further, the broader rise of political and cultural movements centring identity led to Honneth's account capturing the broader academic and activist zeitgeist. Honneth's approach appeared as a means of maintaining the contemporary relevance for critical theory, of advancing normative social research unconstrained by a weighty metaphysics, and of building closer connections to emergent activism. But there are further, less obvious, considerations which need stating, which may have continued relevance today.

For Lois McNay, Honneth's central weakness, his commitment to a unifocal recognition lens, is also crucial to his appeal. McNay's argument is that academics are instinctively attracted to grand theories which promise to capture the entirety of the social world. Once invested in their paradigm, it is both practically and affectively difficult to retreat from the embraced perspective. Through a turn to Bourdieu, McNay suggests Honneth's followers suffer from a bad case of 'scholastic epistemocentricism' (McNay, 2008: 195), where the entirety of the social world is reformatted so that it can become legible within the limited field of vision of a single perspective. Rather than acknowledge the limitations of their monism, recognition theorists have proceeded to reformulate their view of the wider social world so it can be captured within their narrow parameters. As we shall see in the next chapter, this has led to obviously non-intersubjective exchanges being analysed as recognitive; for example, recognition scholars have written on the use of food banks as being a result of 'consumptive need misrecognition' (Schaub and Odigbo, 2019). For McNay, unifocal social theory draws scholars like moths to a flame, and recognition scholars epitomise this tendency. Honneth's followers would sooner doctor their understanding of their entire social world to fit their recognition parameters, than jettison their recognition paradigm.

A further possible reason for the appeal of Honneth's critical theory of recognition is that its focus on the individual chimes with the normative individualism of the neoliberal era. This may seem counter-intuitive; recognition is fundamentally intersubjective in nature. Yet, the entry point to recognition relationships is not the moment of intersubjective praxis: this remains inaccessible to the researcher. One cannot subject abstract intersubjective praxis to empirical analysis; the dyadic recognition moment is intangible and inaccessible. The researcher is only able to rely on the testimony of one-half of the recognition pairing at any given moment, hearing of the affective state of one social subject. The sense of disrespect or misrecognition suffered by the individual is the true foundation of recognition theory, which remains fundamentally individualistic in nature. The analytical currency afforded to the individual's affective response is thus a central feature of the critical theory of recognition. The focus on the individual, and upon the individual's capacity for self-realisation, thus chimes in concert with broader valuation of the individual's status as the methodological unit of social analysis of neoliberal scholarship.

There are thus multiple factors once-removed from the substantive content of Honneth's critical theory which may have aided the positive reception recognition theory received within Frankfurt School circles and within the academy more broadly.

Normative reconstruction

In *Freedom's Right*, Honneth connected the critical theory of recognition with an explicitly 'normative-reconstructive' methodology. From such a perspective, society is viewed as an amalgamation of various norms guiding recognition relationships. Normative reconstruction is a central feature of Honneth's mature critical theory of recognition, and the approach has been subject to considered analysis (Buchwalter, 2016; Schaub, 2015, *inter alia*). As will be discussed at length in Chapter 3, it is this fusion of social pathology diagnosis, recognition theory, and normative reconstruction which has fundamentally 'domesticated' contemporary critical theory, eroding its pathology diagnosing social-theoretical foundations.

Upon first encounter, normative reconstruction may seem similar to the established meta-methodology of Frankfurt School research: immanent-transcendence. Immanent-transcendent critique works by the researcher identifying contradictions within the norms, values, and institutions manifest in the social world (immanent critique) which are unsustainable, and which point towards their sublation (transcendence: pointing towards future development in the form of new norms and practices) (see Strydom, 2020). Central to immanent critique, and indeed to all dialectical forms of social research, is the instability of contradiction, the constant 'ever-becoming', dynamic nature of social reality, and the movement from quantitative to qualitative change. Without a partisan investment in the dominant norms and values of the social world, immanent-transcendent critique enables the identification of possible areas of rupture, of transition, which points towards society's *Aufheben*.

In direct contrast, Honneth's normative reconstructive methodology is predicated on an explicit embrace of dominant social norms and values. In keeping with Hegel's *Philosophy of Right*, Honneth's *Freedom's Right* is founded on the unsubstantiated assumption that the central value guiding the development of Western institutions is the growth of freedom. As such, for Honneth, all social institutions (the market, the family, the law etc.) are examined as having a fundamentally positive foundation, being, at core, oriented towards the freedom of the individual through reciprocal, rational intersubjective relationships of recognition. The goal of Honneth's normative reconstruction is to identify the blockages to said norms coming to fruition more broadly within each sphere of society. For Honneth, society remains in contradiction, in keeping with the immanent-transcendence approach. However, crucially, the contradiction is held to be between the deep norms linked to the promotion of freedom and the contingent instances where these norms are obstructed from coming to the fore. The challenge, for Honneth, is to identify the obstacles to social freedom which prevent the existence of a 'just' society.[8]

In contrast, while immanent-transcendence does not necessitate support for the dominant norms and values of the day, normative reconstruction, à la Honneth, is founded upon an embrace of the guiding norms of existing social institutions. Honneth's approach advocates for modifications to institutional practices where the underlying emancipatory norms of rational recognition are being 'blocked' from manifesting. For example, there may be a need to support new laws to enable more just childcare-sharing practices, same-sex marriage, or minor changes to the market structure. However, ultimately Honneth supports the dominant pillars of Western society, as Hegel did Prussia: the challenge is to mould social institutions, and social subjects, to adjust to the freedom-promoting norms upon which society is predicated. What is required is normative uplift (getting subjects to embrace the deep, emancipating, social norms), rather than normative revolution (identifying fundamental contradictions within society's norms themselves, catalysing their further development).

Honneth's account is obviously at odds with a critical theory of society. First-generation Frankfurt School scholars fought to transform the foundational logics and norms of the social world, rather than seeking to enable their intrinsic norms to flower. To put no finer point on it, Lukács, Adorno, Benjamin, Bloch, Fromm, Horkheimer, et al., desired the abolition of capitalism. They imagined a qualitatively different social formation, where the extractive and reifying capitalist form of life was sublated by a new, rational, and fundamentally socialistic and solidaristic constellation. Progressive critical theory is primarily invested in the impact of irrational and dominating social structures and forms of thought upon the epistemic capacities, proclivities, and desires of the social subject. Honneth's theory of justice, predicated upon normative reconstruction and a perspectival monistic philosophy of recognition, has demonstrably failed to respect this inheritance, deserting critical theory's radical objectives during climatic crisis, insurgent neo-fascisms, and obscene global inequities of neoliberalism. The practical and manifold limitations of Honneth's normative reconstructive method are discussed in the following chapter, where the dominant recognition-cognitive framing of social pathology is critically discussed.

Axel Honneth's critical theory is intellectually unsound, politically problematic, and increasingly divorced from the defining insights of the Frankfurt School tradition. Honneth's most striking claims are (i) that social researchers should view the entirety of social conflict as various subsets of struggles for recognition, (ii) that subjects' experiences of disrespect, or of 'misrecognition', offer a foundational entry point for social analysis, and (iii) that the historical development of institutions has been conditioned by the spread of freedom, manifest through just intersubjective relations. Honneth's first claim is instantly complicated by the myriad counter-examples above, which have been provided from Thompson, Fraser, McNay, and Fanon. Clearly not all social struggles can be framed as struggles for recognition; claims to the contrary are best explained as manifestations of McNay's diagnosed scholastic-epistemocentricism. Honneth's second claim can be dismissed by the reality of 'constitutive' forms of power which shapes the subject, as expressed by Thompson. Simply put, Honneth's theory of power is inadequate as a result of his neo-Idealism. As to Honneth's third claim, the unsubstantiated assertion that the growth of freedom determines historical development, Adorno's *Negative Dialectics* and Amy Allen's (2016) *The End of Progress*, as well as the raft of emerging decolonial and post-colonial theorists, provide a satisfactory rebuttal. What is required is a qualitative revolution in norms and institutions, rather than the inherent value-horizon of Western modernity to reach its zenith.

Politically, Honneth is complicit with neoliberal values, viewing market mechanisms as offering valuable foundations for freedom-producing relations of recognition for the individual. Honneth's critical theory of recognition offers oppressed subjects a manifesto for optimal inclusion within the neoliberal social world, rather offering than aiding in a revolution of its fundamental norms and dynamics. Thus, activists who seek both economic transformation and a fairer status order, who embrace Honneth's politics of recognition, will march for fairer inclusion within a system they wish to overthrow. Sympathetic to the emancipatory potential of market mechanisms and ossifying progressive protest, Honneth's critical theory displaces Marxian, anti-capitalist politics with a strategically inept social liberalism. As such, Honneth's critical theory of recognition barely resembles Frankfurt School critical theory. As presented in the 'Introduction', critical theory explores distortions of social rationality (not injustices), through the interdisciplinary development of Marxian insights (not pro-market), seeking revolutionary change to the guiding dynamics, norms, and values of the capitalist social world (not normative reconstruction).

In Chapter 2, I united and extended the criticisms of Honneth's work present within the existing literature, drawing on the ideas of Michael J. Thompson, Lois McNay, and Nancy Fraser. However, my central contribution in *Critical Theory and Social Pathology* is to focus on the damage which has been done to the social-theoretical foundations of critical theory by the recognition turn, by demonstrating the enfeebled account of social pathology which has emerged. While Thompson, McNay, and Fraser are powerful allies in demonstrating the limitations of Honneth's critical theory, they do not attend to the impact Honneth's work has had on the Frankfurt School's understanding of social pathology. In Chapter 3, I focus on precisely this concern, demonstrating how Honneth has fundamentally denatured critical theory's social-theoretical foundations.

Notes

1 Consider: Kojève (1980 [1947]), Jean Hyppolite (1973 [1955]).
2 It is also debated whether Marx *himself* was influenced by the 'master-slave' dialectic as much as his subsequent admirers suggest (see Arthur, 1983).
3 Laitinen, Särkelä, and Ikäheimo (2015), 5–7.
4 Taylor's account of recognition complimented his broader communitarian critique of liberalism and has been extensively mobilised since in demands for the recognition of socio-cultural differences.
5 Habermas later revised this account, in favour of a 'discourse ethics', derived from the rational presuppositions of argumentation.
6 For example, consider Fraser's support for a perspectival dualism, in *Redistribution or Recognition* (Fraser and Honneth, 2001).
7 Tellingly, in *The Idea of Socialism* (2016) Honneth audaciously reworks the orthodox understanding of socialism (presented as an outmoded relic of the industrial era) in line with his critical theory of recognition.
8 As such, Honneth's account is primarily invested in 'justice', rather than 'rationality', marking a further denaturing of the distinctive roots of critical theory.

3

Pathologies of recognition

With Honneth's *The Struggle for Recognition*, a restrictive and 'domesticated' account of social pathology emerged.[1] In this chapter, I show how variations on the 'pathologies of recognition' framing achieved dominance across social theory which problematically impacted applied social research. As Onni Hirvonen, a leading recognition theorist, succinctly framed it, the term 'pathology' now relates principally to 'failures of realizing recognition relationships successfully' (Hirvonen, 2015: 209). In summary, 'social pathology' has been captured by recognition theory, the casualty of which is the loss of all insights which cannot be grasped through the 'recognition monism' (Fraser and Honneth, 2001: 214). Much of the rich heritage of the Frankfurt School, such as the work of Fromm (Chapter 6) and Marcuse (Chapter 7), has been needlessly displaced. Today, a frosty boundary exists between scholars loyal to Honneth's 'perspectival monist' social theory, and those invested in Frankfurt School research as conceived by its original proponents. To those of us sympathetic to the work of Fromm, Marcuse, and Adorno, all monistic recognition accounts are politically, social-theoretically, and philosophically problematic. Yet, the ascendant 'pathologies of recognition' account is not merely impeded by its monistic focus on recognition (Harris, 2019a). In this chapter, I stress a second limitation, arguing that an even more restrictive 'recognition-cognitive' account of social pathology is in the ascendancy. This approach will be shown to combine a recognition theoretical perspective with a focus on the subject's comprehension of dominant social norms.

Fundamental Marxian insights have been lost to the detriment of critical theory. Insights which, I argue, must be urgently reclaimed. In this chapter, I track the development of the 'pathologies of recognition' framing within Finnish critical theory, and in particular, within the work of the 'Jyväskylä School'.[2] I then trace similar trends within the 'Essex School's' emerging scholarship. Next, I reconstruct and critique Christopher Zurn's influential 'recognition-cognitive' reading of pathologies as 'second-order' disorders, which combines recognition-monism with a restrictive cognitivism. Finally,

I turn to Honneth's magnum opus, *Freedom's Right* (2014 [2011]), which has further transformed how social pathologies are framed, entrenching today's recognition-cognitive orthodoxy. I argue that Honneth's recoding of social pathology is highly restrictive and politically regressive.

The 'Finnish School' of critical theory

While Honneth has written prolifically on both recognition and social pathology, efforts to bring the two into productive dialogue were initiated by other scholars, principally by those based in Finland (Piroddi, 2021).[3] In particular, the 'Jyväskylä School' united these theoretical concerns, closely supported by scholarship emanating from scholars at Tampere. The resultant 'pathologies of recognition' approach has recently been explored by Corrado Piroddi (2021), who places it as central to a 'Finnish school of critical theory'. For Piroddi (2021: 60), the leading advocates of this school are Onni Hirvonen, Heikki Ikäheimo, Arto Laitinen, and Arvi Särkelä. Their scholarship shows a remarkable fidelity to Honneth's work and has been crucial in reshaping the framing of social pathology.

Piroddi maps the Finnish school literature astutely; however, he does so while remaining imbricated within the recognition paradigm. That alternative credible approaches to the study of social pathology exist – à la Fromm, Marcuse, Rousseau, Marx etc. – is left unstated. The fact that these formative figures are side-lined in Piroddi's cartography is indicative of the extent to which social pathologies are now understood solely through a recognition lens. In this regard, Piroddi typifies the 'pathologies of recognition' scholar insofar as he considered it unnecessary to comment on the remarkable transformation social pathology has undertaken. Recognition monism has become hegemonic, and the displacement of Fromm, Marcuse, Rousseau, and Marx entirely normalised.

Three features unite Jyväskylä School scholarship: (a) an investment in a recognitive 'perspectival monism', (b) applying such an approach to research both individual and collective experiences, and (c) a focus on recognition and social ontology. Central to Honneth's debate with Nancy Fraser (2001) was whether a sophisticated recognition perspective could capture the entirety of social processes, granting critical theorists immanently anchored access to the social world. For Honneth, recognition has a remarkable potential to do so; for Fraser, such pretensions are patently absurd and dangerous. Jyväskylä School scholars side decisively with Honneth (see Laitinen, Särkelä, and Ikäheimo, 2015: 3). For Laitinen, Särkelä, and Ikäheimo, recognition theory truly has a remarkable potential to illuminate the totality of the social world, enabling its pathologies to be grasped in their entirety.

Hence, Onni Hirvonen, is able to write that social pathologies today, are, definitionally, 'failures of realizing recognition relationships successfully' (Hirvonen, 2015: 209). In this way, the Jyväskylä School are remarkably loyal to Honneth's critical theory of recognition. For Honneth, the critical theory of recognition captures the entirety of social pathologies; therefore, why would his devoted adherents hunt for further supporting theoretical infrastructure elsewhere? For Finnish School scholars, recognition – and recognition alone – is held to be the 'fundamental overarching' category for social research (Fraser and Honneth, 2001: 2–3). From such a perspective, the role of the critical theorist is radically reframed. The central task of social research is now to analyse 'pathologies of recognition', the obstacles impeding recognition relationships (Hirvonen, 2015: 209).

The continuing fidelity of 'Finnish School' theorists to Honneth's exclusively recognition perspective to social research is remarkable. As discussed in the preceding chapter, scholars across disciplines and traditions have identified limitations in Honneth's account, substantially discrediting it philosophically and politically. However, there is little to no engagement among Finnish scholars with these critical authors. Indeed, there appears to be a remarkable willful ignorance of these alternative positions: there is little to no engagement with Fromm, Marcuse, Marx, or the leading critiques of recognition-centric critical theory – as in the work of Thompson, Kouvelakis, Fraser, or McNay. In short, with Finnish critical theory, a subset of recognition theorists have succeeded in annexing the heurism of social pathology, and now inhabit something of a scholarly echo chamber. Authors critical of Honneth are rarely engaged with, while 'recognition' is imbued with a transcendent clarity and potency.

For the Finnish School, recognition is not merely of use for explaining the pathologies of the ideal-typical subject-meets-subject intersubjective moment, the so-called recognition dyad. Rather, in keeping with Honneth, and Martineau, Meer, and Thompson, Finnish critical theorists adapt the recognitive approach to explore broader inter-group dynamics (Hirvonen, 2015; Elmgren, 2021). For example, Hirvonen has argued that it is entirely possible to 'map out and analyze pathologies of collective recognition' (Hirvonen, 2015: 210) and, through doing so, to outline the 'systemic and institutional problems in providing opportunities for flourishing lives' (Hirvonen, 2015: 209). In more recent work, Hirvonen has focused on the ascent of populist discourses and political campaigns, analysed through the 'pathologies of recognition' perspective (Hirvonen and Pennanen, 2019). Such an approach shows flair and is to be applauded for its originality. However, as demonstrated in the preceding chapter, without a supporting analysis of the market as manifesting distinct logics, which are not merely epiphenomenal to recognition relations, such an account will be forever found wanting.

While social scientists beyond the Finnish School have long connected *recognition theory* and *social research* (see O'Neill and Smith, 2012, *inter alia*), the prevalence of the 'pathologies of recognition' approach for applied social research clearly emanates from Finland. For instance, a leading earlier work, O'Neill and Smith's *Recognition Theory and Social Research*, does not engage once with social pathology. Enter the Jyväskylä School and examples abound. Consider, for example, Petteri Niemi's (2015) extensive research into the normative foundations of social work, which has drawn explicitly on a 'pathologies of recognition' account. Niemi wrote of the 'pathologies of recognition in social work',[4] identifying forms of 'professionalised indifference' (Niemi, 2015: 182), 'professional disesteem', and 'professional disrespect' (Niemi, 2015: 183). This fusion of pathology and recognition in research into social work has since been applied more broadly. For example, Houston and Montgomery have *subsequently* adopted an explicitly 'pathologies of recognition' approach to 'reflect critically on contemporary social pathologies' that pose challenges to 'critical and radical social work' (Houston and Montgomery, 2017).

Clearly Finnish critical theory is making an impact. It is thus worth reflecting on its intentions. As Laitinen, Särkelä, and Ikäheimo (2015: 5) frame it, the aim of Finnish critical theory is simple, it is to 'compliment the Hegel-inspired picture outlined by Honneth and others following him of successful relationships of recognition and their generally optimistic conception of the content, dynamics and results of needs, demands and struggles for recognition with an account of denied, lacking or rejected recognition'. In other words, Finnish critical theorists promote engaging with the entire social world through a 'pathologies of recognition' perspective. In this regard they have been highly successful. Sadly, such success comes at the cost of neo-Marxian critical theory.

An 'Essex School'

The push towards a 'pathologies of recognition' approach to social research did not solely occur in Finland. Academics at the University of Essex, Colchester, United Kingdom, have also written extensively on the theme of social pathology, and often from a strictly recognition-monist paradigm. The Essex School is particularly notable in their attempt to push the heurism to its limits, with various scholars seeking to show that a 'pathologies of recognition' lens can be utilised to research ideal-typical economic maladies, such as poverty, and the increased reliance on food banks (Schaub and Odigbo, 2019). While Fraser, Thompson, McNay, and others have demonstrated the untenability of collapsing market logics into the intersubjective order (see Chapter 2), leading Essex School authors have steadfastly proceeded to do just that. Much like Jyväskylä scholars, the Essex School shows a remarkable loyalty to Honneth's recognition-monist critical theory.

Particularly notable in this regard is the work of Jörg Schaub. For example, in a fascinating paper co-authored with Ikechukwu Odigbo, Schaub (2019) argued that by locating material 'need' (such as the need for food, shelter) within the framing of recognition, the pathologies of the market order can be understood optimally. To those uninitiated in the cult of recognition, such an endeavour may seem extremely counter-intuitive. Yet, Schaub and Odigbo (2019) proceed to outline the 'consumptive' and 'productive' facets in the recognition of 'love, 'respect, and 'esteem, seeking to show how the market order can be comprehended through Honneth's categories. From the perspective of the co-authors, to optimally further Frankfurt School critique today, the diagnoses of social pathologies most focus on exploring the 'variants of misrecognition that … [form] part of the economic sphere' (Schaub and Odigbo, 2019: 117). From such an optic, those who 'have to rely on food and clothes banks' are best understood as being victims of 'consumptive need misrecognition' (Schaub and Odigbo, 2019: 112).

Engaging with people's reliance on foodbanks as a result of failed intersubjective relationships within a broader recognition order seems to me to be absurd. The market order, and the poverty it leads to, simply cannot be reduced to networks of intersubjective relations. As Fraser argued, economic logics are results of a whole variety of factors, including

> the supply and demand for different types of labor; the balance of power between labor and capital; the stringency of social regulations, including the minimum wage; the availability and cost of productivity enhancing technologies; the ease with which firms can shift their operations to locations where wage rates are lower; the cost of credit; the terms of trade; and international currency exchange rates. (Fraser and Honneth, 2001: 215)

This does not register to the co-authors. Like Finnish critical theory, much 'Essex School' pathology diagnosing research is focused on recognition and recognition alone: there is no attempt to see how such pathologies of recognition could be connected to, or utilised alongside, other framings of social pathology. There is one solitary sentence in a footnote which states that 'many argue that other systemic factors not reducible to issues related to recognition also shape outcomes in the economic sphere' (Schaub and Odigbo, 2019: 118). This is highly revealing. Here we see Marxism, in essence, reduced to a footnote, 'haunting' contemporary social theory (see Derrida, 2006), while remaining unnamed. This is worth stressing: critical theory, as understood by its founders, is not even worthy of a second sentence in a footnote.

The preceding analysis may seem unduly harsh or potentially even *ad hominem*. This is not the case. I engage with Schaub and Odigbo as they so eloquently present the pathologies of recognition framework. I find their work revealing and articulate and thus worthy of critical engagement. I consider that the co-authors should also be applauded for taking the approach to its logical conclusion and for attempting to engage with pressing material inequalities. Crucially, the co-authors are also highly indicative of the community of Essex scholarship more broadly, which is passionately invested in recognition theory. Even the work of Fabian Freyenhagen, while in places highly critical of recent developments in social pathology scholarship, retains an implicit fidelity to the pathologies of recognition perspective (Freyenhagen, 2015). Other scholars working within this tradition include Douglas Giles, Timo Jütten, and Robert Farrow. The Essex School produces thought-provoking and original research; however, like the Jyväskylä School, they draw the framing of social pathology further in the direction of a 'domesticated' recognition monism.

Christopher Zurn and pathologies as 'second-order disconnects'

In a significant intervention, published in 2011, Christopher Zurn argued that all social pathologies 'exhibit a similar underlying conceptual structure, that of second-order disorders' (Zurn, 2011: 345). Zurn focused on Honneth's work, and argued that a common thread could be traced across his analysis of ideological recognition, maldistribution, 'invisibilisation', rationality distortions, reification, and institutionalised self-realisation (Zurn, 2011). Precisely what such an endeavour sought to achieve is unclear: the possibility that anything unites all social pathologies (in terms of a shared structure, or otherwise) seems to me highly implausible, and, predictably, Zurn failed to come close to substantiating the claim in his chapter. Yet, Zurn's account precipitated the rise of a 'recognition-cognitivist' framing of social pathology. For Zurn (2011: 348), all social pathologies operate through a 'fundamental disconnect between first-order contents and the subjects' reflexive grasp of the origins and character of those contents, where that gap systematically serves to preserve otherwise dubious social structures and practices'. Such a framing of social pathology is clearly considerably closer to the structure that one would associate with ideology, rather than the breadth of the pathology diagnosing tradition. And indeed for Zurn, ideology does represent the archetypal social pathology, insofar as 'it contributes to deleterious social outcomes through a kind of second-order disorder, a disorder socially patterned and thereby contributes to unwanted social outcomes' (Zurn, 2011: 348).

In this regard, Zurn (2011: 346) argued that 'Marx's articulation of a theory of ideology ... is a good example of the conceptual structure ... central to Honneth's attempts to reinvigorate the practice of social critique through the diagnosis of social pathologies: namely, the grasp of social pathologies as second-order disorders'. From such a perspective, while simple factual inaccuracies (for instance, believing that penguins can fly) often arise from plain mistakes, ideological beliefs can only be 'explained by second-order distortions in the process of belief-formation and stabilisation' (Zurn, 2011: 347–348). For Zurn, only impediments to self-realisation which arise due to this latter dynamic should be understood as a 'social pathology'.

In this framework, all social pathologies are thus cognitive impairments where second-order operations are impeded, precipitating undesired social outcomes in some form or another. It is instantly obvious that Zurn's conception of social pathology is excessively 'cognitivist'; as Fabian Freyenhagen beautifully framed it, Zurn's account is simply far too 'in the head' (Freyenhagen, 2015: 136). For Freyenhagen, Zurn's conception of social pathology holds that 'the problem is how people interpret the world, not that it needs changing at a fundamental level' (Freyenhagen, 2015: 145).[5]

What Freyenhagen does not engage with, however, in keeping with the recognition theoretical approach of the 'Essex School', is the radically recognitive nature of Zurn's account. It is not merely a 'second-order disconnect' which unites social pathologies (if this was not restrictive enough!). Rather, a social pathology can only be said to be present for Zurn when an *ideological act of misrecognition* is present. Zurn thus presents an account of social pathology which is both exclusively recognition-centric and radically cognitivist.

Zurn is explicit: only *ideological* acts of *misrecognition* represent the reality of social pathologies. Zurn (2011: 349) wrote that

> Honneth seeks a way of identifying, in the act of the recognition relationship itself, which markers we could use to say that it is an ideologically distorting, rather than a socially productive, instance of interpersonal recognition. His answer is basically that acts of recognition are ideological when there is a substantial gap between the evaluative acknowledgement or promise that the act centres upon, and the institutional and material conditions necessary for the fulfilment of that acknowledgement or promise.

Thus, from Zurn's perspective, deficient recognition relationships alone are not social pathologies. As Zurn argued, 'without the second-order disorder, what we might generically call "bad" acts of recognition (misrecognition, non-recognition) are not ideological', therefore, they 'cannot count as social pathologies' (Zurn, 2011: 349). This approach has not been universally accepted; far from it. Indeed, Laitinen (2015), Freyenhagen (2015), and my own work to date (Harris, 2019a, 2019b, 2021) have served to demonstrate the limitations of Zurn's approach. However, Zurn's framing has enjoyed remarkable purchase.

While Honneth does not explicitly adopt Zurn's formulation to the letter, his approach to social pathology in *Freedom's Right* has a clear cognitive emphasis. Social pathologies are presented there as being located 'at a higher stage of social reproduction' and working to 'impact subjects' reflexive access to primary systems of actions and norms' (Honneth, 2014 [2011]: 86). While making only limited engagements with social pathology in his more recent *The Idea of Socialism*, Honneth is apparently taking up permanent residence in cognitivist territory. In an intriguing passage from the preface, he wrote,

> It might help to recall that current economic and social events appear far too complex and thus opaque to public consciousness to be capable of intentional transformation. This is particularly true when it comes to processes of economic globalisation in which transactions are carried out too quickly to be understood; here a kind of second-order pathology seems to make institutional conditions appear as mere givens, as being 'reified' and thus immune to any efforts to change them. (Honneth, 2016: 3–4)

By describing the pathology as 'second order', I read Honneth to be lending measured support to Zurn's cognitive framing. But it was with his earlier *Freedom's Right*, rather than his *Idea of Socialism*, that Honneth made his most remarkable intervention in the debate on the foundations of critical theory.

Freedom's Right: normative reconstruction and misdevelopments

No study of social pathology would be complete without engaging with Axel Honneth's *Freedom's Right*. Widely regarded as Honneth's magnum opus (see Schaub, 2015: 108), *Freedom's Right* is a modern recasting of Hegel's *Philosophy of Right* sans metaphysics. Unlike first-generation critical theory, which is rooted in negativity and critique (consider Adorno's *Minima Moralia*), Honneth's project offers a positive referent for critical theory. While *The Struggle for Recognition* provided an anthropologically rooted account of the good life, Honneth's original critical theory of recognition remained focused on the subject, and the intersubjective praxis required for individual self-realisation. In contrast, *Freedom's Right* develops Honneth's intersubjective philosophy through a sweeping macro-sociological analysis of society, identifying how the norms of 'freedom-guaranteeing' mutual recognition are manifest across social institutions (Honneth, 2014 [2011]: 59). Regardless of the multiple flaws in this project (see below), it must be acknowledged that *Freedom's Right* represents a truly remarkable and unique undertaking which has sparked much discussion.

Central to *Freedom's Right* is 'freedom'. For Honneth, there are three kinds of freedom which proliferate in 'Western' societies: negative freedom, reflexive freedom, and social freedom. While 'negative' and 'reflexive' freedom are both integral to social life, it is the superior form of 'social freedom' which is Honneth's primary interest. This 'social freedom' harbours a remarkable warmth and purity, presenting a vision of a social order where individual and collective interests are structurally elided. A certain majesty radiates through Honneth's exposition of this institutional-intersubjective process, bringing 'social freedom' closer to divine 'love' than to juridically insured negative 'liberty'.

As a critical theorist who adores the work of Rousseau, I found myself thinking of *The Social Contract* while reading *Freedom's Right*. The central thrust of Honneth's account is that advanced Western societies possess a set of institutions which enable the subject to be recognised by the collective through their participation in social life. In such a way, the Hegelian dyad of 'subject-is-recognised-through-the-process-of-recognising-another-subject' is extrapolated to 'subject-is-recognised-through-the-process-of-participating-in-recognition-enabling-institutions'. For Honneth, attaining social freedom is thus the objective for critical theory, and can be achieved by supporting institutional arrangements which bring about intersubjective recognition.

Social freedom is the goal. However, Honneth's abstract 'Western' society also manifests two additional, inferior, manifestations of freedom: negative freedom and reflexive freedom. Both are presented as essential preconditions for the development of 'social freedom'. Honneth's account of 'negative freedom' positions it close to Berlin's (1969): defined by the absence of constraint, where the atomistic, calculating individual can pursue their own self-interest. 'Reflexive freedom', in contrast, is the ability to consider one's ethical and moral choices; it is characterised again by the isolation of the individual, however, there is a greater emphasis on the subject's capacity to contemplate their own conception of the good life. In negative freedom the individual is free to do as they please; no consideration is given to where their desires and ethical choices originate. In reflexive freedom, the individual is capable of pondering upon their own desires, reflecting on the genesis of their life choices.

'Negative freedom' is repeatedly presented as sitting close to a form of 'legal freedom', while 'reflexive freedom' sits closer to the subject's ability to make moral and ethical decisions. For Honneth, both forms of freedom have important roles in today's social world; however, they are strictly circumscribed and clearly demarcated. Legal/negative freedom and reflexive/moral freedom will never evolve into 'social freedom' in and of themselves. Social freedom requires a particular kind of intersubjective praxis; it is based on the development of optimal recognition relations being manifest through social institutions. Thus, the challenge Honneth undertakes in the third section of *Freedom's Right* is to demonstrate how 'social freedom' is established in said institutions in contemporary societies.

Crucial to his account, as always, is recognition. For Honneth, recognition remains the antecedent precondition for the individual to attain the good life. Further, recognition now additionally functions as the sole criterion to assess the 'freedom-guaranteeing' (Honneth, 2014 [2011]: 59–61) capacity of social institutions: the market, the family, and the legal system are only seen as sites of 'social freedom' if they enable social freedom *qua* institutionally enabled, mutual recognitive praxis.

Social pathologies in *Freedom's Right*

It is evident that Honneth's understanding of social pathology has undergone substantial revision (Freyenhagen, 2015). Where once Honneth (2000) framed 'social pathology' expansively as the foundation enabling critical theorists to diagnose problems with the form of life and the values it precipitates, the framing of pathology advanced in *Freedom's Right* is remarkably restrictive. To engage with Honneth's latest reframing of social pathology one must first understand his new 'normative reconstructive' method. Normative reconstruction is not unique to Honneth – for example, Jörg Schaub argued that Habermas deploys a similar methodology in his *Between Facts and Norms* (see Schaub 2015: 110, footnote 13). However, *Freedom's Right* offers a particularly extended engagement with normative reconstruction, which substantially informs Honneth's reframing of social pathologies.

Honneth's 'normative reconstruction' has four key premises. The first is 'normative social integration' (Honneth, 2014 [2011]: 4; Schaub, 2015: 110). In essence, this holds that social institutions must legitimate themselves in the eyes of the population. Unless there is some minimal democratic acquiescence to the norms and values of social institutions, they will be unsustainable. Second, Honneth submits that our understanding of *justice* is fundamentally connected to the norms which underpin the institutions central to social reproduction (Schaub, 2015: 111). Third, the critical theorist must select the institutions which are truly central to social reproduction in the normative reconstruction. Finally, normative reconstruction is *reconstructive*: it must identify the disconnects between the norms undergirding social institutions and the limited manner of their manifestation.

One can view normative reconstruction as an idiosyncratic subset of immanent critique which requires abstracting the dominant norms of the institutions central to social reproduction. Such an approach is immanent as it effectively states 'here are the norms which this institution is ostensibly built upon' and thus enables the researcher to compare said norms with the reality in which such standards may not be fully manifest. By comparison, a transcendent approach would be to argue that the norms abstracted from social institutions are *wrong* in reference to some *external* perspective, some higher knowledge. (As I discuss below, at its most effective, critical theory was predicated on an *immanent-transcendent* methodology. This would require the researcher to abstract the dominant norms, and then analyse those abstracted norms themselves, identifying contradictions and possibilities for their sublation).

One might reasonably ask what this has to do with 'social pathology'. Honneth's account of pathology in *Freedom's Right* serves to connect the normative values underpinning social institutions with recognition. As such, pathologies are now framed as 'misinterpretations' of the optimal working of legal and moral freedoms which 'impact subjects' reflexive access to primary systems of actions and norms' (Honneth, 2014 [2011]: 86). For Honneth, pathologies exist when subjects fail to appreciate how the dominant forms of legal and moral freedom function to enable recognition relations to flourish. Pathologies are now defined as a quasi-autistic rigidity (*Verhaltenserstarrung*) in social action (Honneth, 2014: 87); a failure to intuitively grasp the combinatory of social norms and values which are codependent to, and which enable, social freedom. Pathologies are evinced when subjects rigidly adopt a legalistic or moralistic approach to social action, retaining a 'negative' or 'reflexive' approach to freedom.

Honneth provides examples to illustrate his new approach. An archetypal pathology which emerges within the sphere of negative freedom is an excessively legalistic form of social engagement (Honneth, 2014 [2011]: 86–94). For Honneth, the film *Kramer vs. Kramer* is held to typify such a social pathology (Honneth, 2014 [2011]: 90–92). In *Kramer vs. Kramer*, the lead actors Meryl Streep and Dustin Hoffman play parents fighting for custody over their son. In the ever-darkening juridical nightmare of divorce and custody, intersubjective praxis fails, and the family unit suffers immeasurably because of legalistically ossified social relationships. A social pathology exists as both parents fail to understand how the legal norms are meant to operate to enable forms of intersubjective recognition manifest through legal freedom. The 'rigidity' of their social conduct is a manifestation of their disconnect from an optimal understanding of how the social norms should operate to promote recognition.

Honneth also presents an example of an archetypical social pathology which plagues 'reflexive freedom', that of morally inspired terrorism. For Honneth (2014 [2011]: 119), the actions of the Baader-Meinhof Group typify such a social pathology: a rigidity of social action exists which prevents healthy recognition relationships from forming. The possibility of a flourishing intersubjective recognition relationship, enabling communicative praxis, is precluded by the rigidification of a hyper-moralising perspective. One could present this 'rigidity' as a form of moral dogmatism.

Again, Honneth's reframing of 'social pathology' is radically cognitivised. All social pathologies are now said to refer to instances where subjects fail to appreciate how the norms which structure social institutions can enable intersubjective praxis and, through their disconnect, adopt an unhealthy rigidity to their actions. Honneth is also clear that he considers such pathologies to be socially derived; the fact that such a rigidity of thought could have been established within the subject is a result of a problem within the social world.

The limitations of such an account of social pathology are numerous and varied. However, before I engage with the multiple deficiencies apparent so far, a further curiosity of Honneth's *Freedom's Right* must be covered, his short-lived conceptual experiment of 'misdevelopments'.

'Misdevelopments' v. 'social pathologies'

In *Freedom's Right*, Honneth introduces a new species of social malady, distinct from social pathologies, which he terms 'misdevelopments' (*Fehlentwicklungen*). While social pathologies are presented as rigidified forms of thought, impeding 'negative' and 'reflexive' freedom, misdevelopments are held to restrict 'social freedom'. Honneth only presents the framing of 'misdevelopments' in *Freedom's Right*, and he appears to have discarded it in his later work. Following Freyenhagen, I argue that the heurism needlessly complicates social pathology scholarship and is internally inconsistent and unworkable (Freyenhagen, 2015). This is a somewhat complicated charge to prosecute, as Honneth does not offer a particularly clear explanation of how pathologies vary from misdevelopments, beyond the species of freedom they are said to impede. That said, Honneth does attempt to provide clarity in a few short sections. While pathologies are now understood as 'social embodiments of misinterpretations for which the rules of action themselves are at least partially responsible' (Honneth, 2014 [2011]: 128), the origins of misdevelopments must be 'sought elsewhere, not in the constitutive rules of the respective system of action' (Honneth, 2014 [2011]: 129).

So far, we can distinguish between the two as follows: pathologies are impediments to negative and reflexive freedom which occur as a result of the internal breakdown of the norms of those spheres themselves. For example, one can blame particularities internal to the legal order for subjects adopting a rigidly juridical approach to their sociality. In contrast, misdevelopments only impact social freedom, and do not occur due to a decay of social institutions. Rather, 'misdevelopments' are caused by external factors. Schaub (2015: 113) helps differentiate further between the two:

> Let me give you an example for each [misdevelopments and social pathologies]: the socially triggered tendency to withdraw from communicative relationships and to view one's involvements with others almost exclusively from the impersonal standpoint of law is one of Honneth's examples of a legal pathology. Think, for instance, of a husband who, anticipating his divorce, starts to evaluate each and every move he makes strategically according to how it will be evaluated by a judge who has to decide on the custody of the couple's children. The deregulation of the market sphere can serve as an example of a social misdevelopment. For it leads to a situation in which interactions between individuals are less and less about general and reciprocal interest satisfaction.

Like Schaub, but with a subtly distinct emphasis, Freyenhagen understands Honneth's distinction between 'pathologies' and 'misdevelopments' to be based on whether the social malady is due to 'internal' factors within the sphere of freedom (pathologies) or 'external' factors, which serve to retard the emancipatory potential of a social sphere (misdevelopments) (Freyenhagen, 2015). Freyenhagen critiques this distinction on two grounds. First, it is unclear why social maladies might not simultaneously be both 'misdevelopments' and 'pathologies', a possibility Honneth's theoretical infrastructure in *Freedom's Right* seems unable to accommodate (Freyenhagen, 2015: 147). Second, the idea that social freedom does not have any pathologies seems unjustifiable:

> social freedom – roughly modelled on the idea of love, such that the pursuit and realization of your ends is reciprocally implied in the pursuit and realization of my own ends, and vice versa is not just a superior freedom which provides the proper framework and the preconditions for the other two, but is so innocent and pure just like love is often thought to be that it can never be at fault when things go wrong within its practices and institutions. In this way, misdevelopments are reserved for the practices of social freedom, and only legal and moral freedom's deviations are due to their internal structure. (Freyenhagen, 2015: 147)

In this regard, Honneth's framing of misdevelopments is 'domesticating' in that it serves to restrict the framing of social pathologies, and to remove central social-structural logics from its purview. As Freyenhagen (2015: 148) stated,

> A number of social problems that prior to *Freedom's Right* were counted by Honneth as social pathologies ... have now become misdevelopments. This might seem to be merely a rebranding of them. However ... reframing these problems as misdevelopments suggests that the sphere in which they occur – the market – and its associated norms are itself unproblematic and should merely be protected from external influences (rather than overcome or at least contained in virtue of an in-built tendency to generate social pathologies). The sphere and its norms are removed from critical view, with a sole emphasis of critique on external influences.

Freyenhagen's analysis is scholarly, precise, and accurate. However, the remarkable political implications of his assessment need to be shouted from the rooftops. For Honneth, the market is now seen as one of several social institutions which *promote* social freedom (*qua* intersubjective recognition) and thus can no longer suffer from social pathologies. The fact that for Honneth, *the* social institution central to capitalism, its defining feature, is *definitionally* precluded from having 'pathologies', is remarkable. Freyenhagen (2015) is thus correct when he stated this is not merely a 'rebranding'. The reworking of pathologies of the market as 'misdevelopments' matters. It makes clear that failures within the market sphere are caused by 'external factors' and cannot be traced to the innate irrationality of the market order itself. It is hard to conceive of a more efficient way of recalibrating critical theory which discards the entirety of the insights of first-generation scholarship.

As Freyenhagen argued, by including the market within the realm of social freedom, Honneth has 'removed ... [it] ... from critical view' (Freyenhagen, 2015: 148). Critical theorists who adopt Honneth's approach are left unable to analyse the market order as pertaining to intrinsic deficiencies. It is as if Honneth is trying to demolish the theoretical foundations of critical theory: he confuses the meaning of 'pathology' and establishes a rival theoretical infrastructure, which, while purporting to enable critical theory, holds the internal logics of the market order to be beyond reproach. With *Freedom's Right*, Honneth's critical theory of recognition reached the point of absurdity.

Freedom's Wrong: Honneth's betrayal of critical theory

With *Freedom's Right*, Honneth has abandoned the core tenets of critical theory. The understanding of 'pathology' he advanced was confused and restrictive, sitting more as a tacked-on conceptual curio from an earlier era.

Social pathology listlessly haunts Honneth's post-Marxian account, drained of its analytical potency. The account of pathology advanced has none of the 'explosive charge' Honneth himself identified in the work of first-generation scholars (Honneth, 2004: 338).

Significantly, Honneth has parted company with the defining meta-methodology of the Frankfurt School: immanent transcendence. This is a dialectical form of social critique through which researchers explore the contradictions existing within the social world. As a dialectical perspective, immanent transcendence is sensitive to the mediated disunity of the social domain, of the constant transitions which are occurring, and of the movement from quantitative to qualitative social transformations. No 'eternal' essence is posited, no fundamental norms are sought, or adhered to. The guiding principle is the untenability and volatility of unresolved contradictions in social institutions, norms, and relations. Identifying immanent contradictions within the social world enables critical theorists to disclose possibilities for rupture, for emancipatory transition. Honneth's normative reconstruction, in contrast, does not hold true to any of these guiding principles.

For Honneth, the norms which exist within dominant social institutions are held to be stable and positive insofar as they enable 'freedom guaranteeing' forms of intersubjective recognition to develop. The norms of the market, of the family, of liberal democracy, are thus applauded. As Schaub correctly identifies, Honneth does not seek a 'normative revolution' (Schaub, 2015).

In contrast, it would be impossible for an immanent-transcendent approach to anchor itself upon the dominant norms of social institutions. Yet, Honneth does just that: he seeks to abstract the dominant norms (the process by which he completes this abstraction remains somewhat opaque) and holds these norms as a standard from which to judge inadequacies within the social world – where the social order does not live up to its normative aspirations.

In striking contrast, a truly immanent-transcendent account would seek to hold the dominant norms *themselves* to critical scrutiny, identify their contradictions, and disclosing the limitations of the status quo they perpetuate. Honneth, by contrast, embraces the dominant norms guiding social reproduction. First-generation pathology diagnosing critical theorists knew that they must keep a critical distance from dominant societal norms. Immanent critique requires that one anchors one's critique within the social world, not that one has to support its normative order. In total opposition to Honneth, an immanent transcendent approach requires that such norms themselves are held to account, with an awareness of their instability and continual evolution. Irrespective of the political absurdity of a critical theorist embracing the norms underpinning neoliberal capitalism (more on this later), the methodology through which this betrayal is enacted is incommensurate with the defining features of Frankfurt School research (see Strydom, 2020).

Hegel's *Philosophy of Right* was a remarkable achievement regardless of the problem of its substantive normative claim: that the existing institutional arrangements of eighteenth-century Prussia were optimally rational (Knox, 1940). If one were to read Hegel's work as simply an extravagant apologia for Prussian aristocracy, as done by Karl Popper in *The Open Society and Its Enemies* (1945), he could be summarily dismissed. This would, of course, be a mistake. Honneth's *Freedom's Right* makes an equally outlandish case as Hegel's masterpiece: that modern societies have developed in such a way as to promote freedom and that an analysis of the dominant norms structuring prominent social institutions discloses this reality. For his part, Hegel can be explicated from the charge of conservative sycophancy on (at least) two counts: a) when writing, heavy censorship and strident authoritarianism prevented easy dissemination of critical texts, and b) his methodology fundamentally serves to disclose the constant volatility, progression, and mutability of social relations. Honneth, by contrast, has neither defence at hand. His normative reconstructive method is politically quiescent and his support for the emancipatory institutions of modernity uncoerced. Honneth, unlike Hegel, had the option of providing an explicitly anti-capitalist social critique, without fear of imprisonment, or even loss of tenure.

The basic idea that today's world should be viewed as based on the development of freedom, rather than domination, seems anathema not just to Marxism, but to all conflict theoretical approaches to studying society. Honneth's claim places him closer to Parsonian functionalism than to Adornian critical theory. While Fromm (2010 [1991]) claimed that we lived in a 'pathological normalcy', for Honneth the norms dominating today serve to promote liberty. Honneth is encouraging us to take a leap of faith, to follow him in believing that without public support for the dominant norms which structure social institutions, radical upheavals would occur, leading to qualitative change. Such a worldview seems blind to the most basic insight of critical theory: that domination, knowledge, and critical consciousness are closely connected. Social domination serves to create false needs, to obscure contradictions, and to disguise its grip on the subject. Mass acquiescence to social norms does not mean such norms are rational, or in the best interests of the subjects. As Fromm wrote, just as the scholar may identify '*folie à deux*' (folly of two),[6] they may also witness '*folie à millions*' (folly of millions) (Fromm, 1963 [1955]: 15).

Honneth presents a strong normative position, and in today's conditions of normative crisis he should be given credit for offering a bold vision of the good life. However, what he cannot do, in good faith, or with coherent scholarship, is to prevent a functionalist support for dominant social institutions as a contemporary development of Frankfurt School social critique. It is simply untenable. Critical theorists historically would be united in their rejection of Honneth's central claim – as Marcuse wrote, our society is dominated by a 'peculiar unfreedom' (Marcuse, 2007 [1964]: 3), by *domination*, rather than ever by emboldening emancipating norms.

Honneth's hypostatised 'modern world' is also tightly geographically and culturally circumscribed. Like Hegel before him, the focus is European, and he is clearly highly influenced by Germany in particular. This is not necessarily a problem. As Maïa Pal argued, Marxian scholars can productively study European institutions as historical artefacts and as forces of capitalist domination. What is required is to ensure a focus which is sensitive to broader international dynamics and socio-cultural variation. In short, scholarship on Europe remains essential. However, if such research is pursued through a 'methodological Eurocentrism', in which the non-European world is erased, poor research emerges (Pal, 2020).

Honneth falls victim to such 'methodological Eurocentrism': his presentation of the rise of Western freedom fails to account for the dominant role of the 'global South' in the development of European institutions. The continuing centrality of neo-imperial exploitation to the apparent stability of 'Western' institutions is also left unstated. Crucially, possibilities for transition, or rupture of 'Western' norms, may emerge in locales located geographically, and socio-culturally, beyond 'the West'. The harshest effects of climate change, for instance, are already being felt beyond Europe's boundaries. The war in Syria has repeatedly been called a 'climate war' (see Ash and Obradovich, 2019). The reality is that the norms Honneth explores operate within a globalised world, and his 'methodological Eurocentrism' erases this. As R. C. Smith (2017: 2) argued, drawing on Nafeez Ahmed (2010), it is crucial for critical theorists to be sensitive to the interconnectedness of global crises. It is only by focusing on the breadth and reach of social pathologies that their contradictions can be disclosed, and the norms which Honneth seeks to explore meaningfully interrogated.

Honneth and social pathology: a critique

As introduced in Chapter 1, pathology diagnosing critical theory unites insights across disciplines, providing:

(a) a sociological sensitivity to the presence of *negative dynamics* producing 'false needs',

(b) a philosophical awareness that the highest possible form of *social reason* is not manifest,
(c) a Marxian awareness that the *mode of production* substantially determines the above, and,
(d) a psychoanalytic sensitivity to the emancipatory interest embodied in subjects' anxiety and neurotic response to irrational social forms.

One can crudely connect each insight with Rousseau, Hegel, Marx, and Freud, in turn. *Freedom's Right* serves to exclude, or to denature, each of the fundamental principles of pathology diagnosing critical theory identified above.

With *Freedom's Right*, Honneth abandoned all pretensions to interdisciplinarity and broke completely with critical sociology. Today, his work sits closest to ideal-theoretical philosophy, inspired more by Rawls and Kant than by first-generation Frankfurt School interdisciplinary sociology. Honneth does not conduct primary research (he rarely even cites any) to determine the norms which he stated are embodied in dominant social institutions. Rather, Honneth implicitly holds himself as possessing a remarkable ability to seed the normative cloud, to condense the norms structuring the social world into his own analysis. The suggestion that Honneth may have inaccurately abstracted these norms, or that a plethora of opposing norms may be in constant contestation, is not considered. The merits of critical sociological analysis, rather than an approach which sees a philosopher provide a methodologically suspect abstraction of social norms, is not evaluated. Further, the core of critical Marxian sociology is the identification of connections between social pathologies and irrationalities within the structures of the market order. Even if Honneth was interested in conducting primary sociological research, his theoretical infrastructure prohibits sociologists from interrogating the dominant social institutions: the market order is part of 'social freedom', which possesses no internal pathologies.

Curiously, while *Freedom's Right* can be read as a contemporary reworking of Hegel's *Philosophy of Right*, one of the central Hegelian insights driving critical theory, the existence of 'pathologies of reason', is largely absent. Indeed, *Freedom's Right* is effectively a metaphysically abstinent *Philosophy of Right*, demonstrating the freedom guaranteeing capacities of the modern social order, without recourse to any transcendental 'rationality'. In the absence of Hegelian metaphysics, the ethical charge is provided, yet again, by recognition. The social world is held to be just, insofar as its dominant institutions promote norms which enable healthy intersubjective recognition. Honneth has abandoned the focus on social rationality, on the extent to which our form of life is apposite for a flourishing existence, in favour of a theory of justice. For Frankfurt School researchers, the relationship between pathologically irrational social institutions, and the impeded forms of cognition they produce, is a central area of study. The Honneth of *Freedom's Right* appears to be no longer invested in such pathologies of reason.

Indeed, the dominant institution which precipitates reified consciousness – the market – is immune from critical analysis in Honneth's theoretical infrastructure. A Marxian analysis is systematically excluded. In this regard, Honneth truly does sit closer to a form of Parsonian functionalism in his belief that the dominant institutions exist in such a way as to promote freedom, and their internal workings are best left undisturbed. Recall that the market order may suffer from 'misdevelopments', where external forces may bring discord to its harmony; however, as a central factor providing social freedom, the free market is unable to evince its own internal pathologies. This is an absurd hyper-functionalism, predicated on the myth that the dominant value attained by the 'modern world' is freedom, rather than, as Marcuse wrote, 'a comfortable, smooth, reasonable, Democratic unfreedom' (Marcuse, 2007 [1964]: 3).

A primary factor informing Marcuse and Fromm's pathology diagnosing critique is a fusion of Marxism with Freudian psychoanalysis. For Fromm, the critical theorist must be sensitive to how pathologies can become normalised and accepted by social subjects. The theorist must take seriously the proposition that the foundational logics of social 'normality' may themselves be deeply pathological. Anxieties and neuroses which are experienced by subjects must be viewed as normal responses from people to a pathological social order. From such a position, the subject's anxiety response to the conditions of late capitalism indicates not individual pathology, but social pathology. As Adorno (2007 [1966]: 17) wrote in *Negative Dialectics*, the challenge facing the critical theorists is to 'lend a voice to suffering' (*Das Bedürfnis, Leiden beredt werden zu lassen, ist Bedingung aller Wahrheit*); to articulate the social pathologies which are manifest in individual subjects. What is required, for Fromm and Marcuse, is qualitative social change, rather than coercing the protesting consciousness to conform to the normative diktats of the day. Fromm and Marcuse can thus both be read as arguing for what R. C. Smith (2017: 8) calls 'the social connection' – that individual behaviour, including psychic suffering, has social causes. Just as Adorno argued that the 'splinter in your eye is your best magnifying glass', one can provide a powerful critique of the social world by exploring the neuroses, anxieties, and irrationalities evinced in the subject as it struggles to acclimatise to capitalist normalcy (Adorno, 2005 [1951]: 50). In direct contrast, Honneth's understanding of pathology serves to radically cognitivise, rather than to sociologise, research into social pathologies.

A supporter of Honneth's approach might respond by saying that in *Freedom's Right*, the archetypal pathology is a cognitive disconnect which is *socially caused*, that there is something fundamental to the guiding norms of the institutions promoting negative and reflexive freedom which decays. Therefore, they might argue, there remains a sociological and a structural component to Honneth's analysis: the rigidity of thought has a social cause. However, where *Freedom's Right* crucially falters is in failing to carry the insights of 'depth psychology'. The norms and values shaping the subject are created by underlying social-structural forces; 'norms' do not emerge from nowhere. For Fromm and Marcuse, the form of industrial capitalism can be causally connected to the creation of norms, and crucially, to psycho-pathologies. Honneth's account in *Freedom's Right* does not engage in a depth-psychological account, remaining in the psychological shallows of norm socialisation. Rather, as Fromm and Marcuse show, the subject's acceptance of particular norms is an important area of study. Honneth's failure to engage with the complexity of this process is further evidence of his inadequate understanding of power.

The understanding of social pathology advanced in *Freedom's Right* fails to harness the radical explanatory and diagnostic potential of its earlier iterations. Remarkably, Honneth managed to shed the entire critical potential of the framework, which is no small feat. *Freedom's Right* is testament to the liberal ideal-theoretical capture of mainstream Frankfurt School critical theory. The tradition has become 'domesticated', as Thompson powerfully argued. Central to this domesticating process has been the denaturing and debasement of the tradition's social-theoretical foundations, its account of social pathology.

The framing of social pathology has been co-opted by the critical theory of recognition. Fundamental Marxian insights have been jettisoned as the heurism was distorted; first to 'pathologies of recognition', then to 'recognition-cognitivism', and finally to Honneth's understanding of a 'rigidity' of thought in excessively moralistic or legalistic social action. Yet, such Marxian insights can help us comprehend these developments themselves. Honneth's ascent, and the ascent of a 'domesticated' pathologies of recognition framework, occurred within particular socio-economic conditions, reflecting transformations in the broader political economy, and, in particular, within the political economy of knowledge production. As universities around the world neuter critical, and especially explicitly 'Marxist' programmes, Honneth's account appeared harmless and capable of connecting with a liberal post-material politics. The account of pathology advanced in *Freedom's Right* demonstrates the extent of this theoretical castration. The market is repositioned as immune from internal decay. Such an account is a quirky capitalist apologia, harmless and antiquated.

This chapter served to highlight the remarkable recent curtailing of pathology diagnosing scholarship. There exists a desperate need for a post-liberal form of social critique; a genre of social criticism capable of integrating Marxian and psychoanalytic insights in an interdisciplinary social research endeavour. Central to unleashing critical theory is reclaiming this social-theoretical terrain by returning Marxian insights to the centre of Frankfurt School scholarship. To do so, the remaining parts of the book serve to sympathetically reconstruct the foundations of pathology diagnosing critique, which undergird Fromm and Marcuse's account (Part II). In Part III, I argue that Marcuse and Fromm should be read as providing applicable models and concepts through which to advance pathology diagnosing social research today. A battle is raging for the soul of critical theory. If the Frankfurt School programme is to retain a distinctive perspective for conducting social research, it must avoid falling into step with Honneth and becoming yet another theory of justice.

Notes

1 I first made this argument in Harris (2019c).
2 The idea that there is a particular and coherent 'Jyväskylä School' has previously been expressed by Laitinen, Särkelä, and Ikäheimo (2015: 24).
3 It is worth nothing that many of the so-called Finnish School worked closely with Honneth at some point or other, or worked under his supervision.
4 For a comparative paper which *does not* utilise the pathology framing, yet which uses recognition to research social work, consider Houston (2009).
5 Such a critique holds to an even greater extent when one looks at Honneth's *Freedom's Right*, as discussed below.
6 '*Folie à deux*' is a less common term for the psychiatric condition known as 'shared psychosis'. This is also referred to as Lasègue–Falret syndrome.

Part II

Foundations of pathology diagnosing critique

4

Rousseau and the foundations of pathology diagnosing social criticism

In Part I, I argued that Axel Honneth's 'recognition monism' must be dispensed with in favour of a critical theory true to the founding insights of the Frankfurt School. This requires a return to the original social-theoretical foundations of critical theory, characterised by their distinct framing of social pathology. Rebuilding such an account is the purpose of Part II of this book, with Chapter 4 focusing on Rousseau and Chapter 5 focusing on Hegelian-Marxism.

There are several reasons for starting such a reconstructive project with Rousseau. One reason is that it enables an immanent criticism of Honneth's framing of social pathology. Honneth (2007: 10; 2004) has repeatedly presented Rousseau as the 'founder of social philosophy' and as the original 'social pathologist'. It is instructive to reread Rousseau in light of Honneth's work as it enables a targeted criticism of the critical theory of recognition. While, like Honneth, Rousseau's diagnosis centred recognition, Rousseau immediately moved beyond the intersubjective, and did not fall into the trap of neo-Idealism (see Thompson, 2016). In contrast to Honneth, Rousseau demonstrated that a 'polycentric and multilateral' account of social pathology is possible (Fraser and Honneth, 2001: 209), and that recognition insights can sit as part of a broader research endeavour, without overdetermining the theoretical perspective adopted. Engaging with Rousseau shows that the collapse into perspectival monism is contingent to Honneth's critical theory. Crucial insights, which Honneth himself identified as central to the pathology diagnosing tradition, can be located in Rousseau's work, which are absent in contemporary critical theory.

The importance of Rousseau to the development of normative social research is widely acknowledged. For Plattner (1979: 3), Rousseau sits as the 'first great critic of bourgeois society'. For Cullen (1993: 19), Rousseau was unique in engaging with the 'depth of the human problem', while for Noone (1980: 6), Rousseau's work was nothing less than a 'war with society'. Famously, for Della Volpe (1979) and Colletti (1973), one can track proto-Marxian insights within Rousseau's work. Ferrara (2017) has shown that the lineage of theorists culminating in critical theory – Hegel, Marx, Weber, Nietzsche, Freud – are all indebted to Rousseau's insights. Therefore, if one wants to reconvene a pathology diagnosing research programme, true to the urgency and objectives of the original Frankfurt School, retracing the distinctive features of Rousseau's critique seems an intuitive point of departure.

I start this chapter with a short biographical sketch, demonstrating the centrality of pathology diagnosing social criticism to Rousseau's life and work. I suggest that one should read the entirety of Rousseau's corpus as the development of a normative-diagnostic social critique. Next, I demonstrate that Rousseau incorporates recognitive insights within a social theory with normative content, without collapsing into a perspectival monism. I then identify the key features of Rousseau's form of critique, which develop into the Frankfurt School's approach to social pathology. Throughout Rousseau's *oeuvre*, I trace (a) an awareness of socially induced dependence on false needs, (b) pathological vicious circles, and (c) a materially rooted cultural pathology.

Rousseau as social pathologist

Rousseau's entire output was invested in normative social criticism. One can see social pathologies diagnosed in his operas, his *roman à clef*, his musicology, his plays, and his autobiography – in addition, of course, to his social and political theory. I offer this brief sketch to justify my initial turn to Rousseau as a point of departure for reconstructive pathology diagnosing social research.

Rousseau's work can be divided into three periods: a 'young Rousseau' (1743–1761), a 'mid-period Rousseau' (1762–1771), and a 'late Rousseau' (1772–1778). The young Rousseau was the radical pathology diagnostician. The mid-period Rousseau, in contrast, offered iconoclastic palliatives, his potential 'cures' for the ills identified. The late Rousseau was withdrawn and demoralised, and found introspective means of coping with the pathologies of the social.

The young Rousseau: 1743–1761

In 1750, the Academy of Dijon hosted an essay competition, inviting responses to the stimulus 'Has the restoration of the sciences and arts contributed to the purification of morals?' (Wokler, 2001: 23). Rousseau's submission, the famous *Discourse on the Arts and Sciences*, collected first prize, his response was a resounding negative.¹ For Noone (1980: 6), this work marked the beginning of Rousseau's battle with society. Commencing with Horace's epigram, '*Decipimur specie recti*' (we are deceived by what appears to be right) (Rousseau, 1993 [1750]: 3), Rousseau argued that civilisation is 'the bane of humanity' (Wokler, 2001: 34). Drawing on both contemporary sources and texts from antiquity, Rousseau argued that society 'maintained the appearance of all the virtues, without being in possession of one of them' (Rousseau, 1993 [1750]: 5). His indictment remains striking: humanity has been denatured through the civilising process itself, leading to the erasure of mankind's 'natural', child-like innocence (Douglass, 2015). It is interesting to note that from this early stage in Rousseau's work it is the 'natural', and the 'natural world', which is valued, and the city which is castigated (Lukács, 1972 [1923]: 136). Ironically, it is the nations which pride themselves most on their superiority in arts and culture which prove least adept at providing the conditions necessary for humankind to experience their true humanity. Ultimately, civilisations that invest too heavily in the 'perpetual restraint' of arts-driven 'society' will crumble under the weight of their own decadence (Rousseau, 1993 [1750]: 6).

Despite possessing 'neither order, nor logic, nor structure' (Wokler, 2001: 23), *The First Discourse* is significant as a pathology diagnosing text.² *The First Discourse* offered a radical critique of the 'form of life'; in Strong's words, it was perhaps the first essay to really show 'the homelessness' of man (Strong, 1994: 152). Rousseau's critique presents the limitations of 'civilisation' itself (Lukács, 1972 [1923]: 136); crucially, he is not merely attacking 'injustices' or 'illegitimate rule' – his diagnosis is more fundamental. With *The First Discourse*, Rousseau kick-started a remarkable genre of social critique (Damrosch, 2005). In *The Confessions*, Rousseau recalled how it was through the process of writing *The First Discourse* that he first 'saw another universe'; that he 'became a different man' (Rousseau, 1953 [1752]: 327). Rousseau was aware that it was with *The First Discourse* that he found his distinctive critical voice. From this point on, all of Rousseau's published work bore leitmotifs of pathology diagnosis: they castigated the evils of the city, championed the comparative majestic 'purity' of nature, lamented the tragedy of inflamed pride, and disclosed the denaturing impact of alienated labour in 'civilised' society.

While *The First Discourse* and *Le Devin du Village*³ positioned Rousseau as a passionate contrarian, his *Letter on French Music* 1753) sparked outright hostility. Uniting aspects of his pathology diagnosis from *Discourse on the Arts and Sciences* and his earlier fragments on music, Rousseau's essay earned him condemnation unprecedented in the bitter *Querelle des Bouffons*.⁴ Rousseau argued that French music typified the pathological artificiality of the city. All Northern European speech was presented as being staccato and unnatural. In contrast, Southern European speech was more enchanting and animated. The inclement conditions of the 'North' were held to have created languages suited to the efficient communication of needs: 'shrill', 'unpassioned' [sic], equivalence oriented (Rousseau, 1995 [1753]: 380; 407–409). The regulars at *Theatre du Palais-Royal* that Rousseau deplored were condemned for their discourse shorn of 'sweetness' (Rousseau, 1995 [1753]: 425–427). Rousseau's *Letter on French Music* was a clear continuation of the core themes of *The First Discourse*. With his contribution to the *Guerre des Bouffons*, Rousseau focused his pathology diagnosing critique on the lack of humanity an arts driven culture precipitated.

While *Discourse on the Arts and Sciences* led Rousseau's rise to prominence, it was with the *Discourse on the Origins of Inequality*, four years later, that Rousseau's diagnosis reached maturity (see Honneth, 2007: 7–10). Commencing with a fictive anthropology, Rousseau outlined how humanity has passed through three key stages: from a natural, unalienated existence, through an initial early sociality, to the debased, pathologically alienated, social order of his day.[5] Rousseau sought 'to pinpoint that moment in the progress of things when, with right succeeding violence, nature was subjected to the law; to explain by what sequence of prodigious events the strong could resolve to serve the weak, and the people to purchase imaginary happiness at the price of real happiness' (Rousseau, 1984 [1762]: 77–78).

In the first stage, man was initially described as a simple, self-sufficient creature (Rousseau, 1984 [1762]: 81). There existed a brief happy median, of natural but communal sociality, where humans were social but self-reliant. 'People grew used to gathering together in front of their huts or around a large tree; singing and dancing, true progeny of love and leisure' (Rousseau, 1984 [1762]: 114). Yet such harmony was not to last, as 'each began to look at others and to want to be looked at himself; he who was most handsome, the strongest, the most adroit or the most eloquent became the most highly regarded' (Rousseau, 1984 [1762]: 114).

Central to Rousseau's diagnosis was this 'breach of the monological self-relation' (Honneth, 2007: 8). There is a foundational recognition pathology at the core of Rousseau's diagnosis (see Neuhouser, 2008). With civilisation, 'pity suffered ... dilution' at the expense of an ascendant inflamed pride, or '*amour-propre*' (Rousseau, 1984 [1762]:132). The natural innocence of this hypostatised mid-period of human development was tragically displaced by the 'passions and caprices of civilized communities' (Rousseau, 1984 [1762]: 83). Unalienated 'natural' man was lost with the ascendancy of the 'artificial faculties' prized by modernity (Rousseau, 1984 [1762]: 81).

The Second Discourse detailed how the ascent of an inflamed *amour-propre* precipitated relations of unstructured dependency. 'Man is weak when he is dependent' (Rousseau, 1984 [1762]: 99), and modernity precipitated 'universal dependence' (Rousseau, 1984 [1762]: 98). Of equal import was Rousseau's indictment of the pathological cultural apparatus which perpetuated this social conjecture. Based on falsehood, complicity, and alienation, 'it was necessary in one's own interest to seem to be other than one was in reality. Being and appearance became two entirely different things' (Rousseau, 1984 [1762]: 119).

The mid-period Rousseau: 1762–1771

From 1762, Rousseau produced increasingly didactic texts, which can be read as suggested 'cures' or 'palliatives' (Affeldt, 1999). In 1762, Rousseau published two particularly 'incendiary'[6] texts: *The Social Contract* and *Émile*. *The Social Contract* has been read as an explicit attempt to cure the ills outlined in *The Second Discourse* through a radical republicanism. The text presented a blueprint for structuring society in such a way that 'each citizen shall be at the same time perfectly independent of all his fellow citizens and excessively dependent on the republic' (Rousseau, 1968 [1762]: 99).

The Social Contract was an attempt to structure dependency: in Rousseau's formulation, all citizens must depend on the state. Such a polity, theoretically, would encourage a 'moral and communal existence' (Rousseau, 1968 [1762]: 85). *The Social Contract* presented the blueprint for a society capable of existing without the pathologies of unstructured dependency, and could thus cultivate republican virtue. There is a structural beauty in Rousseau's figuration – he attempted to recast *amour-propre* as a source of social cohesion, rather than enmity.[7] Through state-led processes of socialisation, the citizens of the hypostatised republic could learn to direct their desire for recognition and pride towards their shared status as citizens. What was once the greatest source of hostility is transformed into a binding force of solidarity.

Émile, while equally political, and if anything, even more controversial, was a work of critical pedagogy. The core aim of the text was to present a methodology through which a child may be raised to cope in a deeply pathological society. In keeping with Rousseau's earlier critique of the pathological nature of bourgeois culture, Émile is taught that '[t]he rich think so much of ... their possessions ... not because they are useful, but because they are beyond the reach of the poor' (Rousseau, 1911 [1762]: 149). 'The cure' remains consistent with the lessons of *The Social Contract*: invest the general will with a true power, beyond that of any single subject.

Rousseau's work in this period was not solely academic. In 1755, Paoli liberated Corsica from Genoan rule. Rousseau had a pre-existing interest in Corsica, repeatedly remarking of the simplicity and freedom of its way of life (Durant and Durant, 1967: 204; see Damrosch, 2005: 386). On the invitation of Buttafuoco, Rousseau enthusiastically set to drafting a constitution for the Mediterranean island. Rousseau's affective investment in this project cannot be underestimated. In May 1765, he declared, 'for the rest of my life I shall have no other interest but myself and Corsica; all other matters will be completely banished from my thoughts' (Durant and Durant, 1967: 204).

Rousseau saw Corsica retaining the simple way of life he so admired, reflecting the stage in *The Second Discourse* before *amour-propre* corrupted sociality. He was truly horrified when France deposed Paoli, and destroyed the prospect of a rustic Corsican republic. For Damrosch (2005: 387), Rousseau's larger argument was 'that Corsica should resist modernization at all costs in order to preserve its primitive simplicity'. Rousseau's *Constitutional Project for Corsica* is fascinating in that it represents a juridical-political project designed to prevent the onset of the social pathologies he diagnosed elsewhere (Damrosch, 2005: 386–390).

In 1771, Rousseau wrote the last of his main political works, *Considerations on the Government of Poland*. Confounding many readers, *The Government of Poland* is arguably a more conservative text (Durant and Durant 1967: 884). In Durant and Durant's words (1967: 884), 'he advised the Poles to make no sudden changes in their constitution'. And yet traces of the early Rousseau still remain; his most strident demand is for federalisation and for opposing territorial expansion. A small republic might (with luck) defy the pathologising tendencies of modernity. In contrast to the 'flights *in vacuo*' (Durant and Durant, 1967: 884) of *The Social Contract*, *Considerations on the Government of Poland* is short on abstraction. This middle period of Rousseau's output saw a remarkable change in style and scope. But what is clear throughout Rousseau's work in this period is his aim of ameliorating social pathologies, to provide cures to, or to pre-emptively prevent, the onset of the maladies diagnosed in his earlier works.

The late Rousseau: 1772–1778

From 1772 to his death in 1778, Rousseau turned to introspection. Depressed by his failure to achieve institutional traction, and ostracised socially, Rousseau's later scholarship is marked by a change in both style and intent. I frame the works of this 'late Rousseau' as typified by efforts to come to terms with the pathological nature of society through a turn to introspection. In addition to the hugely successful *Dialogues*, this period saw the publication of Rousseau's *Reveries of a Solitary Walker*. Rousseau's bleak frame of mind is well captured by the opening line: 'So now I am alone in the world' (Rousseau, 1979 [1782]: 27). In his despair and isolation, Rousseau turned to a 'total renunciation of the [material] world' (Rousseau, 1979 [1782]: 52), to psychically estrange himself from the evils of the pathological social conjuncture. Seeing nothing but 'human malevolence' (Rousseau, 1979 [1782]: 45) and 'universal conspiracy' (Rousseau, 1979 [1782]: 44), Rousseau mourned 'the sweet liberty [he] ... had lost' (Rousseau, 1979 [1782]: 50). In contrast, nature again triumphed. It is the city which was the epitome of evil: 'I see nothing but animosity in the faces of men, and nature always smiles on me' (Rousseau, 1979 [1782]: 149). In short, in his final years Rousseau turned to nature, to his love of botany, and to quiet introspection.

Throughout this brief sketch I have argued that Rousseau's scholarship as a whole was animated by his 'condemnation ... of modernity' (Plattner, 1979: 5), his diagnosis of social pathology. Rousseau was unique in consistently engaging with the 'depth of the human problem' (Cullen, 1993: 19), his political writings, operas, plays: all were inflected by his normative social critique. It is unsurprising that the social-theoretical infrastructure of his legacy offers a wealth of resources which harbour the potential to revitalise contemporary social pathology diagnosis.

Recognition without myopia

Rousseau's *oeuvre completes* is founded upon his fictive anthropology in which he diagnoses a pathological shift in recognition relationships. *The Second Discourse* is a beautiful evocation of this tragic loss of humanity's natural, 'pure' innocence (Darling, 1994: 6) as a result of a rupture of the original 'monological' self-relation (Honneth, 2007: 8). Before Rousseau's secularised 'fall of man' (Alberg, 2001), life was presented as being rustic and idyllic. The human is simply, 'an animal less strong that some, less agile than others, but taken as a whole the most advantageously organized of all. I see him satisfying his hunger under an oak, quenching his thirst at the first stream, finding his bed under the same tree which provided his meal; and, behold, his needs are furnished' (Rousseau, 1984 [1762]: 81).

Yet, such an Eden was not to last. Rousseau's anthropology has humans slowly becoming more social, increasingly dependent upon each other to survive. In time, '[e]ach began to look at others and to want to be looked at himself; he who was most handsome, the strongest, the most adroit or the most eloquent became the most highly regarded' (Rousseau, 1984 [1762]: 114). The human race began to 'attach importance to the gaze of the rest of the world, and ... [knew] how to be happy and satisfied with themselves [only] on the testimony of others, rather than on their own' (Rousseau, 1984 [1762]: 136).

In short, '[a]s soon as men learned to value one another, and the idea of consideration formed in their minds, everyone claimed a right to it; and it was no longer possible for anyone to be refused consideration without affront' (Rousseau, 1984 [1762]: 114).

The foundational pathology at the core of Rousseau's work is that *amour-propre* has run amok, the consequences of which were both tragic and extreme. Even use-value has been displaced: the proto-bourgeoisie are held to only value that which will further their social standing. Rousseau turns to Petronius's *Satyricon* to further this point: '*nolo habere bona nisi quibus populus inviderit*' (I only want something if others desire it) (Rousseau, 1984 [1762]: 149). Eight years later, Rousseau expresses the same sentiment in his *Letter to D'Alembert*: 'nothing appears good or desirable to individuals which the public has not judged to be such' (Rousseau, 1968 [1758]: 67). Recognitive failure was clearly crucial to Rousseau's work: it was the social pathology which sat at the core of his diagnosis. In this regard, his work is similar to Honneth's: the intersubjective dimension is presented as a vital site for analysis.

Yet, unlike Honneth, Rousseau's social theory does not collapse into a perspectival monism. The analysis of recognition relationships is not presented as capable of explaining the entirety of social reality. Throughout his work, Rousseau presents a sophisticated infrastructure of concepts through which to examine the social world, few of which would be compatible with a monist recognition approach. Crucial amongst these are his analyses of 'need', 'dependency', 'vicious circles', and colonising social logics, which I explore below. In a crucial passage at the beginning of Part II of *The Second Discourse*, Rousseau wrote,

> The first man who, having enclosed a piece of land, thought of saying 'This is mine' and found people simple enough to believe him, was the true founder of civil society. How many crimes, wars, murders; how much misery and horror the human race would have spared if someone pulled up the stakes and filled in the ditch and cried out to his fellow men: 'Beware of listening to this imposter. You are lost if you forget that the fruits of the earth belong to everyone and that the earth itself belongs to no one.' (Rousseau, 1984 [1762]: 109)

Private property clearly needs to be placed at the centre of Rousseau's critique. It is the particular social order in which private property co-exists with unstructured dependency which creates human suffering. This approach was fundamentally materialist: the existing socio-historical conditions shape the subject's capabilities and desires. For Rousseau, the existence of private property was central – it precipitated structural problems, the analysis of which could not be reduced to the intersubjective realm. Rather, pathological dynamics of excessive consumption and exploitation can occur without any intentional intersubjective 'human malevolence' (Rousseau, 1979 [1782]: 45). Rousseau was sensitive to how constitutive power and social structure shaped the subject's social being, determining their needs, cognitive capacities, and inclinations. It is the particularly social fact of modern dependency, the unstructured nature of man's dependence on his fellow man, which is truly pathological (Rousseau, 1984 [1762]: 125; Neuhouser, 1993: 378). For Rousseau, humanity is overburdened by dependence, '[man] has become [a] slave ... for if he is rich he needs [the poor's] services, if he is poor he needs [the rich's] aid' (Rousseau, 1984 [1762]: 116).

The material and relational nature of this pathology was clear to Rousseau: 'anyone must see that since the bonds of servitude are formed only through the mutual dependence of men and the reciprocal needs that unite them, it is impossible to enslave a man *without first putting him in a situation where he cannot do without another man*' (Rousseau, 1984 [1762]: 106 – my italics). It is thus social structural relations which precipitated social pathologies and which legitimated the unnaturally 'excess' 'toil' required for survival in modernity (Rousseau, 1984 [1762]: 84). With Rousseau, we begin to see how bourgeois society shapes the subject. We see a centrality of the role of private property, and the dynamics which are precipitated by its overreach. It is not human malevolence, or the denial of recognition, which explains these particular social pathologies. Rather, their formation is social-structural, cultural, and material. Rousseau is most explicit on this point; his indictment of his own readership leaves little to the imagination: 'your culture and your habits have been able to corrupt [you]' (Rousseau, 1984 [1762]: 79). It is thus worth exploring the particular species of social pathology which bind Rousseau's diagnoses. The wealth of Rousseau's work for critical theory flows directly from the polycentric nature of his critique; recognition relations are never explored in isolation as a basis for social criticism. Rather, 'recognition' functions as a convenient framing for his fictive anthropology, a convenient starting point for a broader, polycentric critique.

Rousseau's theoretical infrastructure

While entire books have been written on the importance of Rousseau's conceptual apparatus for critical theory (see Ferrara, 2017), here I briefly abstract three central components of his diagnostic infrastructure:

(a) a form of socialisation in which the subject develops unhealthy needs,
(b) the presence of negative self-perpetuating dynamics, or 'vicious circles', and
(c) a form of cultural pathology, emanating from flaws within the logics determining social reproduction.

As subsequent chapters will attest, such social pathologies are integral to the diagnostic critique of Frankfurt School critical theorists.

Pathological needs

Rousseau was sensitive to the ease with which people are socialised into a form of life which can be opposed to their true happiness. In Thompson's (2016) terms, for Rousseau, the subject is deeply vulnerable to the forces of 'constitutive power'. This theme, the susceptibility of the subject to fall victim to pathological dependencies, resonated across Rousseau's work. Horace's epigram, '*Decipimur specie recti*' (we are deceived by what appears to be right) (Rousseau, 1993 [1750]: 3), which Rousseau returned to, truly captures his position: we are deceived by the world around us and can easily lose our way. One can even read a proto-ideology critique forming here – Rousseau did not merely reflect on how the subject can be led astray by socially induced *desires*. Rather, following Horace, man is deceived by what 'he thinks to be right'. There is a fundamental second-order error at work: the subject desires X and also believes X to be *good*. It is this second layer of analysis – that the subject believes that possessing X will not merely make them happy, but it is right and good for them. The subject is socialised to believe that attaining X will enable them to achieve self-realisation; however, such a belief is illusory, and self-realisation will be forever deferred.

Rousseau's awareness of the subject's precarious happiness and broader vulnerability is reflected throughout his entire work. Symbolically, in *Reveries of a Solitary Walker*, it is *cerastium aquaticium* that Rousseau is most delighted to encounter: a delicate bloom, immensely susceptible to its conditions (Rousseau, 1979 [1782]: 37). Equally, Vevey, Julie's eponymous 'small village at the foot of the alps', could 'not be further from Paris', although it always appears a hostile force, lurking throughout the pages (Delaney, 2009: 28). The social and cultural world attacks the subject: they are unable to resist the deracinating impact of pathological socialisation. As Lukács argued, for Rousseau, the natural world is championed over the urban as it does not corrupt the subject's humanity; it does not suffer from social pathologies (Lukács, 1972 [1923]: 136).

Rousseau's work provides a crucial focus, alerting the social critic to the reality that the subject is socialised to lust after certain 'unnatural' and unproductive needs. The subject is socialised to depend upon X, which is not essential for their biological well-being, and which will not enable their happiness. Rather, it is a social dependency, a pathological dependency, which is problematic both in the forms of inequality it can precipitate, but also in the very nature of the attraction itself. For Rousseau there is something 'corrupt', rather than merely 'tragic', to this reality (Rousseau, 1984 [1762]: 79). The subject endures a truly illusory, counterfeit existence, dominated by 'artificial faculties' and desires (Rousseau, 1984 [1762]: 81). The subject who seeks to demonstrate their superior material wealth over others typifies this. Purchasing symbolic luxuries – and feeling inadequate without them – is a tragic state of affairs. Yet, one's desperation for such commodities is not merely incidental, it is essential to the reproduction of the social-structural system more broadly. As Rousseau beautifully words it, 'people ... purchase imaginary happiness at the price of real happiness' (Rousseau, 1984 [1762]: 77–78). In short: humanity can be conditioned to desire false needs, which harm the capacity for self-realisation. Rousseau's work teaches us that this can, and must, be a focus for critical social research.

Importantly, the artificiality of such false needs is apparent neither to the subject nor to the orthodox social researcher. The philosophes have also been denatured by the world around them, unable to realise their predicament. As Hulliung (1994) wrote, for Rousseau, the philosophes have been so conditioned by modernity they can no longer see its dangers. To use admittedly anachronistic prose, the academic is interpolated by bourgeois ideology, accustomed to what Fromm (2010 [1991]) termed a 'pathological normalcy'. One can thus understand Rousseau's methodological innovation in *The Second Discourse*, his turn to a fictive anthropology. This functions to enable a 'disclosing critique' (see Honneth, 2000); in Fromm's (1963 [1955]: 14) words, it serves to pierce the 'consensual validation' of conventional social reproduction.

Vicious circles

Noone (1980: 67) rightly views Rousseau as being primarily concerned with exposing 'vicious circles': identifying social dynamics which perpetuated, and which often exacerbated, suboptimal social conditions. Neuhouser (2012) is explicit about the centrality of such negative dynamics to Rousseau's work, identifying such logics as integral to the *Discourse on Political Economy*. Neuhouser is also equally explicit that the term 'pathology' is an apposite signifier through which to capture this genera of social problem (Neuhouser, 2012: 637–640). As with Rousseau's diagnosis of pathological needs, his exploration of vicious circles clearly presents a form of social ill which cannot be adequately presented as a mere epiphenomena to recognition relationships.

With Rousseau's diagnosis, we see the prevalence of dynamics which lead to the social world deteriorating, with negative outcomes for multiple subjects, yet which occur without intentional 'human malevolence' (Rousseau, 1979 [1782]: 45). Such vicious circles 'make a bad situation worse and ... once initiated ... [are] ... exceedingly difficult to break' (Neuhouser, 2012: 637, translation from German). For Neuhouser, such a pathology is most clearly expressed in Rousseau's analysis of what might be called the 'homeland security problems' of Ancient Rome. In the *Discourse on Political Economy*, Rousseau details how,

> in order to raise ... armies, tillers had to be taken off the land; the shortage of them lowered the quality of the produce, and the armies' upkeep introduced taxes that raised its price. This first disorder caused the people to grumble: in order to repress them, the number of troops had to be increased, and, in turn, the misery; and the more despair increased, the greater the need to increase it still more in order to avoid its consequences. (cf. Neuhouser, 2012: 637)

Evidently we see a social problem here, one which is not caused by any intentional malice. However, such a dynamic could potentially cause tremendous social harm. What Neuhouser clearly identifies in Rousseau's work is the existence of vicious circles which can cause tremendous social harm without any participant seeking anything other than free and fair intersubjective praxis. As Neuhouser (2012: 637) wrote,

> Under certain conditions a free market, for example, can systematically produce (and reproduce) undesirable consequences – huge inequalities, widespread poverty, the loss of social cohesion – without any of its participants foreseeing or intending them as consequences of their collective action. And, under easily imaginable circumstances, the inequality, poverty, and social dissolution produced at t1 virtually guarantee that, even when all future exchanges are uncoerced and formally just, those initial ills will only be worse at t2.

While Neuhouser's analysis focuses almost exclusively on *Discourse on Political Economy*, such pathological social dynamics are presented throughout the entirety of Rousseau's scholarship and are integral to his pathology diagnosing infrastructure.

I would suggest that the most obvious pathological social dynamic Rousseau diagnoses is that of the changing relationship between the artist and society. For Rousseau, artists seek to shock and entice their audience with ever-increasing contraventions of the social mores. To succeed, the content presented needs to become ever more extreme, ever more debased. For example, in 2021, an objectifying photograph of a female model in skimpy attire on an advertising billboard will turn few heads as commuters dash around the London Underground. Such an image would have been scandalous in the extreme just fifty years ago. To grab the citizens' attention in the twenty-first century, images must be truly explicit, truly risqué. Likewise, for Rousseau, the more the social body becomes inured to 'depravity' in the arts, the more explicit, the more 'degenerate' the content needs to become to hold society's interest (Rousseau, 1968 [1758]). Arts-driven culture inevitably induces a pathological social dynamic – a 'race to the bottom' – yet no participant intentionally desires this to be the case. Ultimately, the 'market for culture dialectically corrupts both artist and patron' (Noone, 1980: 91).

There are further plentiful examples of negative dynamics in Rousseau's work. For Noone, the central 'vicious circle' diagnosed by Rousseau is the destructive drive towards urbanisation.[8] Throughout Rousseau's work, the 'city is the symbol of just about all evils', and the spread of the city is presented as occurring entirely to the detriment of the 'natural' countryside (Noone, 1980: 197). As established above, this was a consistent theme of Rousseau's analysis: it is the beauty of Lake Leman which is lauded and the Parisian salons which are castigated (Rousseau, 1997 [1761]). Noone draws out the 'vicious circle' well:

> The rural sector, the chief source of population, has no motive to increase itself unless it is guaranteed the fruits of its labour. Any increase in parasitic urban numbers entails a corresponding decrease of peasant surpluses through taxation. When this exploitation reaches a point where the law of diminishing returns leaves a family with no reason to enlarge itself, it merely maintains its present size. Any added increment of taxation reduces the former to subsistence level or below. When it thus becomes unprofitable to work the fields, young agriculturalists are forced off the land and into the city; further augmenting the list of parasites. A *vicious circle* results: the more the city grows, the less agriculture produces. (Noone, 1980: 67 – my italics)

Rousseau therefore cautions his reader to remember 'that the walls of towns are made only from the debris of rural houses. Every time I see a mansion being built in the capital I fancy I can see the whole countryside covered with hovels' (Rousseau, 1968 [1762]: 138).

For Lukács (1972 [1923]: 136), Rousseau's diagnosis of unrestrained urbanisation is invested with the moral imperative to critique the 'growth of mechanisation, dehumanisation and reification'. Crucially, however, there is no intentionality to this dehumanising migration. There is no failure of intersubjective praxis behind the dynamics which lead to rural depopulation. Rousseau is clear: pathological social dynamics can occur, with results which produce real suffering, as seamlessly as 'between the first and last terms of a geometric progression' (Rousseau, 1968 [1762]: 103). Such social ills are clearly forms of social pathology and cannot be captured by a monistic recognition account. The diagnosis of vicious circles is a central theme in both Fromm's and Marcuse's critical theory – a theme I return to in Chapters 6 and 7.

Cultural pathology

While for crude Marxists, 'culture' can be dismissed as part of the 'ideological superstructure', a distraction from the foundational logics at work within the 'economic base', Rousseau pays close attention to the cultural realm and its role in social reproduction. In this regard, Rousseau provides essential theoretical scaffolding for the Frankfurt School's more expansive neo-Marxian engagement with culture. Throughout his work, culture is presented as social-pathological insofar as it functions to stabilise and normalise irrational structures and dynamics.[9] This is the insight which most influenced the Frankfurt School. Principally, Rousseau teaches us that culture can become pathological insofar as it can serve to normalise, to support, or to obscure pathological social structures and dynamics. The cultural domain serves to naturalise the unhealthy 'passions and caprices' of modernity, obscuring the contradictory impacts of systems built upon domination and exploitation (Rousseau, 1984 [1762]: 83). As Rousseau succinctly framed it, Parisian bourgeois culture 'maintained the appearance of all the virtues, without being in possession of one of them' (Rousseau, 1993 [1750]: 5). In this regard, culture serves to invisible the irrationalities of the status quo, and thus functions to perpetuate pathological social dynamics. Through this normalising project, culture is able to balm the subject's feelings of alienation from the irrational logics driving social reproduction. The brutality and horror of the social world can be pushed away by a trip to the opera. Yet culture provides an inadequate substitute to a truly rational social order. By investing in the cultural codes and practices of pathological social systems, 'people … purchase imaginary happiness at the price of real happiness' (Rousseau, 1984 [1762]: 77–78). Culture can stabilise pathological social systems, preventing qualitative social transition to a more rational social world.

Yet, Rousseau presents how culture can also manifest distinct pathologies of its own, originating within the cultural realm itself, not merely sitting as an epiphenomena of broader pathological social foundations. Such criticism can be framed as 'culture as pathology' rather than as 'culture stabilising pathologies'. Rousseau is clear: civilisations which invest too heavily in the 'perpetual restraint' of arts-driven 'society' will crumble under the weight of their decadence (Rousseau, 1993 [1750]: 6). The Parisian culture of Rousseau's period was held to both stabilise extant social-structural pathologies and to evince distinct cultural pathologies of its own, offering a 'constant seduction away from humanness' (Strong, 1994: 156).

Conversely, there are forms of simple sociality and culture which do not serve to corrupt. As discussed above, Rousseau was fascinated with Corsica and was desperate to prevent its modernisation. The 'primitive simplicity' with which Corsicans lived was held to provide a form of unalienated existence (Damrosch, 2005: 387). It was the threat of modernisation and mechanisation which often runs tangential to, if not determining, cultural degradation and pathologisation. What Rousseau truly feared was that Corsica would modernise in keeping with the rest of Europe and, in the process, erase the comparative innocence of its pastoral communities.

Throughout Rousseau's analysis, this is the primal pathology associated with culture – regardless of whether we speak of 'culture as stabilising social pathologies' or 'culture as pathology' in and of itself. In both instances, culture denaturalises the subject, displacing innate sentiments (*pitie*, compassion) with 'artificial faculties' (Rousseau, 1984 [1762]: 81). This artificiality evokes a true contempt in Rousseau, and he provides biting indictments of such behaviour across his work. Ultimately, those engrossed in the cultural domain are left stripped of their humanity, as Rousseau wrote: 'They may very well know a bourgeois from Paris or London but they will never know the human' (Rousseau, 1990 [1761]: 388).

Lukács (1972 [1923]: 136) presents a similar reading of Rousseau, in which culture serves to 'strip man of his human essence … the more culture and civilisation … take possession of him, the less able he is to be a human being'. Ultimately, culture serves to denature the subject and impede collective self-realisation. When attempting to rebuild the Frankfurt School's neo-Marxism it is essential to reconnect with Rousseau's work, to identify the plurality of framings of cultural pathology and their impact upon the subject.

Across Rousseau's *oeuvre* one can identify three distinct social maladies which are integral to his critique: (a) where the subject is socialised so as to develop false, and even self-harming, needs; (b) the presence of 'vicious circles' which retrench and exacerbate social problems, and (c) forms of cultural pathology which typically disguises or stabilises irrational social formations. This engagement with Rousseau demonstrates the importance of what Fraser calls a 'multilateral and polycentric' critical theory, an approach to social research which seeks to explore a plurality of social problems across multiple social registers. While today's critical theory is dominated by Honneth's 'perspectival monism' which views all social problems are being reducible to intersubjective recognition relationships, Rousseau's work demonstrates the complexity of the social world, and the multiple types of pathology which exist beyond recognition.

While Rousseau shares Honneth's interest in recognition, I have shown that Rousseau does not collapse into a recognition monism. Rather, Rousseau is explicit that many of the dynamics he describes have a life of their own, and proceed like a 'geometric progression' (Rousseau, 1968 [1762]: 103), without any intentional malevolence or intersubjective component (Rousseau, 1979 [1782]: 45). What is required is a form of social research which understands that social dynamics – particularly those rooted in the distributional mechanisms of the social order – require a form of analysis which transcends recognition. As Rousseau shows, one can rightly hold that distributional logics impact the recognition order; one may even believe that all social inequities stem from some antediluvian recognition-based 'fall'. However, the critical theorist must not attempt to research all social maladies through the single perspective of recognition; even Rousseau, the 'recognition theorist par excellence', does not even conceive of such a project.

Rousseau offers a powerful reminder that the roots of Frankfurt School critical theory sought to interrogate the 'depth of the human problem' (Cullen, 1993: 19), to seek to explore the limitations on human self-realisation and to see where things had gone astray in societal development. When one reads Rousseau in light of Marcuse and Fromm one feels the contemporary relevance of his writing, the enduring challenge of disclosing and critiquing how 'the people ... [have come to] ... purchase imaginary happiness at the price of real happiness' (Rousseau, 1984 [1762]: 77–78) with terrifying and dangerous results.

Notes

1 This text will also be referred to in this chapter as *The First Discourse*.
2 Rousseau came to dislike *The First Discourse*, regarding it 'as amongst the worst' of his writing (see Rousseau, 1953 [1752]: 328–329).
3 Rousseau's first successful opera, often translated as *The Village Soothsayer*. While the score is musicologically progressive, the libretto is socially conservative.
4 *Querelle des Bouffons* (Quarrel of the Comedic Actors) is the term most often applied to the extended musicological-philosophical debate that took place in Paris between 1752 and 1754. Sometimes known instead as *Guerre des Bouffons* (War of the Comedic Actors), the battle lines were drawn between the respective supporters of French and Italian opera.
5 For an expansive and critical exploration, see Robinson (2008).
6 Both were burned, despite substantial opposition from the philosophes. Voltaire famously stated that the burning of the text was one of the few things as atrocious as the writing of it (see Gay, 2009 [1959]).

7 It is the structural beauty of Rousseau's approach, the conversion of the fundamental 'fall' of pride, into the basis for redemption that animates Neuhouser's *Rousseau's Theodicy of Self-Love*.
8 This may perhaps be better framed as 'rural de-population' and 'urbanisation'. In places, the two seem distinct, while in others they are broadly synonymised. This may be a translation issue; I defer to native speakers.
9 As per the central argument in *Discourse on the Arts and Sciences*.

5

Hegelian-Marxism: pathologies of reason, pathologies of production

Rousseau's awareness that society could develop pathologically, imposing 'structural limitations on … human self-realization', was readily imbibed by his successors (Honneth, 2007: 10). Central to Rousseau's diagnosis was the corruption of the subject's fundamental, viscerally felt, needs. For first-generation critical theorists, the malleability of our needs remained a crucial object of social research, and was central to the work of both Erich Fromm (see Chapter 6) and Herbert Marcuse (see Chapter 7). Yet, before resurfacing in the work of the Frankfurt School, Rousseau's insights were invested with a Hegelian-Marxism (see Bronner, 2011: 37). While Rousseau taught that the subject's needs could be pathologically altered, Hegelian-Marxists such as Lukács (1972 [1923]) stressed that subjects' fundamental forms of thought, not merely their thought contents, could be socially denatured (Held, 1980: 151–153). Following Rousseau's pioneering sociological analysis,[1] the distortion of the subject's consciousness was held to occur without any 'intentional malevolence' (Rousseau, 1979 [1782]: 45) – rather, it was framed as a result of broader socio-economic logics. In this way, Hegelian-Marxism served to 'philosophise' Rousseau's proto-sociology, connecting it to a unique form of social epistemology (Bucher, 2012).

In keeping with the objective of this project as a whole, this is not a chapter of 'Marxology', nor a micro-treatise on German idealism. Connoisseurs of Marx and Hegel will not find an analysis of dense Hegel quotations, nor lengthy exegeses of extracts from *Capital*. Rather, the unashamedly reductive intention of this chapter is to further outline the distinctive vision which condensed into the social-theoretical foundations of the Frankfurt School's research programme. While Adorno, Fromm, Marcuse, Benjamin, and Horkheimer were sensitive to Marx's insights, they were not dogmatic in their Marxism. Rather, they sought to develop Marx's thought to understand the circumstances of their day,[2] to explore the peculiar and distinct species of 'smooth, reasonable, democratic unfreedom' which had come to pass (Marcuse, 2007 [1964]: 3). Therefore, it is important to stress that while first-generation critical theorists built upon Hegelian-Marxian foundations, these ideas were mediated by other insights, notably from both Lukács and Weber. First-generation critical theorists sought to learn from, and build upon, Hegel and Marx, without collapsing into either hagiography or economism (Horkheimer, 2018 [1931]: 119).

However, times change. Today, there are loud voices which explicitly reject both Marxism, for its perceived 'productivism' (see Jay, 2008: 5), and Hegelianism, for its 'partisan' metaphysics (Honneth, 2000: 119). Thus, after outlining the influence of Hegelian-Marxism upon pathology diagnosing social research, I engage seriously with such criticisms. I show why such rejections of Hegelian-Marxism are immanently incoherent and counter-productive. I conclude this chapter demonstrating that the foundational insights of Hegelian-Marxism for social pathology scholarship are wilfully neglected by Honneth's recognition monism. This is shown to be to the detriment of a critical theory of society. Honneth's work erases the foundational materialist inversion of Hegelian idealism, eroding the Frankfurt School's social-theoretical foundations. By revisiting the Hegelian-Marxian origins of the original Frankfurt School project, I demonstrate that Honneth's approach to social pathology actually sits closer to a form of Kantianism than to critical theory.

From Kant to Hegel

Hegel's (1770–1831) philosophy is best introduced as a response to the work of Immanuel Kant (1724–1804). At the core of Kant's philosophy sit his 'three critiques': *Critique of Pure Reason* (1787), *Critique of Practical Reason* 1788), and *Critique of Judgement* (1790). United by his Enlightenment investment in autonomy and the power of critical thought, Kant's work placed a primacy on reason,[3] understood as the subject's capacity to engage with the universal 'moral law' (Wood, 2007). Hegel's critique of Kant is primarily focused on the first of his three critiques, *The Critique of Pure Reason*. This work was introduced as a meditation on the very possibility of metaphysics – as to whether a 'faculty of reason in general' might exist. Kant's analysis in this 'first critique' focused on transcendent ideas, which were discernible *a priori*, that is, ideas which did not derive from the subject's lifeworld experiences. Kant divided such *a priori* knowledge into two distinct groups: 'synthetic' and 'analytic'. It was the existence of 'synthetic *a priori*' knowledge which fascinated Kant, and which drove his investigation.

A textbook example of an *analytic a priori* claim would be that 'all bachelors are unmarried men', as further knowledge can be attained by analysing the known information. By definition, a 'bachelor' is a man who has not entered wedlock. As such, we can determine that all bachelors are unmarried men by critical reflection alone; we do not need to conduct empirical research to garner this information. The claim is also valid in all places and at all times, providing the signifier/signified relationship remains stable. In contrast, synthetic *a priori* statements are typified by *prediction*, rather than by forms of syllogistic reasoning. A typical example of an *a priori* synthetic would be determining the date of a future eclipse. The specifics of such an event are ascertainable through an analysis of existing data, without requiring further sensory or empirical input. Astronomers can predict exactly where and when an eclipse will take place on the basis of existing information. Yet such an analysis goes beyond demonstrating what is already extant within the world, in the form of a syllogism. Rather, such synthetic *a priori* statements are typically future-oriented, predictive, a reliable forecast. For Kant, such *predictive* forms of knowledge were essential to the metaphysics undergirding the Enlightenment project more broadly.[4]

Kant argued that such *a priori synthetics* were dependent on the existence of *a priori* perceptive abilities. By this, Kant means that subjects have an innate capacity to perceive space, time, quality, and quantity. Such *a priori* perceptive capabilities manifest in a plurality of permutations; for example, subjects can locate objects in space and time, and can distinguish between quality or quantity. Due to the presence of our *a priori* perceptive capacities, all events and objects are locatable within time and space. As such, we can predict the future based on requisite data; we can contemplate what *will* happen, in terms of prognoses of motion and progression. Without such foundational capabilities, basic geophysical considerations would be impossible. For Kant, such abilities were universal and fixed and were central to the power of human reason. As such, the presence of meaningful *synthetic a priori* statements demonstrated the existence of a remarkable cognitive capacity – of perceptive abilities which enable predictive forecasting – central to the development of the Enlightenment project.

Hegel's philosophy marked a radical departure from Kant's. With Hegel, 'reason' was reframed as a metaphysical 'spirit' or 'mind' (*Geist*).[5] In Hegel's formulation, 'reason' was, importantly, no longer simply cognitive and static. Rather, *Geist* was held to be 'unfolding' historically across both the social and the natural world. While Kant's critique of reason was universal, timeless, and noumenal, Hegel liberated reason from the confines of cognition, and analysed *Geist* as an explicitly social and historical process (Marcuse, 1969b: 251–257). The subject's perceptive capabilities were reframed as being historically dependent on the development of socio-historical *Geist*.

With Hegel, the critique of reason became a critique of society itself: how far *Geist* had developed within society impacted the rational capacities of the subject. Hegel's broader project sought to demonstrate the historical evolution, or 'unfolding', of reason over time, across societies. As a result, an idiosyncratic form of 'Reflective History', which he christened 'Universal History', was central to Hegel's work. Such a discipline focuses on one metaprocess, the inexorable unfolding of *Geist*. This progression of *Geist* is the true force propelling Hegel's philosophy. Crucially, the innate *a priori* conditions of perception, essential to the subject's capacity for critical thought, the key to Kant's enquiry into *a priori* synthetics, had been repositioned by Hegel as a product of the unfolding of *Geist*.

Hegel's account is totalising: all culture and history can be understood as the process of abstract *Geist* finding form ('being actualised' (*Verwirklichung*)) in institutions and in modes of cognition.[6] It is through overcoming ('sublating' (*Aufheben*)) the internal contradictions of the present (inadequacies in societal organisation and forms of thought) that *Geist* unfolds. In this process, irrational forms of thought and societal organisation are displaced by more coherent institutional arrangements and forms of consciousness. There is also an eschatological inflection to Hegel's work (Tucker, 1964: 45–48); spirit continues unfolding until the 'rational universal' is reached, until all contradictions are worked through. The ultimate destination of the Hegelian social-philosophical (*Rechtsphilosophie*) project is a grand 'reconciliation' (*Versöhnung*): of *Geist* with the world (see Hardimon, 1992).

Controversially, Hegel argued that such 'reconciliation' had occurred with the Prussian state of his day. The existing social institutions were held to be internally coherent, Prussian society was presented as reflecting the highest possible standards of reason available. There were thus no extant social pathologies.[7] Rather, the challenge was simply for individuals to realise the rational perfection of the social system: for the individual to be reconciled with the 'modern world' (Hardimon, 1992: 165–167). Through reading Hegel's text, the subject could attain similar perfection in their own thought, reshaping their *a priori* perceptive capabilities so as to be in communion with the rational structure of society. Hegel's two most famous books, *Philosophy of Right* 1820) and *Phenomenology of Spirit* 1807), might, therefore, both be considered deeply conservative. When the reader has read (and understood) *Phenomenology of Spirit*, they will (allegedly) be able to achieve the highest possible standard of consciousness. Equally, through a reading of *Philosophy of Right*, the reader will be able to comprehend the perfection of the extant (Prussian) social world.

Pathologies of reason

Yet conflicting interpretations abounded (see Pippin, 1981; Roberts, 2013). While conservative elements, the so-called right-Hegelians, utilised Hegel's work to justify the political conjuncture of their day, many progressives saw utility in Hegel's method, rather than in his conclusions (Harris, 1958). These so-called left-Hegelians, or 'young Hegelians', re-energised the Hegelian project. Such figures included Ludwig Feuerbach, Arnold Ruge, Bruno Bauer, and most famously of all, Karl Marx (see McLellan, 1969). In direct opposition to conservative readings of Hegel, the young Hegelians repurposed Hegel's work as a foundation for revolutionary social transformation. For left-Hegelians, '[t]he existence of ... social suffering ... is explicable only as the given social world exists as an "insufficient appropriation" of an "objectively" already possible reason' (Honneth, 2007: 23). From this perspective, the fact that suffering continued meant that *Geist* could not possibly have completed its unfolding; 'reconciliation' had not yet been attained (Harris, 1958). As such, both the form of consciousness embodied by social subjects, and the dominant form of social organisation, required sustained critical inquiry.

With this awareness, the task became furthering the development of the unfolding of spirit, by engaging with, and critiquing, the obstacles preventing the unfolding of *Geist*. Such impediments were 'pathologies of reason', the social-structural limitations obstructing subjects from attaining a good and happy life. Strydom presents such 'pathologies of reason' as the 'Gordian knot' which left-Hegelians forever unpick, their Sisyphean challenge (Strydom, 2008). It thus becomes possible to understand the limitations of the contemporary capitalist world in purely Hegelian terms, where the 'pathological deformation by capitalism may be overcome only by initiating a process of enlightenment among those involved' (Honneth, 2007: 21). The critical theorist is able to provide such enlightenment by diagnosing the pathologies of reason in the present, by exposing the areas of the social world, and of the subject's consciousness, where the highest available standard of reason is impeded. Such an effort includes disclosing the distortion of subject's *a priori* perceptive capabilities (see Chapter 7 on Marcuse).

Left-Hegelians identify where the 'rational universal' is yet to be attained, and where the social world falls short of the standards of objectively possible reason. The task is to 'practically remedy' the gulf between the organisation of the social world and the rational potential latent within it (Honneth, 2007: 21). Such pathologies in the development of reason can exist in any social domain: in the organisation of sexual relations, in the modes of economic exchange, or in the forms of aesthetic appreciation (Hegel, 1953 [1822]: Part 3, Section C; see also Honneth, 2007: 23–27). Thus, the challenge is to subject society as a 'totality' to continual, rigorous critique (Honneth, 2007: 24), to remorselessly 'look the negatives in the face' (Hegel, 1977 [1807]: 36). In Marcuse's (1969b: 11) words, 'As long as there is any gap between real and potential, the former must be acted upon and changed until it is brought into line with reason'.

Hegelian-Marxism

To briefly recap: Kant held that all subjects were born with fixed *a priori* perceptive capabilities. Hegel, in contrast, considered the subject's cognitive capacities were historically and culturally dependent, a result of a metaphysical social process: the unfolding of *Geist*. It was against this backdrop that Karl Marx presented a radical reorientation of the German philosophical tradition. Marx 'turned Hegel on his head', arguing famously that 'it is not the consciousness of men that determines their existence, but their social existence that determines their consciousness' (Marx, 2010 [1859]: 92). This materialist inversion of Hegel's idealism is crucial to first-generation critical theory, centrally informing the Hegelian-Marxian understanding of 'pathologies of reason'. Marx's argument is thus worth unpacking to demonstrate its impact on the social-theoretical foundations of Frankfurt School social research, and to highlight the divergence between Hegelian-Marxism and Honneth's approach today.

While Hegel considered *Geist* to be unfolding over time, determining both the subject's cognitive capacities and the institutional structure of the social world, Marx reversed the causality. For Marx, the cognitive capabilities of the subject were a result of the development of the material world, rather than a result of the unfolding of *Geist*. As such, 'pathologies of reason' were held to derive from the material organisation of society; the world shapes our ideas and our consciousness, rather than our consciousness shaping our world. This insight marked a crucial moment for Frankfurt School scholarship to come: that our capacity to engage with the world, including our *a priori* conditions of consciousness, can be deformed by societal logics. Forms of societal domination can impede our capacity for critical engagement with the social world. As Schecter (2019: 12) succinctly framed it, for critical theorists, following Marx, 'epistemological issues have political ramifications'.

For Marx, the social existence of subjects, including the *a priori* conditions of their consciousness, was impacted by the system of production. Marx's broader dialectical materialist philosophy famously found form in a particularly *historical* materialism, which demonstrated a sensitivity to changing class dynamics over time. This productivism is justified both anthropologically and sociologically. Labour is presented as being a fundamental quality of human life: we are productive creatures, who make our mark upon the world. Labouring is what makes us human, making the 'externalisation'

(*Entäußerung*) of the worker from his product all the more harrowing (Marx, 1975 [1844]: 324). Sociologically, the dynamics imbedded within production are held to have a causal primacy upon all aspects of social life: in a crude reading of Marx, the working of the economic 'base' are held to substantially determine the contents of the socio-cultural 'superstructure' (Harnecker, 1976: 32–35). Thus, while Hegel argued that the dialectical clash of competing ideas drove social development, Marx presented a historical materialism, in which the contradictions inherent within productive forces drove social change. For Marx, these contradictory forces were manifest over time in different class configurations, each possessing competing – and mutually irreconcilable – interests, within the given economic structure. With his historical materialism, the clash of competing class interests displaced Hegel's dialectical sublation of contradictions within unfolding *Geist*. Critical theorists thus retain an interest in the 'fundamental problem about knowledge' (Schecter, 2010: 51), which drove Kant's inquiry; however, the idealism is seeded into a historical materialism. The mutability of our *a priori* perceptive capacities is reframed by Marx as epiphenomenal to the clash of class interests within the dominant mode of production.

Lukács and reification

While first-generation critical theory was anchored in a fusion of Hegelian and Marxian ideas, it was György Lukács (1885–1971), in *History and Class Consciousness*, who produced the foundational work of a distinctly 'Hegelian-Marxism' (Bartonek and Burman, 2018).[8] As Lukács (1972 [1923]: 84) expressed in the essay 'Reification and the Consciousness of the Proletariat', his research was based 'on Marx's economic analyses … proceed[ing] from there to a discussion of the problems growing out of the fetish character of commodities, both as an objective form and also as a *subjective stance corresponding to it*' (my italics).

Lukács (1972 [1923]: 84) was adamant that '[o]nly by understanding this can we obtain a clear insight into the ideological problems of capitalism'. His work thus focused on the 'subjective stance' induced by, and corresponding to, a world dominated by the 'fetish character of commodities'. Expressed plainly, he focused on determining the relationship between the irrationality of the capitalist system and the cognitive capacities of the subject. This inquiry was developed in both Lukács's own work, and in the extensive research programme advanced by the Frankfurt School, the fruits of which were remarkable studies on the pathologies of reification, instrumental reason, and the deformed subject of modernity. While the Frankfurt School developed Lukács's work to build their own social research agenda, they did so critically.⁹ Lukács's work should be read as a vital waypoint between a direct conflation of Hegel and Marx and the fully fledged Hegelian-Marxism of the mature Frankfurt School.

Reification is a multifaceted concept, encompassing ossified forms of thought ('reified consciousness'), petrified forms of sociality ('reified social relations'), and, perhaps most intuitively, the reduction of the entire external world to object status ('reification of nature').[10] While present within Marx's writings, Lukács truly developed the concept and presented it as a crucial concern for critical study. A textbook definition of 'reification' is offered by Petrovic, as

> The act (or result of the act) of transforming human properties, relations and actions into properties, relations and actions of man-produced things which have become independent (and which are imagined as originally independent) of man and govern his life. Also transformation of human beings into thing-like beings which do not behave in a human way but according to the laws of the thing-world. Reification is a 'special' case of alienation, its most radical and widespread form characteristic of modern capitalist society. (Petrovic, 1983: 411)

Reification is clearly thick with both Hegelian and Marxian motifs and directs a critical focus upon pathologies within the social world which remain underexplored in classical liberal philosophy. The root cause of reification is held to be the capitalist form of life. In *Negative Dialectics*, Adorno refers to reification as explicitly 'epiphenomenal', as symptomatic of the underlying contradictions of the socio-economic order (Adorno, 2007 [1966]: 189–192). The analysis of reification is crucial – it marks a fundamental pathology within the social world, however, it stands as secondary feature, precipitated by the fact that 'capitalist relations of production have come to dominate society as a whole, leading to extreme, albeit often invisible, concentrations of wealth and power' (see Adorno, 2007 [1966]: 189–192). The precise lineaments of theories of reification are increasingly debated, with Žižek arguing that the current form of capitalism is so brazen about its form of social relationality that one can no longer utilise the framing of reification in 'the classic Lukácsian sense' (Žižek, 2010: 221). However, critical theorists of all stripes remain invested in the notion of reification. Honneth (2008) has even offered a controversial reworking of the concept as a further justification of his recognition monism. This demonstrates the enduring appeal of reification as an important concept for critical theory. Reification remains a central vector in critical social research, and marked a vital original development of Hegelian-Marxism into a viable research agenda.

Lukács was focused on the reification of consciousness, as reflected by the title of his most famous essay in *History and Class Consciousness*. For

Westerman, this stems from Lukács's keen reading of Edmund Husserl's phenomenology (Westerman, 2019). With a Husserl-inflected reading of Lukács, the reification of consciousness can be understood as the creation of an artificial distantiation between the subject and the external world, where the subject considers the world in a disengaged and dispassionate register. The capitalist mode of production served to break the subject out of their natural world, and instead presented the world to them as a mixture of dead objects and fixed relations. The natural fluidity and dynamism of social reality is replaced by a barren, 'quality-less', standardised order.

Likewise, Adorno and Horkheimer focused extensively on the impact of capitalist society on consciousness. However, unlike Lukács, they linked reification to a broader metanarrative, viewing capitalism as the manifestation of underlying 'barbaric' Enlightenment logics. Sharing Lukács's understanding that capitalism reified consciousness, the co-authors wrote in *Dialectic of Enlightenment* that the bourgeois individual is left unable to comprehend qualitative values and individual essences. Rather, Enlightenment thought served to induce a form of 'identity thinking' in which the lifeworld was understood through a division of 'concepts'. All particular realities, subjects, thoughts, emotions, hopes, or lives could be 'perceive[d] ... only as one case of the general' concept (Adorno and Horkheimer, 1997 [1944]: 84–85). 'Identity thinking' thus serves to reinforce reified consciousness, birthing subjects unable to feel a connection to the qualitative and the particular. Rather, the reified consciousness experiences the 'elimination of qualities' (Adorno and Horkheimer, 1997 [1944]: 39), viewing the social world through a petrified fixity of relational categories. The particular, individual X is understood merely as a singular, exchangeable instance of a broader conceptual category.

For Lukács (1972 [1923]: 6), this reification of consciousness inevitably led to 'the reification of all human relations'. The subject's relationship to the Other, as well as their relationship to self, had become fundamentally distorted and pathological. The subject engaged the Other through the rationality of the market, inflected by dominant logics of exchange and equivalence. Capitalist society had served to reify intersubjectivity itself, ruthlessly engendering a 'conversion into functions' of social relations (Adorno and Horkheimer, 1997 [1944]: 36). Subject X viewed and enacted their dyad with subject Y in keeping with the relational necessities of the market. Such a deformed relationship occurred through the degeneration of the subject's perceptive *a priori* capacities: the reification of consciousness manifested in a destruction of the innate sociality of the subject. Likewise, the external world, nature, even the beauty of a sunset, is reduced to its 'functional' value. For Horkheimer (1993: 81), the natural world thus becomes 'dead matter – a heap of things'. A 'phantom objectivity' and equivalence emerges. For example, the marketable 'attention-value' of a photograph of said sunset on Instagram is implicitly equivalent to X commodity. The natural and human world is robbed of its majesty, of quality, of distinction. An equivalence-oriented instrumentality achieved hegemony.

Instrumental reason

The analysis of exactly such an 'instrumental' relation became a central feature of the early Frankfurt School's pathology diagnosing research. This focus on an ascendant 'instrumental rationality' served to connect Marxist and Hegelian insights with the work of Max Weber. In contrast to Durkheimian sociologists, Weber (1947) famously stressed the importance of the subject's understanding and interpretation (*Verstehen*) of their social world. For Weber, positivistic analyses of the scientifically observable 'social facts' failed to capture the complexity of the human condition, the core of what makes humans distinct social animals: our capacity for understanding our lifeworlds. Yet, Weber analysed how this crucial distinguishing factor of our humanity was being eroded by the processes of 'rationalisation' connected to capitalist imperatives (Weber, 1992 [1905]: xviii). For Weber, modernity was increasingly typified by the supremacy of a formal, 'instrumental rationality', dominating over the pre-existing substantive, qualitative, and affective forms of thought. Processes lodged deep within the formations of 'European' modernity were held to have pathologically denatured the subject's cognitive capacities.

Ultimately the dialectical working through of contradictions was meant to be liberating and inexorable. Yet, for Weber, reason itself had become pathological, instead of serving to sublate its contradictions, the dialectical unfolding had taken a wrong course. Instead of working through its contradictions and producing a more rational society, modernity showcased a 'rationalisation' marked by the streamlining of social processes, the redundancy of all forms of thought and behaviour which impeded optimal production. The dialectical progression of *Geist* had been deformed by capitalist modernity. The contradictions being sublated within society were increasingly the obstacles to optimal market efficiency.

For Weber, advanced bureaucratic systems typified the pathologically 'purposive' or 'instrumental' rationality, where the space for critical reflection, or qualitative input, was lost. In place of quantitative transitions (changes within the system) leading to qualitative transformation (a new system), as per the basis of Hegel's logic, Weber presented modernity as the ever-advancing march of a mono-perspectival rationalisation.

Thought was becoming trapped in a purposive instrumentality; an 'iron cage' was being placed upon the consciousness of the social subject (Weber, 1992 [1905]: 123).

Weber's insights were thus crucial to the Hegelian-Marxism of Adorno and Horkheimer, and this fusion was further developed by Marcuse and, to a lesser extent, by Fromm. For critical theorists, the unfolding of *Geist* was no longer something which could be seamlessly nursed through its sublations. Rather, Weber's work obliquely drew out how the unfolding of *Geist* is not merely retarded by stubborn contradictions, but that the actualisation of reason within society can be blocked by institutional imperatives colonising social learning processes.

For Lukács (1972 [1923]: 6), aggressive instrumental reason dovetailed with the 'phantom objectivity' of false equivalences. For Adorno and Horkheimer (1997 [1944]: 7), the qualitative and the affective were devalued, 'written off as literature', as indulgent and antiquated. Reification and instrumental rationality thus united to further exploitative, pathological capitalist imperatives. For Schecter (2010), one can thus identify a legacy of the critique of instrumental reason as a crucial trajectory for critical theory more broadly. From such a vantage point, one sees the Frankfurt School's research agenda to be foregrounding the Hegelian-Marxian insight that there exists a relationship between the structural imperatives of social institutions and the forms of thought which dominate amongst social actors. The idea that social learning processes can thus become deformed, can manifest pathologies, becomes central to the research objective. The diagnosis of social pathologies thus argues that society is dogged by an irrationality which cannot be sublated, which is fundamentally imbricated within the capitalist system.

Enter psychoanalysis

As such, the understanding of the subject which first-generation Frankfurt School scholars operated with was truly Marxian. Frankfurt School scholarship saw the subject as impacted by complicated forces, with a form of consciousness which was reified and distorted by social-systemic logics. In this regard, Fromm and Marcuse were particularly alive to the utility of marrying Freudian and Marxian insights. The cocktail of ideas thus became even headier: Freud and Marx worked alongside Weber and Hegel.

Marx had written about the bifurcation of the social world induced by the ascendant commodity form at the start of Book One of *Capital*. The market is based on logics of equivalence and 'exchange value', rather than on 'use value' (Marx, 1976 [1867]). This produces a damaging discordance for the social subject, who is naturally aware of both ontologies existing within the social world. According to the Marxist account of human nature, we are anthropologically inclined to utilise the social world on its functional merits: to intuitively think in terms of 'use value' (Mehrotra, 1991). For example, when we see a spade in the garden shed, we think of it first and foremost as an instrument which can be used for digging, rather than as a commodity worth £16.99 new at Tesco, with a potential second-hand value of £3 on eBay. Yet, as Adorno and Horkheimer wrote in *Dialectic of Enlightenment*, capitalism compels the subject to deny this basic 'instinct', and to engage primarily calculatedly (Adorno and Horkheimer, 1997 [1944]: 69). The world of external objects is shattered into equivalences and exchange values. The spade must increasingly be seen as an asset, worth £3.

For Lukács, this 'fragmentation of the object of production' led inexorably to the 'fragmentation of ... the subject' (Lukács, 1972 [1923]: 89). The market-socialised subject is forced to consider that the time spent aiding a co-worker carrying books into their new office, for instance, is counter-productively wasting twenty-five minutes of their productivity. This is an unhealthy and unsustainable attitude for a creature which is, at core, social. The crucial point to underscore here is that the Hegelian-Marxian insight – that the subject's cognitive capacities are fundamentally impacted by institutional logics which can impede social learning processes – can manifest in forms of *psychopathologies*.

The subject's experience of neurosis and anxiety is thus fundamentally connected to the pathological irrationality of the social world (see Chapters 6 and 7). A critical psychoanalysis and psychiatry thus discloses the importance for social-structural change, rather than medicating and reformatting the subject constantly to be 'resilient' (Flick, 2016) in the face of pathological institutional imperatives. In a world where 'happiness is obsolete', as Adorno framed it in *Minima Moralia*, the disclosing power of the somatic manifestations of the unconscious offers a powerful entry point to social research. The pathologies of the social world can, and must, be connected to the psychopathologies manifest within the capitalist subject (Fromm, 1963 [1955]).

This Freudo-Marxian insight returns to the broader Hegelian-Marxian animus of Frankfurt School research into social pathologies. The irrational structure of the social world is intimately connected to the forms of thought dominant within social subjects. Schecter powerfully draws out how, in keeping with Marx's materialist inversion of Hegelian idealism, the dominant forms of irrationalism required a political solution: a revolution in the form of qualitative social organisation and the transcendence of identity thinking. For Schecter, reification and social neuroses are not individual failures of cognition or resilience, rather they are reflective of a broader social pathology, located in the contradiction between the interests of the social subject and the imperatives of the capitalist social system. The irrational nature of the social world and of the subject's forms of cognition and consciousness is thus 'an epistemological problem which can no longer be solved philosophically ... [I]t is ... an absolutely fundamental problem about knowledge which *requires a practical political solution* because the moment for its theoretical resolution as a knowledge problem has been made redundant by history' (Schecter, 2010: 51 – my italics).

As Schecter argued, it is not possible to provide a solution to these forms of irrationality simply through a correction of the 'knowledge problem' they represent (Schecter, 2010: 51). Rather, it is essential to understand such reificatory logics as requiring a 'practical political solution' (Schecter, 2010: 51). Marxism had fused with Hegelian in a manner that prioritised material, qualitative transformation. Or, as Marx (1998 [1932]) more famously worded it, 'the philosophers have only interpreted the world, the point, however, is to change it'. This Hegelian-Marxian animus guided first-generation pathology diagnosing critical theory. The idiosyncratic fusion of Marx and Hegel, Weber and Freud, drove the research programme and was crucial to the work of Fromm and Marcuse (see Chapters 6 and 7).

Honneth's rejection of Hegelian-Marxism

Honneth's recognition monism contrasts starkly with the Hegelian-Marxism of first-generation critical theory. For Lukács, Adorno, and Marcuse, the subject is fundamentally shaped by what Thompson terms 'constitutive power', which modifies the subject's *a priori* perspective abilities, inducing a form of 'reified consciousness'. From such a viewpoint, power clearly precedes subjectivation; the subject's cognitive and intersubjective capabilities are determined by the external world. In contrast, recognition relationships occur after the subject has been denatured by capitalism. For Hegelian-Marxists, social-structural imperatives, which are themselves the manifestation of a certain development of historically mediated reason, impact the cognitive capacities of the subject. As such, said logics must be the centre of analysis, as they determine and precede intersubjective relationships. Indeed, *all* cognitive processes are shaped by social-structural power. Our capacity to understand the Other, to engage with the world around us, to appreciate, and to view the natural world, or to perceive qualitative values, is determined, and can be vitiated by, overbearing logics and social-structural imperatives impacting our *a priori* conditions of consciousness. That is what the German-idealist legacy teaches: from Kant to Lukács, we learned that the preconditions for consciousness are socio-historically variable, and that no 'pure' prelapsarian capacities reside, lodged deep within the psyche. For Hegelian-Marxists a primary (but not sole) factor which pathologically distorts the subject's cognitive capacities derives from the logics which 'pulse' within the market (Thompson, 2016: 7). As such, market dynamics are held to deform subjectivity and to reify consciousness. The commodity-driven society serves to perpetuate a pathological form of reason.

For Honneth (2007: 20), for today's reader, nothing would sound 'more foreign' than the above sketch. In direct contrast to Hegelian-Marxian accounts of pathologically deformed social rationality, Honneth (2008) redefines 'reification' as a sub-species of denied recognition. For Honneth, reification is a 'forgetting' of the real content of the object of cognition: be it a sunset, or lover, or colleague, or woodpecker. At first glance, this appears close to Adorno's framing. However, this 'forgetting' is not due to a socially induced decay of the subject's *a priori* perceptive capabilities, as this would admit to the ontological primacy of the structural relations of capitalism over intersubjective praxis. This is something anathema to the critical theory of recognition, and would be fatal to Honneth's broader project, which is predicated on consistently placing ontological and causal primacy on the recognition moment. Rather, for Honneth, such a 'forgetting' refers to the loss of an original, deep-seated form of interpersonal relation, or self-relation, which is held to *precede* such socialisation. Honneth's reframing of reification serves to entrench the erroneous ontological primacy of the recognition moment within his programme.

Such an effort lapses plainly into a clear neo-Idealism. Honneth's account is again predicated on the idea there are some *a priori* capacities which exist which are pure and can form the basis of our sociality, which are immune from the deracinating impacts of social structural power. But Hegelian-Marxism teaches us that our cognitive capacities develop within the power-strewn complexity of the social world. Reification must be understood as a result of social-structural imperatives.

As Berlant, Fraser, Thompson, and McNay argued, Honneth's account is, yet again, shown to be predicated on a false account of power. In contrast, Hegelian-Marxian insights demonstrate that our capacities for social engagement, intersubjective and reflexive, are impacted by social structural logics which are coeval with subjectivation: there is no pristine prelapsarian knowledge – this is the primary insight which Marx and Hegel offer Frankfurt School critical theory. Power and knowledge are connected. Hegel's critique of Kant is that both our thought contents and the manner of our thinking are impacted by social reality. What is thus required is the rigorous analysis of everything before us – both of our external world and of our thought contents. We must not invest in some fictive pure moment of praxis. Honneth has returned to a Kantian belief in some constant *a priori* capacities, ignoring the foundational lessons offered by the founding fathers of critical theory.

Habermas and the rejection of metaphysics

Since Habermas, social theory has been expunging metaphysics from its texts in favour of a move to formal pragmatics and critical hermeneutics (Honneth, 1995 [1992]: 1). As Habermas (2017) expressed in *Post Metaphysical Thinking*, the reliance of the 'first generation' on a metaphysically weighty left-Hegelianism was to henceforth remain unambiguously in the past. There are three related claims to consider here: (i) that Hegelian-Marxism is inescapably tied to a metaphysics, (ii) that this is philosophically unjustifiable/undesirable, and (iii) that 'third-generation' critical theory has managed to avoid all metaphysical claims. I contend that all assumptions can be questioned, and that there is an immanent incoherence to a rejection of Hegelian-Marxism on the basis of its perceived unjustifiable metaphysics. I stress this contribution is but an invitation for further dialogue, and the full scope of such a discussion is far beyond this present book. However, I contend that these considerations are pressing and important for the broader discussion on the state of pathology diagnosing critical theory.

While an orthodox Hegelian-Marxian approach holds to a concept of 'reason' which is 'thick' and 'social', it does not necessarily need to accede to a substantive grand metaphysics. While it is entirely the case that Hegel's approach is predicated on the unfolding of a metaphysical *Geist*, this does not mean that all subsequent framings have to retain an identical Hegelian metaphysics. The (undeniable) insight that the organisation of the social world serves to further particular forms of thinking can be productively engaged with without needing to believe a singular 'spirit' drives all nature and humanity on its predetermined unfolding. It is possible to redact the metaphysical understanding of *Geist* while arguing that normative value positions are implicit within, and reinforced by, various forms of social practice, which serve important functions in the acculturation of social subjects to broader societal goals and which can impact the subject's cognitive capacities – as repeatedly demonstrated above.

This leads to the second rejoinder: I argue that it is not *necessarily* ideal for critical theory to seek to dispense with all metaphysical content. I stress this claim is made as a provocation, and I admit to the complexity of such a charge. However, there is an extensive and growing literature, which takes such a position. Indeed, Thompson's (2016) *Domestication of Critical*

Theory is very clear on the merits of re-centring a critical social ontology as a pivotal component of a reinvigorated critical theoretical endeavour. For Thompson (2016: 179–180),

> an essential aspect of the neo-Idealist turn in critical theory has been its turn away from metaphysics and towards a pragmatist conception of social practice ...
> ... By detaching itself from the ontological questions that Hegel and Marx had pursued, neo-Idealists are unable to secure a rational, universal understanding of the dynamics of a rational social order structured by truly free agents.

In keeping with Thompson's broader project, one can see how a return to a critical social ontology *could* be of merit for comprehending the impact of social structures on processes of socialisation (in Thompson's terms, their 'constitutive power'). Thompson (2016: 180) further justifies his position, 'we obtain rational (i.e. critical) cognition about the world only by estranging ourselves from it, not by being folded into its immediacy. Only conceptual thought can mediate the object domain, and as concept-users, the central task is to find those concepts that can mediate the world rationally.'

One may thus question whether it is indeed desirable to show how one can discard the metaphysical heritage of a pathologies of reason approach. While above I argued that a pathologies of reason perspective can be adopted shorn of a burdensome metaphysics, following Thompson (2016: 180), I am tempted to agree that one is able to discover 'a much more comprehensive and more critically engaged form of social critique' *with* a critical metaphysics. That stated, such a discussion is vast and beyond the scope of this volume.

One can also question whether third-generation critical theory has actually achieved its objective of a metaphysically abstinent approach to social research. Intersubjective praxis, while framed through the optic of pragmatics and recognition, purports as being empirical, 'grounded', terrestrial. However, from a certain distantiation, 'recognition' is an exceedingly metaphysical construct. 'Intersubjectivity' and 'subjectivation' cannot be empirically tested; all that can be researched is the affective experience of a singular subject, a monad of the dyad. The subject's feeling of 'disrespect' or 'misrecognition' is the raw material of the critical theory of recognition. The purported focus is on the 'recognition moment', and on 'recognition relations' – the actual moment of praxis is illusory, it remains inaccessible, hypostatised, and abstract. Again, such a claim would need to be much further developed; however, I present it as a provocation, an attempt to show how the established certainties of post-metaphysical critical theory are less secure than one might think.

The central claim I wish to make here is that one does not need to dispense with the central Marxian-Hegelian insights because of their perceived partisan metaphysics. Rather, the core tenets which push left-Hegelian research can be productively furthered *with or without* a metaphysical foundation. The desecration of the Hegelian-Marxian legacy cannot be justified by arguments to the established viability of transitioning critical theory to a metaphysically abstinent research agenda and the necessity to do so. The insight that the structural imperatives of the social world may impact our cognitive capacities does not require a partisan metaphysics: merely a belief in the power of socialisation more broadly. As such, there is a clear incoherence in the core rejection of the left-Hegelian framing on three grounds. One, left-Hegelian insights can continue to shape critical theory without the need for a metaphysics; two, such a metaphysics is no longer seen as being *universally* unjustifiable; and three, Honneth's critical theory, with its investment in some prelapsarian intersubjective capacity, seems highly partisan in its metaphysical presuppositions, and has thus rightly been referred to as neo-Idealist.

Hegelian-Marxism provided crucial foundations for the social-theoretical base of the Frankfurt School's research programme. Such a perspective served to take insights and research interests from Rousseau's proto-sociology and produced a radical, interdisciplinary framework. As the following discussion shall demonstrate, the fusion of Marx, Hegel, Rousseau, Freud, and Weber provided a unique and idiosyncratic basis from which Fromm and Marcuse were able to advance their pathology diagnosing social research.

Hegelian-Marxism may seem dated. Honneth is correct to write that many of the insights from Lukács may seem far from the presuppositions of critical sociology, let alone liberal philosophy, dominant today. Yet, the fundamental insights carried by the Hegelian-Marxist paradigm remain valid and the reasons for their dismissal seem increasingly suspect in retrospect. That Adornian critical theory had reached a 'dead end', and that metaphysics was toxic, no longer seem forceful arguments to reject the idea that how we think within, as well as about, our social world, is fundamentally impacted by our social world. In contrast, and with a certain irony, today Thompson and others have demonstrated that a belief in some inviolable cognitive capacity which enables a just and equitable society to emerge, seems ultimately more unjustifiable and idealist.

As the following chapters on Fromm and Marcuse shall present, these bickering heirs to Freud advanced forms of social research which served to explore the social world with the full force of the pathology diagnosing imagination. In contrast to further investment in an unverifiable inviolable cognitive capacity for sociality, in defiance of the entire trajectory of German idealism, I submit it makes more sense to consider the possibility that our social being is impacted by our social world. In short, in the following chapter, I argue for the continued relevance of a fusion of Marcuse and Fromm's work to advance a framing of social pathology apposite to the challenges of the day; a framing which captures the Hegelian-Marxist insights of the first generation.

Notes

1. Durkheim famously considered Rousseau to be the first sociologist (see Durkheim, 1960).
2. Which, as McKenzie Wark reminds us, was also Marx's objective (see Wark, 2021: 7).
3. Although Kant rarely uses the word 'reason' explicitly, leading to debate on the precise focus of his enquiry and best translational practice.
4. For a broader discussion of Kant's view, see Dupré (1998).
5. While *Geist* is famously hard to define, it is perhaps best understood as an amalgam of the English words 'reason', 'self-understanding', and 'spirit' (see Houlgate, 2012).
6. As Tucker words it, for Hegel, 'world history is thus the unfolding of Geist in time, as nature is the unfolding of Geist in space' (see Tucker, 1964: 47).
7. For a wider reaching discussion, see Knox (1940).
8. Karl Korsch was another important figure in the development of a distinctly Hegelian-Marxism, however due to space considerations I focus solely on Lukács here.
9. Indicative of the Frankfurt School's productive, yet critical, relationship with Lukács is their work on reification. For instance, Adorno, in *Negative Dialectics*, explicitly critiqued Lukács' theory of reification as lapsing into a form of idealism (see Adorno, 2007 [1966]: 191).
10. For an extended and contemporary taxonomy, see Gunderson (2021).

Part III

A Fromm-Marcuse synthesis

6

Erich Fromm and pathological normalcy

Lukács (1971 [1920]: 22) famously derided Adorno for enjoying the pleasures of the 'Grand Hotel Abyss', for observing the horrors of the modern world with a detached, almost nihilistic, indifference. Histories of the Frankfurt School tend to echo this stance, holding Adorno to have written critical theory into an 'ivory tower' irrelevance (Višić, 2020). In response to activist demands for revolutionary praxis, Adorno warned against an ascendant 'actionism' and 'left-fascism' (Richter and Adorno, 2002: 11). While the protestors sought insurrection, Adorno advocated for the emancipatory possibilities of abstract art (Jarvis, 1998: 90–123). The discordance between Adorno's appreciation for Berg and the *soixante-huitards*' barricades could not have been more striking. In the eyes of his militant students, Adorno was increasingly seen as a bourgeois irrelevance, and even as an obstacle to socialist transition (see Müller-Doohm, 2005: 475). Habermas is typically presented as 'rescuing' critical theory from this impasse, offering a much-needed reshaping of the research programme with his rejection of metaphysics and investment in communicative action (Alexander, 1985). Honneth's critical theory of recognition is held to have further developed this trajectory (see Ivković, 2017). However, this narrative fails to tell the full tale.

True, Adorno's work did become increasingly inaccessible and removed from the protestor's demands for immediate material praxis. He had distanced himself from existing radical movements, even calling the police on student protestors occupying his office (Adorno and Marcuse, 1999: 125). Yet, the Frankfurt School was always larger than Adorno; simultaneously, other critical theorists, such as Herbert Marcuse and Erich Fromm, took different stances. Marcuse famously supported the student activists, encouraging their fusing of theory and practice (Marcuse, 1969). He also presented a (relatively) more accessible diagnosis of the social pathologies rooted in the technological realities of the day (see Chapter 7). Erich Fromm, likewise, did not pale into abstract contemplation. While Adorno was accused of an excessive intellectualism and a failure to get his hands dirty, Erich

Fromm was discredited for the obverse, for being too relatable. For some on the academic left, Fromm was simply too accessible to be taken seriously, and was dismissed as more of a 'simplistic populizer' and 'self-help guru', rather than as offering a sufficiently weighty critical theory of society (McLaughlin, 2021).

Habermas certainly 'revitalised' critical theory, but at the cost of surrendering large portions of its distinctive Hegelian-Marxian heritage, a policy expedited by Honneth (see Thompson, 2016). In contrast, Marcuse and Fromm developed Frankfurt School research in different – and underexplored – directions, while retaining a central investment in Hegelian-Marxism and Freud. In this final part of *Critical Theory and Social Pathology*, I bring Fromm and Marcuse into dialogue, demonstrating that a productive framing of social pathology can be reconstructed through a sympathetic rereading of their work.

While both Marcuse and Fromm offer sophisticated social-theoretical foundations for conducting social research, Fromm is most explicit about his investment in 'social pathology'. For Fromm, the 'pathological normalcy' of capitalism must be central to the Frankfurt School's research agenda, and his conceptual apparatus is explicitly constructed to enable the diagnosis and disclosure of social pathologies. Yet Fromm does not provide easily operationalisable avenues for applied social research; his work remained more macro-sociological and abstract. In this regard, Marcuse provides an ideal counterpoint. Marcuse offers equally promising foundations from which to conduct pathology diagnosing research; however, unlike Fromm, he does not make an explicit investment in the language of 'pathology'. However, with his framings of the *technical a priori* and *repressive desublimation*, Marcuse offers easily operationalisable avenues for normative social research. As such, in this final part of *Critical Theory and Social Pathology*, I outline Fromm's pathology diagnosing critical theory which I then bring into dialogue with Marcuse (in the succeeding chapter). I argue that when reading Marcuse and Fromm together we can find the social theoretical foundations required for a renewal of critical theory's pathology diagnosing heritage, which sits in keeping with the research programme's original Hegelian-Marxian insights.

Fromm the stranger

Fromm typifies the prodigious intellectual that never really 'fitted in', both in his social relationships and in his disciplinary practices. As Annette Thompson astutely framed it, 'the theme of the *stranger*, of not quite belonging ... played an important part throughout his life' (my italics). Fromm was never embraced as a member of the Frankfurt School; for Stuart Jeffries, Fromm suffered an effective 'anathematization from Critical Theory' as a result (Jeffries, 2017: 294). I argue that when one considers the failure of Fromm's work to achieve prominence on a par with his contemporaries, certain facets of his biography must be taken into account.

Fromm suffered from catastrophically poor social relationships with his fellow critical theorists (Friedman and Schreiber, 2013: 48). Indeed, as early as 1939 his ties with the Institute for Social Research were officially severed (Bronner, 2011: 73). The origins of Fromm's eventual intellectual ostracism can be traced to his initial meeting with Theodor Adorno; Rainer Funk (2000: 97) wrote that from their 'first acquaintance, Fromm ... developed a marked aversion' to the philosopher. Their mutual, spiralling dislike is well charted (Thompson, 2009: 12), and added a piquancy to their intellectual debates; consider Adorno's (2018 [1946]) savage criticism of Fromm in 'Social Science and Sociological Tendencies in Psychoanalysis'. However, perhaps the 'bloodiest' of his Frankfurt School 'civil war' spats was the 'bitter dispute' with Herbert Marcuse that played out in the pages of *Dissent* in the second half of the 1950s (see Jeffries, 2017: 289).

For Witenberg (1997: 334), *The Dissent* debate damaged Fromm's reputation internationally, and with it, diminished substantive scholarly engagement with his work. Marcuse's disagreement with Fromm arose from their diverging readings of Freud (Jeffries, 2017: 289). Fromm considered that capitalism had reshaped the subject's primal libidinal drives, while Marcuse held fast to a more doctrinal Freudianism, viewing the subject's drives to be universal and unchanging (see Rickert, 1986). Fromm had limited collegiate support, and the bulk of the Frankfurt School circle held his approach to be an 'assault on metapsychology' and 'a revision of Freud's radical legacy' which 'threatened to obliterate the legitimacy of ... [an] anthropological critique of civilization' (Bronner, 2011: 73). The debate became truly acrimonious, with Marcuse suggesting 'that Fromm has smuggled capitalist values into his critique (Jeffries, 2017: 289). For Burston, the brutality of the debate can be attributed to 'sibling rivalry' between Freud's heirs (Burston, 1991: 226–227). Fromm was by far the worst off from this fraternal duel and made no efforts to hide his dislike from Marcuse. Years after the *Dissent* dispute, Fromm 'saw Marcuse on a train and studiously ignored him' (Jeffries, 2017: 294). This is obviously not an ideal policy for forming productive relationships and bolstering one's intellectual profile.

Beyond the Frankfurt School, Fromm's works were attacked with similar hostility. For the psychoanalytic mainstream, his approach lacked focus on 'real life choices', which was considered an essential prerequisite for clinical application (Margolies, 1996). By the mid-1960s Fromm was truly an outsider; he was disliked by critical theorists and was seen as 'too provocative and disturbing to be readily assimilated into the analytic mainstream' (Burston and Olfman, 1996: 321). In part, this dismissal arose out of Fromm's accessibility and unrepentant hostility to capitalism which left the 'traditional academic and psychoanalytic' elite predictably 'wary' (Thompson, 2009: 20). As a result, Fromm died in 1980, aged seventy-nine, as 'the forgotten intellectual' (Braune, 2014: 3). While there is an increasingly powerful Fromm renaissance underway, a recent paper in *The European Journal of Social Theory* presenting itself as articulating a complete typography of conceptions of social pathology, failed to engage once with Fromm (Laitinen and Särkelä, 2019). This typifies the extent to which Fromm's work remains on the periphery. For Jeffries, the 'deck was stacked against him' from the very start (Jeffries, 2017: 294). I consider that there exists a rich and promising social-theoretical infrastructure provided by Fromm which was never seriously engaged with when the perceived Adornian 'dead end' was reached. Had Fromm been more central in the Frankfurt School, had his social connections led to the triumphing of his work, rather than its denigration, the supplanting of original Hegelian-Marxist insights by Habermas may have never occurred. Fromm may have been, intellectually, a more intuitive direction from which to rekindle critical theory after the Adornian cul-de-sac – an option I retrace here as I draw out his impressive framing of social pathology.

A (short) introduction to Erich Fromm's critical theory

While Fromm's most popular book remains *The Art of Loving* (1956), his critical theory was developed across *The Fear of Freedom* (1941),[1] *The Sane Society* (1955), *Beyond the Chains of Illusion* (1962), *To Have or to Be?* (1976), and a lecture series, published as *The Pathology of Normalcy* (1991). These texts are all distinguished by Fromm's fusion of Marxian and Freudian ideas. In this regard, Fromm's work can be read as a radical 'sociologising' of psychoanalysis and as providing an equally radical injection of psychoanalysis into sociology. To understand Fromm's investment in this unlikely marriage, one needs to grasp the importance of Georg Groddeck (1866–1934) to his work.[2]

Fromm read Groddeck closely and developed his central claim that it is the 'objective social conditions' which precipitate 'neurosis', and therefore, it is the 'objective social conditions' which require considered critique (see Groddeck, 2012 [1913], 1977; Fromm, 1983 [1962]: 56).[3] Groddeck wrote that 'many illnesses are the product of people's lifestyles. If one wants to heal them, one has to change a patient's way of life; only in very few cases can the illness itself be tackled through so called specifica' (Will, 1984: 22).

This point is worth expanding upon as it is something Fromm repeatedly stresses throughout his own work: that it is the 'insane society' which produces 'insane subjects' (Fromm, 2010 [1991]: 86). Indeed, the anxious or neurotic subject's response to the 'insane society' is in fact perfectly 'normal' (Fromm, 1963 [1955]). The problem is the pathological nature of the 'normal' operations of the capitalist society; what Fromm termed the 'pathological normalcy' of capitalism (Fromm, 2010 [1991]). Central to Fromm's critical theory is this awareness that society itself is pathological. Curing patients of course matters, but it is inadequate in isolation; what is truly vital is to advance a powerful social critique which can propel qualitative social change towards a more 'sane society'.[4] A critical depth psychology necessitates a critical sociology; and vice versa.

Fromm was thus at pains to stress that his critical theory was 'not at all a psychological theory' (Fromm, 1983 [1962]: 38). Rather, as Carl Ratner (2014: 300) framed it, it is always evident that Fromm was more invested in understanding 'macro-cultural forces' and their impact on the subject. In keeping with the Hegelian-Marxian foundations of critical theory, in Fromm's account, the subjects' cognitive capacities, their mental well-being, even their personality development, are all consistently framed as being deeply *socially* constituted. Fromm (1941: 20) captures this when he wrote that 'individual psychology is fundamentally social psychology'.

Fromm held the irrationality of the social world and the irrationality of the social subject to be intimately connected. Capitalist subjects are complicit in deluding themselves so they may forget their 'dependency, … [their] alienation, [their] … slavery to the economy' (Fromm, 1983 [1962]: 14). People are complicit in their own alienation and irrationality insofar as they perpetuate illusions about their own conditions as a desperate palliative, to help them survive the horrors of modernity. As Fromm stated, for both Marx and Freud, 'man lives with illusions because these illusions make the misery of real life bearable' (Fromm, 1983 [1962]: 15). The maintenance of the illusion of liberty and of meaning enables a smoother, happier life, and prevents a descent into crippling anxiety. The challenge, therefore, is to change the organisational structures of society itself so that such illusions are no longer required. Fromm's critical theory thus powerfully reanimates Marx's sentiments in the *Contribution to the Critique of Hegel's Philosophy of Right*, where he offers the famous chiasmus: the 'demand to give up the illusions about … [our] condition is the demand to give up a condition which needs illusions' (cf. Fromm, 1983 [1962]: 105).

Throughout *Beyond the Chains of Illusion*, Fromm places his faith in 'truth' as a weapon to promote change.[5] Fromm makes a connected, broader, anthropological point, which, while factually contentious, underscores the strength of his conviction. He stated that 'all the human race has achieved, spiritually and materially, it owes to the destroyers of illusion and to the seekers of reality' (Fromm, 1983 [1962]: 152). The goal of his entire project is hence framed as the effort to 'enable [the reader] ... to wake up and act as a free man' (Fromm, 1983 [1962]: 16). In this regard, there is a parallel between Fromm's work and Hegel's *Phenomenology* – when one has read, and understood, Fromm's critical theory, the reader purportedly attains a higher 'freedom'.

The Freudo-Marxian core of Fromm's critical theory is also well captured in his *Fear of Freedom* 1941). While focusing on the rise of Nazism, his analysis is more wide ranging and remains relevant today, inspiring various contemporary studies.[6] Fromm's central argument is that 'negative freedom', or 'freedom *from*', typified by the absence of constraints, is a weak and volatile form of liberty, and can easily descend into authoritarianism and destructiveness. In contrast, 'freedom *to*', or 'positive freedom', centres a sociality and a creativity, which enables the subject to achieve a connectedness with their wider social world. What is required is a society structured to enable positive freedom, rather than one which simply enables capitalistic 'freedom *from*'. Fromm connects his analysis to developmental psychology: as the infant grows and they mature they are slowly given increased 'freedom *from*', as parental constraints are removed. For the child to develop healthily, it is crucial that they have positive outlets for this freedom; spaces where the child can explore their humanity and creativity. In the absence of suitable outlets for 'freedom *to*', the child can regress, seeking alternative sources of authority. Similar patterns can be traced culturally, with entire societies craving authoritarian rule.

While Freud clearly plays a central role in Fromm's critical theory, it is Marx's diagnosis of alienation which consistently drives Fromm's analysis. Citing liberally from the *Economic and Philosophical Manuscripts*, Fromm argued throughout *Beyond The Chains of Illusion* that the capitalist system of production produces a totally alienated subject: alienated from themself, from the process of production, from their fellows, so that 'life itself appears only as a *means of life*' (cf. Fromm, 1983 [1962]: 44). Fromm reads Marx as arguing that man's total alienation arises from 'alienated work' (Fromm, 1983 [1962]: 43). Fromm wrote that the alienation of capitalist society, 'follow[s] from the fact that the worker is related to the *product of his labor* as to an *alien* object. For it is clear on this presupposition that the more the worker expends himself in work, the more powerful becomes the world of objects which he creates in face of himself, the poorer he becomes in his inner life and the less he belongs to himself' (cf. Fromm, 1983 [1962]: 42–43).

The antidote to alienation is 'the complete change of the economic-social constellation' (Fromm, 1983 [1962]: 56). The ultimate destination of Fromm's critical theory is the Hegelian-Marxian imperative of moving towards a more rational society: qualitative social change so that the 'chains of illusion' can be cut. To do so requires transformation at both the cognitive and the social level. Through his union of Marx and Freud, Fromm demonstrates that the capitalist world induces forms of impeded cognition and distortions at the level of depth psychology. The epistemic concerns of Hegelian-Marxism are accompanied by, and somewhat transposed into, respective insights within the psycho-analytic register. In both domains, the subject's pathologically distorted cognitive functioning (belief in illusions about their conditions) is crucial to social reproduction. As I shall demonstrate in the next chapter, by bringing Fromm and Marcuse into dialogue, the potency of both the epistemic and the psychoanalytic strengths of the Hegelian-Marxist reading can be combined in a framework for pathology diagnosing social research. The foregoing sketch was exceeding reductive; however, it is presented to enable a reader who is new to Fromm's work to see how and where his pathology diagnosing infrastructure fit within his broader critical theory.

Erich Fromm's 'pathological normalcy'

Fromm's framing of 'pathological normalcy' succeeds in simultaneously carrying the two central insights which drive Frankfurt School research: that the objective social world is pathologically malstructured and that 'sociocognitive'[7] obstacles exist which impede progressive transformation (Harris, 2019c). Rooted in a Marxian critique of the alienating impact of the capitalist economy, combined with a Freudian sensitivity to the deracinating effect of such a social world on the subject's depth psychology, Fromm's framing of social pathology is rich in possibilities for further development. In the following abstraction of the social theoretical foundations which undergird Fromm's account of 'pathological normalcy', I identify three key conceptual-analytical tenets. The first is Fromm's analysis of the pathological social world, which is held to be inadequate relative to the demands of a 'normative humanism'. Second, I expand on Fromm's account of 'consensual validation', which is central to his analysis of the mechanisms which impede social transformation. Finally, I comment on the presence of what Fromm terms 'socially patterned defects', which serve to entrench irrational forms of social organisation, restrict cognition, and maintain 'objectively unhealthy' psychological states and drives. Fromm's pathology diagnosing infrastructure is thus worthy of serious consideration and is shown to offer the possibilities for rebuilding Frankfurt School social research, beyond the monistic recognition programme advocated by Honneth. Having expanded upon the core features of Fromm's social theory, I demonstrate that his approach carries the explanatory-diagnostic insights central to 'the explosive charge' of pathology diagnosing critique.

While the 'recognition-cognitive' framing of social pathology advanced by Zurn and Honneth exclusively examines 'second-order disconnects' (Zurn, 2011: 345), limitations within the subject's understanding of dominant social norms, Fromm's account is anchored in the problems within the social world itself. The current material organisation of the socio-economic system is presented as being objectively inadequate and injurious to social subjects. In both the 'Individual and Social Origins of Neurosis' (1944), and more extensively in *The Sane Society*, Fromm argued for a social world structured by the requirements of 'normative humanism' (Fromm, 1963 [1955]: 12).[8] For Fromm, there are simply 'right and wrong' solutions to the question of 'human existence'.[9] There are clear, discernible 'laws which govern ... mental and emotional functioning' (Fromm, 1963 [1955]: 12). As a result, for Fromm, there were certain societies that are fundamentally more or less compatible with the requirements for a happy and meaningful ('sane') human life. The core of Fromm's framing of pathological normalcy is his analysis that the accepted, 'normal' objective social conditions are found wanting, relative to the attainable superior conditions dictated by normative humanism (Funk, 2000: 9).[10] Such an analysis was presented as simultaneously normative, 'objective', and universal. Fromm's work is built on this unapologetic foundation, that one can, and must, speak of objectively inferior social conditions. Fromm teaches that the critical theorist must be intellectually brave enough to advance an ethical, normative, and partisan form of social critique.

Crucially, unlike the Zurn-Honneth understanding of social pathology, Fromm holds social reality itself to be found wanting, rather than merely the subject's (mis)understanding of it. Fromm focuses his critique on the market system, which is diagnosed as pathological on the basis of the alienation it induces in the subject. All the time the subject is alienated from their labour, from their fellows, and from themselves, the social world can be said to be 'insane' and 'pathological'. Material social transition is held to be the essential solution. By grounding his social critique on the objectively pathological conditions created by capitalist imperatives, Fromm offers a strong, normative form of social research, in keeping with the original spirit of the Frankfurt School programme, while his investment in the critique of alienation serves to further Marxian, Freudian, and Hegelian motifs.

Fromm's substantive diagnosis is one of pathological *alienation*: he wrote throughout his *oeuvre* that in capitalist societies 'we are aliens to ourselves' (Fromm, 2010 [1991]: 46), that alienation is '*the* sickness of man' (Fromm, 1983 [1962]: 45 – my italics), and that 'every neurosis can be considered an outcome of alienation' (Fromm, 1983 [1962]: 53). For Fromm, the market 'has reached such proportions' that 'all participants have been moulded by it', that 'all experiences' have 'become [as] abstract as commodities' (Fromm, 2010 [1991]: 63). As he wrote in *To Have or To Be*, and develops further in *The Anatomy of Human Destructiveness*, the unalienated 'biophilic' approach to life has been jettisoned, in place of a materialistic desire for 'possession', for domination, and 'ownership' (Fromm, 1979). Fromm thus argued that the market order is objectively 'insane' insofar as it induces this pathologically alienated form of life. It is worth seeing how Fromm's critical theory is reliant on both Freud and Marx in his foundational critique of the objective social order. Alienation appears both '*within* productive activity' (cf. Fromm, 1983 [1962]: 43) and excludes man from *productive* activity. Fromm extends this analysis, arguing Marx is concerned with 'man's alienation from life, from himself, and from his fellow man' (Fromm, 1983 [1962]: 44). As such the capitalist system is systematically impeding the capacity for forms of positive freedom, of 'freedom *to*', rather than 'freedom *from*'. It is essential for the healthy development of the subject for society to be structured in such a way that each subject relates to, and works for the benefit of, the social whole.

Fromm presents an explicitly normative critique of the social world. Of course, such an account was submitted before the rise of post-modernism and post-structuralism and seems entirely out of place in today's academy. After having presented the totality of Fromm's pathology diagnosing social theory, I return to engage with such objections, which, like Ratner, I ultimately present as resolvable.

There are two levels to Fromm's 'pathological normalcy'. His framing captures both the diagnosis that in its 'normal', 'everyday' operation society is pathological, but crucially, it also captures the idea that the nature of this 'normalcy' itself is pathological too, serving to counteract the forces of progressive social change. Central to Fromm's analysis of these obstacles to transition are his framings of 'consensual validation' and 'socially patterned defects', both of which provide powerful and underexplored entry points for conducting critical social research.

'Consensual validation' refers to the fact that social subjects tend to 'follow the herd', believing that the routine behaviour of the multitude is valid and rational. The more people there are that hold a certain view, or that behave in a certain way, the more likely other social subjects are to follow in kind. There are crucially two components here: (i) an apparent 'consensus' on X typically leads to subjects unquestionably following said social practice, but also (ii), in addition to inducing a blind conformity, consensus serves to induce the belief that X is a *valid* way to act. In short, a perceived 'consensus' around X makes the subject both more likely to follow in said social behaviour, but also it carries a false form of validity: a 'consensual validation'.

For Fromm, 'conceptual validation' is truly 'deceptive', 'it is naively assumed that the fact that the majority of people share certain ideas or feelings proves the validity of these ideas and feelings'. However, 'nothing is further from the truth' (Fromm, [1955]: 14). Fromm continues that '[j]ust as there is *"folie à deux"* there is *"folie à millions"*. The fact that millions of people share the same vices does not make these vices virtues. The fact that they share so many errors does not make the errors to be truths, and the fact that millions of people share the same forms of mental pathology does not make these people sane' (Fromm, 1963 [1955]: 15).

In one of his earliest lectures at the New School, Fromm retells H. G. Wells's *The Country of the Blind* (1904), to support his analysis of the power of consensual validation (Fromm, 2010 [1991]: 17). Paraphrasing Fromm's own paraphrasing of Wells, with a light creative licence of my own, the story proceeds thus: a healthy stranger lost in a rainforest stumbles into a village which is home to an isolated tribe. Due to a genetic defect among the population, the local population is needlessly blind, and a small, harmless operation can enable them to see. When encountered, they have clearly defined smooth, silky skin growing over their eyelids, which could be easily and safely removed. None of the tribe has ever heard of sight. However, in the country of the blind, the two-eyed man is not king, rather he is an insane lunatic, with phantasmal, unhealthy visions. Further, he is stigmatised for the unseemly nature of his pupils, rather than the desirable, smooth skin to which the populace are accustomed. In place of enabling a palliative operation, a 'hysteria of hate' is whipped up against the hapless traveller (Fromm, 1983 [1962]: 6). The villagers are mutually reassured of their factual accuracy, and remain ignorant to the possibility they are living a less than optimal existence. Even if the stranger was exceptionally persuasive, and unprecedentedly biologically insightful, people are unable to simply 'look at the facts' (Fromm, 1963 [1955]: 3). By supporting their fellow tribespeople, and reinforcing the legitimacy of their worldview, the tribesfolk serve to reassert their sense of community, and each benefits from their solidarity. Yet, this does not enable them to live an optimal, healthy life.

For Fromm, 'the irrationality of human mass behaviour', evinced through the proclivity of the social subject to conform to consensual norms, is an antecedent, almost anthropological flaw, and is a stubborn obstacle to social transition (Fromm, 1983 [1962]: 8). What is required is a considered analysis of the mechanisms of such consensual validation and the identification of means to interrupt and challenge it. A foundational scepticism to 'common thought' must be promoted by academics and activists, with the distorting effect of consensual validation rigorously exposed (Fromm, 1983 [1962]: 14). Such an approach continues the Hegelian-Marxian approach of unpicking Strydom's 'Gordian knot' of social contradictions (Strydom,

2008). Returning explicitly to Marx, Fromm deploys Marx's favourite motto, *de omnibus dubitandum est* ('above all, one must doubt'), as an epigram capturing this need for critical thought (McLellan, 1985: 457).

A research focus on the logics of consensual validation enables the critical theorist to identify the forces which pathologically induce adherence and conformity to the irrational social world. Fromm is convincing: these particular logics are worthy of considered investigation. This sits in keeping with the broader Frankfurt School research programme, and Fromm's insights are shared in places by both Marcuse (see Chapter 7) and Walter Benjamin. For example, Benjamin (1982: 592) famously wrote, 'that things are "status quo" is the catastrophe'. With Fromm's awareness of the pathological nature of logics of consensual validation the social researcher can focus on the manner in which both thought contents, and the manner of thinking, as well as broader patterns of social behaviour, are reinforced and 'normalised'. Such an analysis can help disclose and, through disclosing, resist the social-pathological impediments to transitioning beyond the pathological objective social world.

Fromm's study of 'consensual validation' led him to identify 'socially patterned defects' (Fromm, 1963 [1955]: 15). The subject can be conditioned to ignore contradictions and inconsistencies in their social world and to forget modes of being. While 'consensual validation' in itself 'has no bearing on reason or mental health', it is frequently accompanied by dynamics which instil such 'defects' that serve to both reinforce conformity and protect the subject from developing a personal manifestation of the social pathology (Fromm, 1963 [1955]: 14–15). For example, in late capitalism the subject is conditioned to think exclusively in an instrumental, reifying manner. A crucial part of this process is the development of a socially patterned defect: where the subject's mimetic and erotic proclivities are repressed. This functions to protect them from the pathological dominance of instrumental rationality, preventing a descent into neurosis and anxiety. By obscuring the subject's broader cognitive capacities, the irrationality of the social world is obscured, and the possibility for the subject to experience this loss is nullified. Crucially, the subject which suffers from said 'socially patterned defect' is 'not aware' of this reality (Fromm, 1963 [1955]: 15). Indeed, often the 'very defect ... [is] raised ... [as] a virtue' (Fromm, 1963 [1955: 15); consider the praise and awards heaped on 'high achievers' who focus obsessively on key performance indicators in the course of their employment, at the cost of all else.

For Fromm, this is an important factor which explains the subject's acceptance of pathological capitalist norms and practices. 'Socially patterned defects' have a double action: they function as both a powerful 'opiate', comforting the subject (Fromm, 1963 [1955]: 15), but they also serve to preclude the subject's critical faculties, obscuring the pathologies of social reality. The typical labourer works too many hours a week, in mind-numbing conditions, for low pay. The possibility of a more rational, more 'human' existence, is constantly deferred. In Fromm's (1963 [1955]: 15) words, 'What he may have lost in richness and in a genuine feeling of happiness, is made up by the security of fitting in with the rest of mankind – *as he knows them*'.

Yet such an empty sense of communion with society will be forever found wanting; the subject's manifestation of the broader social pathology as a personal neurosis is simply deferred, the psychic trauma merely repressed, rather than evaded. Such socially patterned defects can be powerful impediments to social change. Like religion for Marx, the subject's defective cognition serves to soothe the subject, to balm their suffering. Yet, this will be forever inadequate, the only way of truly 'curing' the subject's neuroses is radical social transformation. Ultimately, such defects serve to provide an opiate relief; paralysing the subject in the sorrows of the moment, impeding possibilities for emancipation. Fromm's framing is thus rich in possibilities for further exploration. While the analysis of 'socially patterned defects' is convincing, the full range of forces which facilitate consensual validation is worthy of considered investigation.

Pathological normalcy as the epitome of 'explosively charged' critical theory

If it were not for the biographical contingencies presented above, Fromm's account of pathological normalcy might have offered an alternate source for the programmatic renaissance of the Frankfurt School in the late 1960s, in place of Habermas. Rather than instigating a retreat from a direct confrontation with the social-structural forces of production, Fromm's account places the critique of the capitalism at its centre. Pathological normalcy carries the radical 'explosive charge' of pathology diagnosing critical theory, holding the rich cocktail of concepts in a stable theoretical structure.

From *The Republic*, through to the work of Rousseau, Hegel, Marx, and Adorno, a central constituent of 'deeper' social criticism is a focus on the deformation of the subject's needs and cognitive capacities. Likewise, Fromm's critical theory states that there are certain objective social conditions which are more suitable than others for meeting the subject's anthropologically determinable needs. Discernible through a so-called Science of Man, the requirements for a 'normative humanism' are held to be objective and present a series of foundational needs which must be met by the social world to prevent the subject from spiralling into anxieties and neuroses. Expressed most reductively, society is pathological and 'sick', as these basic needs are not met; society is rife with alienating dynamics and logics, and the subject is left 'estranged from themselves' and from 'their fellow man' (Fromm, 1983 [1962]: 44).

The immanent anchor of Fromm's account of pathological normalcy is that the social world does not enable the subject's foundational needs to be met. But, in keeping with the tradition of thought outlined above, Fromm's account goes further. It is not merely the failure of the subject's needs to be met which constitutes the social pathology; rather it is the 'deformation' of their desires, the ascent of pathological needs, which will not enable the subject to enjoy an optimal existence. In place of a 'biophilic' appreciation of life, and enjoying the 'freedom *to*' engage in interpersonal activities and to experience the joy of the natural world, the subject is socially conditioned to feel a need to possess rather than to live, to 'have', rather than 'to be' (Fromm, 1979 [1976]). Fromm's concept of alienation does substantial work here, and it binds his diagnostic critique together. The subject's alienated existence is held as proof that their foundational needs are not met, and that society is pathological. But equally it is the subject's alienation from themselves, and from their wider world, which instigated their desire for possession, and for 'having'.

A crucial feature of Fromm's analysis of alienation is a vicious-circular logic; the more the subject is alienated from their social world, the more they invest in their possessions ('having'), which is unsatisfactory, so they invest further in their possessions – the more one is alienated, the more one becomes alienated. This again follows the lineage of Rousseau and Hegelian-Marxism, with the identification of pathological negative dynamics being a central feature of their social critique. Importantly, it is not merely the objective social world which is plagued by negative self-perpetuating dynamics. Rather, the mechanisms which impede progressive transition, a co-equal concern for Fromm, are also held to be pathologically reinforcing. Consider the account of consensual validation: the more people who uncritically engage in capitalist processes, the more people follow suit. The more subjects that enact a capitalist life, the harder it is to gain traction for a diagnostic critique. The failure of a diagnostic critique to achieve purchase will lead to proportionately more people embracing, or at the very least, acceding to the diktats of capital. Such vicious-circular logics are a distinctive feature of pathology diagnosing social theory, and typify the 'fevered' nature of advanced industrial society.

The dialectical relationship between the irrational organisational structure of society and the dominant forms of cognition is a central productive insight for pathological diagnosing social research. Such an account of pathological normalcy enables social research to focus on the impeded capacities of the subject, with a focus on *both* the epistemic impediments of an alienating social world and the denatured depth psychology engendered by a purely negative freedom. The 'socially patterned defects' which Fromm identifies are explicitly related to the condition of the material world. For Annette Thompson, their development is explicitly seen as part of 'a process of dynamic adaption between social structures and individual psyche' (Thompson, 2009: 101). The irrational social world produces irrational subjects: *mens sana in societate sana*.

And, of course, Fromm is sensitive to the psychoanalytic insights which are contained within the pathology diagnosing framing; that the subject manifests the irrationality of the social conjuncture in the form of neuroses and anxieties. Fromm is the Frankfurt School's most articulate exponent of the insight that a healthy subject requires a healthy society. It is the 'insane society' which produces 'insane subjects'. Fromm, as a psychoanalyst, however, develops this framing further. It is not merely the presence of anxieties and neuroses which are induced by the irrational social world. Rather, the desire for authoritarian leadership, or sadistic or masochistic relations, can be held to be a precipitant of the objective social world. The pathological normalcy can serve to normalise both the irrationality of the social structure, but can also obscure the dominance of unhealthy personality traits and proclivities.

Fromm's framing of pathological normalcy, while not 'perfect', is certainly worthy of further investigation. The social-theoretical apparatus he presents provides a way of carrying forth the central insights of the Frankfurt School into social research. As I argue in Chapter 7, what is truly required is a critical theory of society which is capable of developing Fromm's foundational understanding of 'pathological normalcy' into a grounding for applied interdisciplinary research. In this regard, I argue for a marriage of Fromm and Marcuse.

In defence of Fromm

Before advancing such a Fromm-Marcuse synthesis, it is important to attend to the criticisms which have dogged Fromm's work. Obviously, if Fromm's account suffers from irredeemable weaknesses it would be simplest to dispense with it entirely. There are two main criticisms which are directed towards his critical theory today. The first focuses on the perceived gendered nature of his work. The second focuses on the explicitly normative-objective anchoring of his critique. While both criticisms deserve engagement, I argue that neither undermines Fromm's social theory.

Today, Fromm may seem 'almost archaic' at first encounter, both substantively and stylistically (Thompson, 2009: 25). Progressively minded academics have thus been 'wary' about engaging with Fromm's work, viewing it as potentially regressive and antiquated (Thompson, 2009: 20). In particular, concern is often raised about Fromm's use of gendered language which is at odds with the lexicon consciously adopted by critical theorists today (Thompson, 2009: 43). Two concerns exist here: one, through the problematic signifiers he adopts, Fromm is accused of showing no sensitivity to the realities of gendered oppression, and he appears to have been outmoded by the lessons of third-wave feminism. Second, and more troublingly, the concern has been raised that Fromm's work is not merely 'gendered' in its use of language, but that his problematic syntax reflects deeper patriarchal and essentialising sentiments (Chancer, 2020).

As to the first charge, it is undeniable that Fromm repeatedly uses the word 'man' where his meaning is actually 'people' or 'humanity'. This is indeed discomforting for the contemporary progressive reader (Thompson, 2009: 25–26). Consider his titles: *Man For Himself*; *Marx's Concept of Man*. While a charge of gendered prose could be levelled at the majority of thinkers within the sociological canon, Fromm espouses explicitly 'humanist principles', which makes this apparent syntactic 'sexism' all the more jarring (Thompson, 2009: 25). Annette Thompson, a respected Fromm biographer, explains the focus on Fromm's gendered prose as stemming from the fact that his apparently 'sexist' language' is so clearly 'at odds with his humanist principles' (Thompson, 2009: 25).

Fortunately, for scholars invested in Fromm's work there is an explanation at hand. Fromm was raised in the German canon, and there is a curious German word, '*mensch*', which has no direct 'appropriate' translation in English. The word is best translated as 'humanity' or 'humankind'; however, because all nouns are either masculine, feminine, or neuter linguistically in German, it is masculine in German syntax. This is not to suggest that the word signifies a masculine nature to humanity more broadly. Crucially, when one wishes to explicate Fromm from the charges of an unthinking masculinist nature to his prose, Fromm addresses this charge himself. In *To Have to Be?* Fromm claims that he deliberately uses the word 'mensch' out of a conscious desire to 'restore' its 'non-sexual meaning' (Fromm, 1979 [1976]: 10). One can thus read Fromm as actively attempting to recode the term, and to further an explicitly humanist prose, rather than adopting an exclusively masculinist lexicon. Annette Thompson stresses that such a use of 'mensch' was 'common' when Fromm was writing, suggesting that this explanation should be satisfactory (Thompson, 2009: 25).

However, while this explanation for the signifier may seem acceptable, the more serious question remains as to whether Fromm's entire output is tainted by an implicit masculinist bias. Fortunately, while I believe a convincing argument could be made to the contrary, this is of no concern to an investment with Fromm's social-theoretical foundations. Fromm's insights are (i) that one should be able to diagnose objective failings in the social world, (ii) that such logics can be connected explicitly to the market system which alienates the subject, and (iii) that an analysis is needed of the mechanisms which perpetuate this pathological normalcy, which involve exploring logics of consensual validation, and which can produce the socially patterned defects within the subject. Such insights remain valid social-theoretical foundations to explore regardless of whether aspects of Fromm's substantive critical theory are suspect today. In short, one can find real use in the social-theoretical resources Fromm provides, without fear of said social-theoretical foundations being tainted by patriarchal undertones.

The rebuttal of the gendered criticism of Fromm's work is sound. One can demonstrate (a) that it is not 'gendered' in the sense suggested. Further, even if this counter is not accepted, one can parry with (b), that even if Fromm's work was problematically gendered it would not impact Fromm's social-theoretical foundations. It is somewhat more challenging to provide a rigorous response to the charge that Fromm's social theory is predicated on an unjustifiable normativity and universalism. This is a concern which has been levelled at all pathology diagnosing social theory, as per my discussion in Chapter 1 (see Honneth, 2000: 121). With regards to Fromm's work, however, this accusation is particularly common, as Fromm is explicitly normative and universalist in his account. This is part of Fromm's theoretical appeal and is intrinsic to his rhetorical flourish. Fromm's critical theory thus sits in a striking contrast to the dominant 'ethico-cultural relativism' of today's post-modern and post-structuralist academy (Ratner, 2014: 301). While the question of the normative justification for a critical theory of society is mammoth, and worthy of book-length study of its own,[11] three brief rejoinders can be made to the charge, which, in tandem, I find a sufficient rebuttal to the post-structuralist critique.

The charge against Fromm is clear. The claim made by post-structuralist and post-modern theorists is that Fromm unjustifiably presents his critical theory as 'objective' and 'normative'; stating that there are discernible 'right and wrong ways' of living, and, accordingly, right and wrong social formations. Such claims are held to be unviable in light of post-structural and post-modern scholarship. In place of Fromm's confident normative humanism, such scholars suggest that there is a plurality of alternate understandings of the good life, and, as such, no single account of the 'sane' society can be justifiably prioritised. Further, Foucauldian scholars would be critical of any attempt to demarcate a singular template for a 'healthy society' as politically coercive and theoretically unsophisticated. In contrast to such grandiose claims, the 'constructivist-relativist' would acknowledge the complexity of providing a normative foundation to social research (Ratner, 2014: 301).

In response to this charge, one can return to the very origins of critical theory as a distinctive research programme. For Horkheimer, critical theory is definitionally aware of its normativity; but further, it is aware that all scholarship is a manifestation of forms of thought, reason, and norms. For Horkheimer, this was inescapable. All scholarship reproduces values, and attempts at an 'objective' scientific research programme are not merely futile but counter-productive. The 'savants' of 'impartial' positivistic research are not merely deluding themselves, but they are impeding their analytic and explanatory efforts. Critical theory, in contrast, acknowledges its normativity, aware that all thought contents are socially constituted and serve to either reinforce or to challenge the dominant form of reason. Critical theory is thus explicitly normative, seeking to challenge the social world, and to do so on the basis of a critique of the present as inferior to alternate possible social realities. In this regard, the fact that Fromm's critical theory is normative is simply just part of what critical theory is. One may reply to the charge of Fromm's normativity with a shrug: as Neuhouser effectively says of pathology diagnosing critique, it is all normative – get over it (Neuhouser, 2012). In place of spending an eternity squabbling over the normative foundations of critical theory, however fascinating this might be, one should simply 'get on' with the job of conducting pressing social research. We are living through various existential crises; it is patently obvious that the conditions for human survival are themselves being threatened. A crude anti-theoretical and political response might be that the precise, optimally justifiable foundations of critical theory, while intellectual fascinating, need not detain us from conducting urgent social research. To do so would have a certain irony: the objective of critical theory is to explore why desperately needed radical social change is not happening – *now*. To be delayed by pedantic scholars seeking philosophically perfect foundations for engaging in any research at all would seem beyond irony.

However, in response to this political and anti-theoretical rebuttal, it could be countered that social research predicated upon an unjustifiable set of normative assumptions remains unjustifiable social research. No superior moral and temporal objective based on the unfolding socio-environmental crises will turn 'poor theory' into 'good theory'. Poor theory, in turn, may produce poor praxis. Thus, in keeping with Axel Honneth's approach of adopting a 'weak formal anthropology' to respond to the normative challenge, I proffer a defence of Fromm's normative foundations on the basis of his diagnosis of the alienating effects of the social world on the subject. While Honneth locates the importance of recognition anthropologically through a turn to Winnicott, Fromm can anchor his normativity in the objective analysis of the psychopathologies within the subject as proof of the objectively 'unhealthy' social reality.

Thus, if it is acceptable for Honneth to produce a critical theory with normative content in today's post-metaphysical conditions based on the subject's foundational need for recognition, Fromm can be read as predicating his critique on the subject's foundational need for a biophilic and non-alienated existence. As Fromm repeatedly stated, the primary causal ill is alienation, and this is produced by the 'abstractifying' mechanisms of the market. In keeping with Honneth's fusion of developmental psychology and intersubjective social theory in *The Struggle for Recognition*, or Habermas's investment in psychoanalysis in *Knowledge and Human Interests*, one can read Fromm as anchoring his normative judgement in the fact that the social subject is unable to live an 'unalienated' life in capitalist societies, which precipitates a host of neuroses and anxieties. The 'objective' failure of the social world to enable self-realisation is determined by the presence of pathological alienation manifesting in psychopathologies. The sick subject is 'proof' of the sick society.

Such an account does not necessitate, although Fromm gestures towards it, a strong ethical understanding of the good life. In keeping with Adorno, and first-generation critical theory more broadly, the investment can be in negativity – in the power of critique. Such an approach has the advantage of further distancing Fromm's work from post-structuralist and postmodern criticism. That an alienated existence is 'wrong' objectively can be stated without requiring Fromm to provide an unjustifiable account of the 'good life'. Negativity and critique have value for their own sake. Just as it is of merit to argue that a helicopter is not airworthy, and such an analysis can be conducted without knowing precisely how to fix it, so too, with social critique. A powerful critique of society can be constructed from Fromm's social theory without requiring allegiance to a strong and substantive formal ethics, beyond the requirement for an 'unalienated' existence.

Finally, in keeping with my second rebuttal of the criticism of Fromm as tarnished by gendered prose, one can simply sidestep the issue, by restating that the primary engagement with Fromm's account of social pathology is with his social-theoretical foundations, rather than with his substantive critical theory. The foundational basis – that there are objective problems which exist within the social world – does not have to be tied to a diagnosis of alienation. Rather, the normative anchoring can be found from an alternate source of social critique. Or, as I propose in the succeeding chapter, from a fusion of Fromm's diagnosis and that of other critical theorists, such as Marcuse's more explicitly Hegelian account.

While Fromm's account of social pathology remains underexplored, there is a growing research output utilising Fromm's broader critical theory to explore pressing social concerns today. The work of Kieran Durkin (2014) and Carl Ratner (2017), *inter alia*, show the real strengths of deploying Fromm to pursue contemporary social research. Fromm's work is also re-emerging in fields more removed from the traditional concerns of critical theory.[12]

However, my focus here remains firmly upon the pathology diagnosing foundations of the Frankfurt School. In this regard, Fromm's work has much to offer which has not been fully explored. There is substantial scope for further critical development. Just as critical theorists are not blind devotees to Marx, neither do I suggest an account of social pathology which is purely derivative of Fromm's substantial critical theory. While Fromm's account of pathological normalcy has much to offer, I contend it must be brought into dialogue with Marcuse's work. Just as the Habermasian turn from Adorno neglected Fromm's insights, Marcuse was also largely ignored by the 'second' and 'third' generations of critical theory. Curiously, Marcuse was not neglected in other fields, and his work remains influential in Science and Technology Studies (STS), and is key to the prodigious output of Andrew Feenberg (2005, *inter alia*). In the following chapter, I serve to recentre Marcuse the critical theorist. By bringing Fromm and Marcuse into dialogue I demonstrate the possibility of a pathology diagnosing social critique for conducting social research today. Fromm's account of 'pathological normalcy' can be easily operationalised by uniting it with Marcuse's social theoretical infrastructure. I contend that such a Fromm-Marcuse synthesis can enable the researcher to critically explore today's pathological normalcy.

Notes

1 This was published in the United Kingdom as *Fear of Freedom* and in the United States as *Escape From Freedom*.
2 For more on Groddeck, see Foster, Hristeva, and Giefer (2016).
3 Freud (1930: 142) argued in *Civilisation and Its Discontents* that the fundamental 'system of civilization' has become 'neurotic'.
4 The title of Fromm's 1955 text.
5 This is reminiscent of the more problematic Lenin quote, 'The Marxist doctrine is omnipotent because it is true' (Lenin, 1977: 21).
6 As an indicative example, see Braune (2020).
7 I use this term to capture both epistemic and depth-psychological impediments to transition.
8 For an extended sympathetic discussion on normative humanism, see Thompson (2017a).

9 Fromm's universality, his normative essentialism, and his clear rejection of social constructivism place him in obvious opposition to the post-structuralist currents dominant within contemporary social theory. I engage with these concerns later in the chapter.
10 The substantive content of these conditions was to be explored through Fromm's 'Science of Man'. Such a project never achieved sufficient institutional traction.
11 For an excellent review of earlier literature engaging this problem, see White (1983).
12 See Fuchs (2020).

7

The pathological normalcy of what? Towards a Fromm-Marcuse synthesis

In the last chapter, I argued that Erich Fromm's work can form the basis for a reconceptualisation of social pathology, enabling Frankfurt School researchers to move beyond their current 'recognition-cognitive' approach to social research. In place of the dominant vein of critical theory which invests in the norms of neoliberalism (as criticised in Chapter 3), I suggest rebuilding pathology diagnosing social research on Erich Fromm's insight that the very 'normalcy' of today's social world is itself deeply pathological.

While Fromm's account holds remarkable potential, in this chapter I bring it into dialogue with the writings of his contemporary, and erstwhile rival, Herbert Marcuse. By bringing the two into conversation, I seek to unite their distinct insights. I believe that a Fromm-Marcuse synthesis can enable a 'polycentric and multilateral' diagnosis of the 'pathological normalcy' (Fraser and Honneth, 2001: 209) and offer a productive way for Frankfurt School social research to progress. In this chapter, I demonstrate that Marcuse's account offers the specificity and precision needed for an operationalisable interdisciplinary research programme today.

I advocate the merits of combining Fromm's account of pathological normalcy with two central framings presented by Marcuse: (a) the pathological development of a *'technical a priori'*, and (b) a social-systemic nexus of *'repressive desublimation'*. Both insights serve to provide important ways of understanding the most pressing question driving Frankfurt School research: why do subjects 'put up with' the irrational and exploitative social world? Why has revolutionary social change seemingly been deferred indefinitely? Through a fusion of Fromm's account of pathological normalcy and Marcuse's phenomenological and social-systemic framework, I present productive avenues for future normative social research. Taken together, Fromm and Marcuse offer a radical redirection for social research, away from the 'domesticated' intersubjective and norm-supporting critical theory of third-generation scholars.

Fromm and Marcuse have much in common, perhaps this explains their bitter 'sibling rivalry' (see Burston, 1991: 226–227). Famously they engaged in a heated and unsavoury personal exchange in *Dissent* (see Jeffries, 2017: 289). Yet, from the perspective of hindsight, the two were remarkably similar, both seeking to unite insights from Freud and Marx to produce a depth-psychological account of the subject's response to their irrational social world. Both sought to move beyond the 'ivory tower' scholasticism which gripped Adorno. Both remained in North America after the Second World War, and became involved in the socio-political lives of their adopted homes. Their scholarship has remarkable overlaps, with Marcuse's *One Dimensional Man* sharing Fromm's 'objective' and 'immanent-transcendent' critical standpoint. Marcuse famously wrote, 'the fact that the vast majority of the population accepts, and is made to accept, this society does not render it less irrational or any less reprehensible' (Marcuse, 2007 [1964]: xliv), and that 'the insanity of the whole absolves the particular insanities and turns the crimes against humanity into a rational enterprise' (Marcuse, 2007 [1964]: 55). The parallels with Fromm's diagnostic approach, and style, are striking. Similarly, where Fromm wrote of the denial and corruption of our basic needs in *The Sane Society*, Marcuse wrote in *Eros and Civilisation* that, 'whatever Liberty exists in the realm of the developed consciousness, and in the world it has created, is only derivative, compromised freedom, gains at the expense of the full satisfaction of needs' (Marcuse, 1998 [1956]: 18).

Yet, meaningful differences do exist between the two thinkers. While there is clear overlap in many of their philosophical and political commitments, where Fromm's work endorses Groddeck, Marcuse's writings are inflected with a Heideggerian investment in phenomenology, ontology, and the role of technology (see Feenberg, 2013a; Wolin, 1991a, 1991b). Marcuse's phenomenological sensitivity was particularly important to the development of his understanding of the 'technical *a priori*', which I discuss at length below. For Marcuse, the subject's own lived reality has been pathologically distorted by capitalism so that 'the tangible source of exploitation disappears behind the facade of objective rationality' (Marcuse, 2007 [1964]: 35). With Marcuse, we see a Hegelian-Marxian outlook productively united with a phenomenological sensitivity – there is a materialist 'objectivity' driving a critique of the subject's phenomenological engagement with the lifeworld. Like Fromm, Marcuse anchored his diagnosis within the social world, but rapidly sublated its dominant norms to present an immanent-transcendent and disclosing form of critique (see Veita, 2016).

Marcuse's writing unites a critique of the pathological deformation of the subject's consciousness with a diagnosis of the social-systemic logics which perpetuate the irrational social order. For Marcuse, the 'liberty' which is offered by advanced industrial society, where the subject enjoys a choice between qualitatively indistinct forms of alienating labour, enabling one the freedom to purchase commodities that are socialised to appear essential, 'is the pure form of servitude: [enabling the subject] ... to exist as an instrument, as a thing. And this mode of existence is not abrogated if the thing is animated and chooses its material intellectual food, it does not feel it's being a thing, if it is a pretty, clean, mobile thing' (Marcuse, 2007 [1964]: 36).

Today this may seem unduly deterministic, but I argue Marcuse's social-systemic account provides a valuable resource for restoring the original research animus of critical theory. In addition to providing a useful epistemic-phenomenological framing through the 'technical *a priori*', Marcuse offers a critical psycho-social account of 'repressive desublimation'. Both of these help to substantiate some of the more implicit and abstract content of Fromm's work on pathological normalcy.

As discussed in the previous chapter, a central obstacle which has impeded academics from uniting Fromm and Marcuse has been their intensely divergent readings of Freud. However, I do not consider this to be an obstacle to combining their respective *social theoretical apparatuses*. Marcuse's more classical reading of Freud does not serve to discredit the utility of adopting a perspective invested in diagnosing features of a 'pathological normalcy'. Rather, by combining Marcuse and Fromm, the critical theorist is able to explore how 'new, more effective, and more pleasant forms of social control and social cohesion' (Marcuse, 2007 [1964]: xlvi) are enabled by the technological capabilities of advanced industrial society in a way which pushes beyond Fromm's work.

My interest here remains the social-theoretical foundations of Frankfurt School scholarship. By marrying the central theoretical apparatus from both thinkers, I present a way of operationalising a critical social research programme with clear normative content. While Fromm's account of pathological normalcy can be developed as a theoretical foundation to explore the logics through which the irrational social world is perpetuated, Marcuse's work on the *technical a priori* and *repressive desublimation* enables a tighter focus and more targeted avenues for inquiry on the social-systemic and psychological nodes of domination. In what follows, I argue that a Fromm-Marcuse synthesis offers a social-theoretical, political, and philosophical recalibration of Frankfurt School research, capable of realigning critical theory with its original emancipatory ambitions.

Marcuse and Habermas

An obvious question arises: if Marcuse had a sophisticated and operationalisable framework for conducting social research, which was sociologically embedded, why did Frankfurt School scholarship not move in his direction?[1]

Why did Habermas's intersubjective turn follow Adorno? Again, as with the quasi-exile of Fromm from the Frankfurt School, to understand the substantive developments of critical theory one must look at both intellectual and interpersonal realities, as well as the many contingencies of the critical theorists' biographies.

Perhaps the most obvious response lies in the difference between Habermas's and Marcuse's relationship with Heidegger (see Wolin, 1991a). Marcuse initially attempted to create a Heideggerian form of Marxism, a project which he eventually discarded (see Wolin and Abromeit, 2005). In contrast, Habermas wrote consistently, and at times aggressively, against Heidegger (Habermas, 1977 [1953]), with his mature critical theory providing a radical alternative to Heideggerian hermeneutics (see Lafont, 2020). Ultimately, Habermas's account was more influential, reflecting both philosophical and political currents. In broader intellectual tides, Marcuse was increasingly adrift. While Marcuse's work remained utopian and grand in scope, Habermas's mature critical theory appeared more measured and timely (Feenberg, 1996). For example, in contrast to Marcuse's sceptical engagement with technology, which was seen as always being explicitly political, Habermas moved to located technical-instrumentality as belonging within a designated sphere of social reproduction (see Kunneman, 1990). If technical-rationality remained in its 'box', so to speak, within its correct 'domain', it possessed something approaching political neutrality. In contrast to the Heideggerian ontological critique of modernity, and the Marcusean awareness of technology as inherently political, Habermas provided a nuanced embrace of modernity and progress, as having important rational, communicative, and emancipatory potential. This was a clear divergence from Habermas's (1971 [1967]) more critical engagement in *Technology and Science as 'Ideology'*. While Heidegger's ontology, and Marcuse's fusion of an ontology and dialectical materialism, offered rich and stimulating grounds for theoretical development, Habermas's later, more 'measured' and 'demystified' approach won the hearts and minds of the day (Feenberg, 1996: 46).

This cursory sketch, however, is far from exhaustive. Like Fromm, Marcuse opted to remain West of the Atlantic after the Second World War. His scholarship and politics became increasingly US-centric, as evinced by various sections from *One Dimensional Man*.[2] Yet, Marcuse's engagement with American politics was not merely academic. Rather, in 1968 Marcuse took an entirely divergent stand to Adorno. Where Adorno warned against 'actionist' students engaging in 'left-fascism', Marcuse was adopted as 'the father of the new left' (Marcuse, 1998 [1956]: i). He was delighted by students seeking to unite 'thought and action', which previously had no obvious point of synthesis in the second part of the twentieth century (Marcuse, 2007 [1964]: xliii).

While late-Adornian critical theory was thrown 'back to a high level of abstraction' (Marcuse, 2007 [1964]: xliii), Marcuse encouraged politically educated students to confront the totalising system of domination in a 'great refusal' (see Lamas, Wolfson, and Funke, 2017).

However, as the protests of 1968 fizzled out, and as the Vietnam war continued, Marcuse's politics evolved, with his 1969 text *An Essay of Liberation* championing the possibilities of a non-subsumptive, 'erotic' engagement with the external world. Typically, Marcuse, contra Adorno, spoke directly to the protesting students, and actually led forms of direct action, functioning as a paragon public intellectual, even participating in a public-off with Richard Nixon. However, the move to 'hippie' culture, 'free love', and mind-expanding substances associated with the new social movements of the late 1960s were far from the cultural politics associated with Frankfurt intellectuals. Culturally, Marcuse was out of step with the more measured Habermas. To understand the triumph of Habermasian inter-subjective pragmatics over new sensibility, one must consider cultural and interpersonal factors, in addition to scholarly divergences.

Finally, to understand why Habermas's critical theory ultimately took precedence over Marcuse's work, one must acknowledge the theoretical sophistication of Habermas's project. While today, authors like Michael J. Thompson (2016) rightly identify Habermas's intersubjective turn as precipitating a 'domestication of critical theory', for scholars reading Habermas for the first time, seeking the return of an institutionally backed critical social research programme, Habermas's conceptual and disciplinary syncretism was genuinely astounding.

Marcuse's insights may have fallen by the wayside in contemporary critical theory because of his Heideggerian inflection, his expansive and unyielding utopianism, his belief in a liberating form of non-subsumptive 'erotic' praxis, and his relative cultural and geographical distance from Frankfurt scholarship. In contrast, Habermas spoke more to the concerns, culture, and mores of the Institute for Social Research at that time. However, considering the direction Habermas's critical theory has taken, and the 'domesticated' state of contemporary critical theory today, it is now high time to reconsider the social-theoretical infrastructure provided by Marcuse's substantive critical theory. As such, I outline Marcuse's critical theory as presented in *One Dimensional Man* and *Eros and Civilisation*.

Marcuse's critical theory

In *Eros and Civilisation*, Marcuse described his project as the 'development of a theoretical construction which aims, not at curing individual sickness, but at diagnosing the general disorder' (Marcuse, 1998 [1956]: 8). In keeping with first-generation critical theory more broadly, this diagnosis carried both a critique of the objectively inadequate social formation and an identification of the obstacles which prevented progressive social transformation. Marcuse's central theoretical innovations, the technical *a priori* and repressive desublimation – which I elaborate below – harbour both facets: a diagnosis of the objective inadequacy of the present and an explanation for the untenable stasis. Crucially, such observations arose from an analysis of the existing social world, seeking to examine 'society in the light of its used and unused or abused capabilities for improving the human condition' (Marcuse, 2007 [1964]: xl). In stark contrast to Honneth's critical theory, Marcuse perspective enables the researcher to engage in immanent-transcendent critique while retaining a critical disdain for the dominant institutions and norms of the day.

In keeping with Fromm, and again, reflecting academia before what Carl Ratner (2014: 301) calls the 'cultural-relativist' turn (read: post-modernist and post-structuralist), for Marcuse there existed objectively 'better' and 'worse' social configurations. This insight forms the very basis for Marcuse's investigation. He wrote at the start of *One Dimensional Man* that

> The established society has available an ascertainable quantity and quality of intellectual and material resources. How can these resources be used for the optimal development and satisfaction of individual needs and faculties with a minimum of toil and misery? Social theory is historical theory, and history is the realm of chance in the realm of necessity. Therefore, among the various possible and actual modes of organising and utilising the available resources, which ones offer the greatest chance of an optimal development? (Marcuse, 2007 [1964]: xli)

Crucially, the inadequate reality of the historically contingent, existing social formation is obscured through both cognitive impairments and social-structure forces so that the social world seemed not merely 'normalised' but 'rational'. It is exactly such institutional pressures and norms which Marcuse considered worth disclosing and transcending. In contrast to the recognition-cognitive framework, Marcuse is incredibly sensitive that 'there is a lot to be criticised in the social reality as it is' (Laitinen, 2015: 48). Marcuse is particularly sensitive to the form of domination which typified advanced industrial society – a regulating, normalising force, which encouraged 'comfortable' conformity; a one-dimensionality which impeded the subject's phenomenological awareness of their social world and which undergirded the imperatives of the social order. Marcuse wrote,

> We are again confronted with one of the most vexing aspects of advanced industrial civilization: the rational character of its irrationality. Its productivity

and efficiency its capacity to increase and spread comforts, to turn waste into need, and destruction into construction, the extent to which the civilization transforms the object world into an extension of man's mind and body makes the very notion of alienation questionable. That people recognise themselves in their commodities; They find their soul in their automobile, hifi set, split level home, kitchen equipment. The very mechanism which ties the individual to his society has changed, and social control is anchored in the new needs which it has produced. (Marcuse, 2007 [1964]: 11)

As such, the subject is ultimately left unaware of their fundamental exploitation, their critical faculties are degraded, and their awareness of the precarity and tragedy of their condition is lost. The 'tangible source of exploitation' is obscured, hidden 'behind the façade of objective rationality' (Marcuse, 2007 [1964]: 35). The subject is preconditioned to accept the totality of the social order, with every facet of the social world reflecting the 'belief that the real is rational, and that the established system, in spite of everything, delivers the goods'(Marcuse, 2007 [1964]: 82). As Marcuse witheringly put it, advanced industrial society exists as a 'realistic caricature of dialectics' (Marcuse, 2007 [1964]: 92).

Pushing Marcuse's critical theory is in investment in revolutionary praxis: in arresting the repressive dynamics of capitalist modernity. Marcuse is famously aware of two problems here: first, those who are 'within' the system are unable to develop the required revolutionary consciousness organically – they have been too conditioned to accept the norms and values of the system. As such, the revolutionary actor must come from without – in the form of students, the homeless, and migrants. Second, Marcuse advocated for an 'education' programme – aware that the effectively totalising conditioning of the masses means that external catalysts are required for any transformative movement. As Marcuse (2007 [1964]: 44) words it, 'to the degree to which the slaves have been preconditioned to exist as slaves and be content in that role, the liberation necessarily appears to come from without and from above. They must be "forced to be free", to "see objects as they are, and sometimes as they ought to appear."'

As such, the theoretical infrastructure provided by Marcuse is deeply hostile to the established order, seeking to offer a disclosing and radical critique. This is exactly what critical theory requires today, in light of mass acquiescence to neoliberal imperatives, even as evidence piles higher as to the impact of unchecked growth on the climate crisis. As such, the lineaments of Marcuse's critical theory must be understood as being part of this broader project, of a desire to comprehend the social-structural pathology, and the place of the 'deformed', 'conditioned' subject within it. The two central theoretical constructions advanced to further this endeavour – his framings of the *technical a priori* and the system of *repressive desublimation*, both of which can be utilised to develop a pathological diagnosing social research program today.

Marcuse's account of social pathology

Distilling Marcuse's critical theory into two social-theoretical contributions is patently reductive. But, the purpose of my engagement with Marcuse, as with Fromm, is not to offer a comprehensive review of his work. Rather, my objective is to identify key resources which can inspire a new approach to diagnosing social pathologies *today*. In this regard, Marcuse's framings of the *technical a priori* and his analysis of *repressive desublimation* offer real potential for revitalising interdisciplinary pathology diagnosing social research.

Marcuse was a gifted Hegelian, and wrote a seminal introduction to Hegelian-Marxism, *Reason and Revolution* (1969b). Engaging with Marcuse's framing of the *technical a priori* thus requires a brief return to the development of German idealism (as discussed in Chapter 5). Recall that for Kant there existed certain fixed parameters through which the subject comprehended the reality of their world: the so-called *a priori* conditions of consciousness. These fixed capabilities enabled the subject to consider objects in time and in space, and, crucial to the Enlightenment project, to make predictions about future events. For Kant, discovering the specifics of such *a priori* capabilities was the foundational epistemological endeavour.

As discussed in Chapter 5, Hegel offered a radical reworking of the Kantian imagination, suggesting that these fundamental conditions of consciousness are not permanent and universal but socially contingent and variable. Marcuse followed Hegel's 'sociologised' approach to consciousness, viewing the subject's cognitive capabilities as being historically variable. While Hegel saw the development of the subject's rationality as being tied to the inexorable unfolding of *Geist* (or spirit/reason), Marx held that the development of the subject's rational capabilities is fundamentally determined by their social-historical circumstances. Marx famously inverted the Hegelian idealism, offering instead a dialectical materialism. For Hegelian-Marxists, the preconditions of consciousness are held to be supremely impacted by the socio-economic conditions of the day; this is the 'historical materialist' understanding of subjectivity.

For Marcuse, following Marx and Hegel, the conditions through which the subject engaged with, and comprehended, their social world were truly socially contingent. What concerned Marcuse in particular was the way in which advanced technical societies had instituted a deformation of the subject's cognitive capacities – had eroded their abilities for non-instrumental thought. For Marcuse, the particular relationship which existed between science, technology, and capitalism had served to fundamentally reconfigure the foundational striations of consciousness: the *a priori* conditions through which the subject engaged with, and lived, their social lives, had been pathologically deformed by advanced industrial society. This new worldview was framed as the *technical a priori*.

Marcuse was influenced by a plurality of rich philosophical and psychoanalytic traditions. As such, the account of 'one-dimensionality' in *One Dimensional Man*, where the framing of the technical *a priori* is most clearly explicated, draws on a rich medley of ideas (sadly there is not space to explore them all here). Uniting phenomenology, psychoanalysis, and left-Hegelianism, Marcuse submitted that the world is increasingly viewed through an 'instrumentalist' lens (Marcuse, 2007 [1964]: 161), which is induced by the relationship existing between modern science, technology, and the capitalist subject. For Marcuse, there is nothing, in itself, which is problematic about science; rather, it is the particular relationship which existed in advanced industrial societies between the three which developed the pathological manner through which the subject experienced their lifeworld. Marcuse commented that 'the principles of modern science were *a priori* structured in such a way that they could serve as conceptual instruments for the universe of self-propelling, productive control' (Marcuse, 2007 [1964]: 162).

Enlightened thought served to enable humanity to thrive, to erase fears and suspicions, and to gain mastery over the natural world. Yet, 'the scientific method which led to the ever-more-effective domination of nature thus came to provide the pure concepts as well as the instrumentalities for the ever-more-effective domination of man by man through the domination of nature' (Marcuse, 2007 [1964]: 162).

As such, the development of modern science, in view of the particular relationship existing between science, technology, and capitalism, spiralled into barbarism. As Marcuse wrote in *Eros and Civilisation*, 'Concentration camps, mass exterminations, world wars, and Atom bombs are no "relapse into barbarism", but the unrepressed implementation of the achievements of modern science, technology, and domination' (Marcuse, 1998 [1956]: 4).

Socialisation within the particular nexus of science, technology, and capitalism led to subjects experiencing and understanding the world in a pathologically instrumentalist and reductive manner. The innovations of science and technology had fused under the capitalist formation to produce a 'political rationality', a pathologically limited way of viewing the world (Marcuse, 2007 [1964]: xlvii). Science and technology had been 'welded together' to produce a new form of consciousness, conducive to the capitalist form of life. This new way of looking at the world was deeply supportive of the capitalist formation and functioned as a 'new form[s] of social control' (Marcuse, 2007 [1964]: 149). Viewed through the technical *a priori*, the outside world was one of 'universal quantifiability' (Marcuse, 2007 [1964]: 168) in which the domination of nature was naturalised. Crucially, 'technology' is thus understood is a number of different ways, some very different from its colloquial usage today.

Marcuse's theoretical complexity is necessary to explain how inducing such an attitude to the natural world ultimately rebounds upon the social subject. He wrote (Marcuse, 2007 [1964]: 170),

> science, by virtue of its own method and concepts, has projected and promoted a universe in which the domination of nature has remained linked to the domination of man – a link which tends to be fatal to this universe as a whole. Nature, scientifically comprehend and mastered, reappears in the technical apparatus of production and destruction which sustains and improves the life of the individuals while subordinating them to the masters of the apparatus. Thus the rational hierarchy merges with the social one.

Marcuse's lesson is that 'there is no such thing as a purely rational scientific order; the process of technological rationality is a political process' (Marcuse, 2007 [1964]: 172). Yet this political process is potent and corrosive, aggressively recoding the subject's essential cognitive patterning. As a result of the technical *a priori*, the subject has no space left to reflect on the mores and values induced by the imperatives of the capitalist order. This space has been 'invaded and whittled down by technological rationality', '[m]ass production and mass distribution claimed the entire individual, and industrial psychology has long since ceased to be confined to the factory. The manifold process is of introjection seemed to be ossified in almost mechanical reactions' (Marcuse, 2007 [1964]: 12).

There is no longer any space left of 'inner freedom', no private domain for reflection (Marcuse, 2007 [1964]: 12). As a result, the technological *a priori* manifests in acquiescence to reification and the widespread logics of equivalence across social domains. The 'quantification of nature' is triumphant (Marcuse, 2007 [1964]: 150), both internal and external. The subject is left with no value horizon beyond the instrumental and scientific-technical, 'exchange value, not truth value counts', when the technical *a priori* is hegemonic (Marcuse, 2007 [1964]: 61). Concerns as to the contradictory and unstable nature of the constellation are unable to take root in a purely quantified and reified consciousness. There is no space to analyse contradictions, dialectical thought is revoked as 'critical content evaporates into the ethical or metaphysical atmosphere' (Marcuse, 2007 [1964]: 151). The technical *a priori* fundamentally recodes the subject's engagement with the world, revoking vital aspects of their humanity. As

Marcuse exquisitely framed it, 'the music of the soul is [now] also the music of salesmanship' (Marcuse, 2007 [1964]: 61).

The pathological onset of the technical *a priori* serves to impede social critique and to prevent social transformation. The contradictions of the social world are obscured; the subject is left unable to grasp their contents when the external world is comprehended through a solely instrumental and quantifiable perspective. The technical *a priori* thus enables the perpetuation of the unstable system, the possibilities for rupture are obscured, and the system is presented as fundamentally rational.

Marcuse argued that the operationalisation of the technical *a priori* so as to enable social control occurs through administration. In this regard, Marcuse can be seen to echo Weber themes. The 'mute compulsion' of the market (Mau, 2019) is depersonalised, 'objective forces' are calculated, with rational 'objective' responses to be delivered in turn. As such the domination of the capitalist over the worker is 'transfigured into administration … The capitalist bosses and owners are losing their identity as responsible agents; they are assuming the function of bureaucrats and the corporate machine' (Marcuse, 2007 [1964]: 35).

The relationship between technology, science, capitalism, and administration thus requires careful attention. For Marcuse, the 'rationally organised bureaucracy' (Marcuse, 2007 [1964]: 74): serves to perpetuate and reinforce the destructive status quo, the subject is unable to see the contradictions manifest within the dominant societal form of rationality. As a result, the 'tangible source of exploitation disappears behind the facade of objective rationality' (Marcuse, 2007 [1964]: 35).

This aspect of Marcuse's analysis has not lain dormant. For example, Andrew Feenberg, whose work intersects critical theory and STS, has written extensively on the technical *a priori* (Feenberg, 2013b). This is indicative of the interdisciplinary potential the framing holds: just as Marcuse unites a plurality of philosophical approaches, from Hegelianism to phenomenology to ontology, the idea of the technical *a priori* unites science and technology scholars with psychologists, psychoanalysts, and cognitive scientists, in addition, of course, to critical theorists. In terms of the possibilities for advancing pathology diagnosing social research, Marcuse's notion of the technical *a priori* thus offers a potential rich harvest for interdisciplinary research.

In keeping with Fromm's foundational framework – that the everyday 'normal' operations of societal are pathological and are reproduced through logics of consensual validation – Marcuse's account provides an operationalisable perspective through which to explore the impact of the dominant scientific-technical attitudes on consciousness. The pathological reshaping of subjectivity by the social constellation is crucial to left-Hegelianism. Marcuse's account of the technical *a priori* opens the possibility for a redirection of social research, one which is capable of instigating a truly interdisciplinary research endeavour, seeking to explore and expose the pathological nature of the social conjuncture. Applied research, from sociologists, psychologists, and clinicians, can be productively united to explore the deracinating impact of the capitalist formation on the development of consciousness. In direct contrast to a recognition monist and excessively cognitivist and norm-acceding critical theory, Marcuse's framing of the technical *a priori* offers the possibility for a radical rebirth of pathology diagnosing social research.

Marcuse's diagnosis of a pathological restructuring of the *a priori conditions* of consciousness helps explain the perpetuation of the irrational and exploitative social order. The subject is conditioned so as to conform to the diktats of the bureaucratic-technical systems in place, viewing their social world as entirely rational and as one which 'delivers the goods' (Marcuse, 2007 [1964]: 82): they are left unable to experience the loss of qualities, or to critique the contradictions inherent within the social world (Marcuse, 2007 [1964]: 168). Marcuse supports this analysis with a complimentary diagnosis of a pathological social-systemic logic which he refers to as a system of 'repressive desublimation'. While the technical *a priori* serves to obscure the irrationality of the status quo from the subject, a system of repressive sublimation serves to guarantee the subject's investment in the social order itself. With his account of repressive desublimation, Marcuse presents a view of the social world as a 'totalitarian' system (Marcuse, 2007 [1964]: xlvi, 5, 16, 162) in which the primal needs and desires of the subject are artificially induced so as to perpetuate an exploitative political economy (Marcuse, 2007 [1964]: 5).

'Sublimation' is a concept with derives from Freudian psychoanalysis and connects to the foundational 'civilising' process itself. At its most simple, 'sublimation' refers to the conversion of a socially unacceptable urge, or lust, into an acceptable behaviour. For instance, after a heated phone call with a rude colleague, instead of going around their house and slapping them about the face, I might instead angrily hoover my flat. In such a way sublimation may even be healthy and productive and can enable peaceful coexistence (Freud, 1930). Yet, Marcuse speaks of a *repressive de*sublimation – a situation in which the original impulse or urge is not resolved or dissipated. In contrast to hoovering out one's anger and productively moving on, with hopefully a cleaner house and some good cardio, logics of repressive desublimation serve to further exacerbate the original urge in the long term and have a repressive, rather than transcendent, function. Ultimately, the process of repressive desublimation is a system in which the subject engages in an action which serves to protect, stabilise, and embolden an irrational and destructive logic.

While the example of an interpersonal dynamic in which a colleague 'hoovers out' their tension may be a textbook example of sublimation, Marcuse is more interested in the broader socio-cultural and political-economic institutions, principally the exploitative and alienating market system. As is the concern with critical theory more broadly, the question driving Marcuse's analysis is the failure for a revolutionary class to emerge (Marcuse, 2007 [1964]: 22, 35). In keeping with Horkheimer's original lecture, the challenge driving critical theory was to ascertain why the proletarian revolution had seemingly been deferred indefinitely.

In this regard, repressive desublimation offers an excellent and productive avenue for interdisciplinary-sociological research into social pathologies. The system of repressive desublimation is a paragon example of a pathological 'vicious circle', as explored in Part I (Marcuse, 2007 [1964]: 37, 255). For Marcuse, as for Fromm, the worker is fundamentally unhappy in their employment – alienated, reified, exploited. At a psychoanalytic level, there exists an impulsive, libidinal response against such conditions. The subject feels neurotic, anxious, angry. As Adorno (2007 [1966]: 203) worded it in *Negative Dialectics*, 'The physical moment tells our knowledge that suffering ought not to be, that things should be different.' For Marcuse, repressive desublimation helps explain the containment of such libidinal urges, and the ultimate stability of the contradictory system. While the worker feels fundamentally used and abused by their labour, instead of achieving a productive transcendence of their situation – instituting a qualitatively different political-economic arrangement – they seek to sublimate their frustration through *consumption*. This process is neither natural nor incidental nor therapeutic. Rather, Marcuse explains how it is intrinsic to the exploitative system itself and is crucial to the perpetuation of the market order, which should be understood as a totalitarian whole.

In this regard, the analysis of *advertising systems* becomes crucial to critical theory (Marcuse, 2007 [1964]: 52). The worker is aggressively presented with various opportunities to consume – to find pleasure and escape from the drudgery and misery of their exploitation. As a result, their viscerally felt 'needs' are socially constituted. The 'true' desire for a better life – and resultant anger at their exploitation in which the majority of their hours are spent in exploited tedium – is sublimated by the desire to purchase a new hi-fi set, for example (Marcuse, 2007 [1964]: 11). As such, the worker continues, even desiring overtime, to ensure the possibility of future consumption, as prescribed by the advertising systems. However, tragically, while consumption provides a temporary respite, it is never adequate – it is never a satisfactory sublimation. The anger, the resentment rapidly returns. Yet, instead of instigating socio-political transformation, a new opportunity for consumption is dangled before the worker. If that hi-fi set didn't do it for you, why not try this new car? The desire for further consumption perpetuates the status quo, while the fundamental resentment builds over time, only increasing the neuroses and psychopathologies within the subject. The more disillusioned the worker becomes with the work, the more they seek escape in the socially prescribed consumption, which requires more work, which requires more escapism by socially prescribed consumption, which requires my work.

For Marcuse, a central pathology which is connected to this system of repressive desublimation is thus the shaping of the subject's needs. Marcuse is clear that the advanced industrial society induces a desire for false needs within the subject:

> 'False' are those which are superimposed upon the individual by particular social interests in his repression: the needs which perpetuate toil, aggressiveness, misery, and injustice. Their satisfaction might be most gratifying to the individual, but this happiness is not a condition which has to be maintained and protected if it serves to arrest the developments of the ability (his own and others) to recognise the disease of the whole and grasp the chance of curing the disease. The result then is euphoria in unhappiness. (Marcuse, 2007 [1964]: 7)

Crucially, Marcuse contends that these false needs are prescribed by the same system which exploits the worker – it functions as a totalitarian whole, perpetuating itself and the exploitation of the worker. As a result, '[i]n this society, the productive apparatus tends to become totalitarian to the extent to which it determines not only the socially needed occupations, skills, and attitudes, but also individual needs and aspirations' (Marcuse, 2007 [1964]: xlv–xlvi).

The framing of a system of repressive desublimation helps explain the perpetuation of the exploitative status quo – the subject's frustration at their exploitation and alienation is used as grist to continue their labour – by pointing them in the direction of a false sublimation in the form of material consumption. For Marcuse, this must be understood as having a central psychoanalytic dimension; it is not merely a clear 'persuasion' tactic, in which something pleasant is dangled in front of the worker, who is persuaded by its appeal. Rather, the advanced industrial society is typified by the 'mobilisation and administration of libido' (Marcuse, 2007 [1964]: 79). The social system serves to harness the libidinal drive in such a way as to stabilise the critical forces leading towards transcendence. As a result, to understand the 'voluntary compliance, the absence of terror, the previous stabilised harmony between individual needs and socially required goals', one must look at the socialised recoding of the libidinal drive (Marcuse, 2007 [1964]: 79). There is a social adjustment of what the subject finds pleasurable which 'generates submission' (Marcuse, 2007 [1964]: 79).

Crucially, the negative forces pushing towards transcendence and revolution are thwarted as they are integrated within the systemic logic itself. There is a qualitatively distinct mobilisation of desire which is status quo affirming. The system of 'institutionalised sublimation thus appears to be an aspect of the "conquest of transcendence" achieved by the one dimensional society' (Marcuse, 2007 [1964]: 82).

While there has been substantial interest in the framing of the technical *a priori*, sparked by Andrew Feenberg's excellent work, there is less contemporary scholarship on the framing of repressive desublimation. Finn Bowring (2012) and Alexander Stoner (2020) are notable exceptions; however, this more social-structural aspect of Marcuse's account remains underdeveloped today. Potentially, this may be due to three reasons, which I briefly discuss and show are insufficient to dissuade critical theorists from investing in the perspective.

First, one may argue that repressive desublimation is socio-historically outmoded. While in the 1960s the prospect of consumption providing a sublimation preventing revolution was tenable, today the normalcy is for the working class to struggle on zero-hour contracts. The social-democratic settlement of the 1960s has been displaced by the wild inequities of neoliberalism. The idea that the radicalism of the precariat can be been 'bought out' by consumption seems far less tenable. In response, two rejoinders can be raised. First, that the recoding of the libidinal drives is seen across all sections of society – including those suffering from in-work poverty and racial and class discrimination. In the London riots of 2011, for example, rioters did not burn the Conservative member of Parliament's local office, rather they looted the local tech and sports shops (Wearden, 2011). This suggests that the drive and desire remains for these products, rather than for a more rational political economy. Secondly, one can suggest that the material reward offered needs to be substantially less than first thought to maintain conformity from the labouring classes. Indeed, increasingly social-cultural factors, such as immigration policy, have led to a mass partisan realignment in the United Kingdom, with traditional 'red wall' Labour voters moving to the Conservative Party (Rayson, 2020). Partisan dealignment has persisted post-2010, and the myth of the materially self-interested tactical voter can no longer be tenable in light of mass support for neoliberal parties. Thirdly, one might reply that actually there remains a substantially well-heeled population within the core; neoliberalism has served to primarily expedite relative core-periphery inequalities. The desperately poor, who may no longer tenably be described as fitting within the setting of repressive desublimation, were never those targeted by Marcuse's framing in the first place – today, they would be the sweatshop workers in South Asia, for example. Such locales were never the focus of Marcuse's account.

The second reason one might argue that the account of repressive desublimation gained less traction today is because it fails to provide 'adequate' scope for the agency of the subject. Increasingly approaches to social research which do not provide a sufficiently nuanced account of agency fail to be taken seriously (Madhok, 2013). However, one might comment that this trend is not something which has been adequately justified theoretically. True, Marcuse's approach may seem to be leaving little scope for the actor and presenting a deterministic functional whole. This may be less attractive in contemporary currents in this regard; however, that does not mean it is not accurate. The task of adequately defining and affirming the precise nature of the subject's agency is far from complete and is increasingly accepted despite being an unquestioned metaphysical assumption of exactly the kind which is otherwise dismissed today. The implicitly more deterministic account is not necessarily any more problematic than the implicitly agentival account. In fact, the belief in agency is a positive belief, which would require further justificatory argumentation.

Third, there is a broader distaste for macro-sociology in the post-structural age. Since the 1980s, the sociological orthodoxy has moved to study pragmatics, taste, culture habits, and intersubjective praxis (see Delanty, 2020). Marcuse's sweeping social-systemic and quasi-deterministic account is wildly out of step, it could hardly be any less 'micro-sociology'. Yet, as with the above reason for its fall from favour, this is not a justifiable reason to avoid it either. Rather, in light of the 'domestication' of contemporary critical theory, a sea change to a more structuralist and social-systemic analysis may be exactly what critical theory requires.

Using Marcuse for pathology diagnosing critique

Clearly, Marcuse's work offers the foundations for a rich and interdisciplinary critical theory of society. However, this does not in itself demonstrate that the social-theoretical infrastructure which can be abstracted from his work carries the true potency of the pathology diagnosing approach to social research as identified in Part I. I demonstrate how, through the diagnosis of the technical *a priori* and of logics of repressive desublimation, Marcuse provides the foundations for an optimal renaissance of an explicitly *pathology diagnosing* critical theory. In keeping with the analysis provided in Part I, I argue that Marcuse's framings carry the rich tapestry of ideas which combine in pathology diagnosing critique, offering a means to diagnose

(a) the pathological deformation of the subject's 'needs' and the failure of their 'true needs' to be met,

(b) the presence of pathological vicious-circular social logics,
(c) the pathological deformation of the subject's cognitive and psychic capabilities, which
(d) are traced to the historical-material economic conditions.

Marcuse's diagnosis of a system of repressive desublimation which impedes progressive social transformation forces the critical theorists to remember that 'the established universe of needs and satisfactions is a fact to be questioned' (Marcuse, 2007 [1964]: 8). Marcuse is explicit that it is possible to 'extend liberty while intensifying domination' (Marcuse, 2007 [1964]: 76); that the 'choice' of which commodity to consume, or which identically monotonous and exploitative job one should take, is a 'peculiar form of unfreedom' rather than liberation. Through an analysis of the logics of repressive desublimation, the social researcher is able to diagnose a social world in which 'the production of "affluence" [is] ... delaying the satisfaction of still unfilled vital needs' (Marcuse, 2007 [1964]: 56). What repressive desublimation articulates is that the 'productive apparatus' can 'become totalitarian', determining 'not only the socially needed occupations, skills, and attitudes, but also individual needs and aspirations' (Marcuse, 2007 [1964]: xlv–xlvi).

Pathology diagnosing research drawing upon the framing of repressive desublimation can be consciously attuned to the fact that 'the most effective and enduring form of warfare against liberation is the implanting of material and intellectual needs that perpetuate obsolete forms of the struggle for existence' (Marcuse, 2007 [1964]: 6). That the subject being granted their apparent desires is no guarantee of the good life, that,

> Free choice among a wide variety of goods and services does not signify freedom if these goods and services sustain social control over life of toil and fear – that is, if they sustain alienation. And the spontaneous reproduction of superimposed needs by the individual does not establish autonomy; it only testifies to the efficacy of the controls. (Marcuse, 2007 [1964]: 10)

> Their satisfaction might be most gratifying to the individual, but this happiness is not a condition which has to be maintained and protected if it serves to arrest the developments of the ability (his own and others') to recognise the disease of the whole and grasp the chance of curing the disease. The result then is euphoria in unhappiness. (Marcuse, 2007 [1964]: 7)

As discussed in earlier chapters, from Plato to Rousseau, to Fromm, a central feature of 'thick' social criticism has been the identification of pathological social dynamics, which 'once initiated ... [are] ... exceedingly difficult to break' (Neuhouser, 2012: 637, translation from German). Such vicious-circular logics should be at the forefront of social critique yet have no natural place within traditional liberal scholarship. The identification of such vicious circles is a crucial constituent of pathology diagnosing social research and is vital to its exploratory potency. Marcuse's social theoretical framework is highly sensitive to such social pathologies. Both in the framing of repressive desublimation and in the analysis of the one-dimensionality induced by the technical *a priori*, Marcuse is clear that the social order is pathologically 'perpetuating ... its own pre-established direction – driven by the growing needs it generates and at the same time contains' (Marcuse, 2007 [1964]: 37). Marcuse is actually explicit that he is describing a 'vicious circle' which is 'indeed the proper image' for such a social pathology (Marcuse, 2007 [1964]: 35). The pathology is thus 'being built into the system as a cohesive power' (Marcuse, 2007 [1964]: 55). Liberties are granted which serve merely to 'strengthen the repression' (Marcuse, 2007 [1964]: 249). The technical *a priori* means that the individual is conditioned to think that their fundamental needs are met. Crucially,

> if the individuals are satisfied to the point of happiness with the goods and services handed down to them by the administration, why should they insist on different institutions for a different production of different goods and services? And if the individual is a precondition so that the satisfying goods also include thoughts, feelings, aspirations, why should they wish to think, feel, and imagine for themselves? True, the material mental commodities offered may be bad, wasteful combat rubbish – but Geist and knowledge or no telling arguments against satisfaction of needs. (Marcuse, 2007 [1964]: 53)

Marcuse's framing provides the researcher with the foundations to identify logics which serve to perpetuate the irrational status quo, increasing domination and restricting critical capacity. As such, research into the technical *a priori* and logics of repressive desublimation can disclose how the possibilities for transcendence are increasingly foreclosed.

Marcuse's account also satisfactorily captures the denaturing of the subject's cognitive capacities and psychic state. The analysis of the subject's recoded *a priori* conditions of consciousness provides a productive avenue for such social research, while the framing of repressive desublimation serves to combine a psychoanalytic sensitivity to the impact of constitutive power on the subject's libidinal drives. Taken in tandem, the critical theorist is able to determine how 'the organism is ... preconditioned for the spontaneous acceptance of what is offered' (Marcuse, 2007 [1964]: 77). The 'voluntary compliance' of the subject to the pathological social order should be grasped as partly a result of the 'mobilisation and administration of libido' (Marcuse, 2007 [1964]: 78). As Marcuse framed it, 'pleasure, that's adjusted, generates submission' (Marcuse, 2007 [1964]: 79). But the richness of Marcuse's syncretism needs to be stated: it is a fusion of a Freudo-Marxianism and a

Hegelian-Marxism which produces Marcuse's radical insights. Not merely is the subject now desirous of the status quo, but they are unable to see the irrationality of its imperatives. The technical *a priori* serves to obscure all that cannot be reduced to number. The particular form of 'democratic unfreedom' is 'administered by a rationally organised bureaucracy' so as to appear optimally efficient and rational (Marcuse, 2007 [1964]: 74).

Fundamentally, Marcuse's account is rooted in an analysis of the historical-material conditions, and in an explicit critique of the capitalist market order (Marcuse, 2007 [1964]: 234). Ultimately, the deformation of consciousness of the technical *a priori*, and the totalitarian system of repressive desublimation are both products of the capitalist mode of production. The central pathology lies in the fact that subjects cope with 'the wrong organisation of society', a social order which is totalitarian and exploitative (Marcuse, 2007 [1964]: 148). The social theoretical frameworks which can be abstracted from Marcuse's critical theory thus clearly carry the central insights of pathology diagnosing social research.

Fromm and Marcuse

While Fromm's account of pathological normalcy is philosophically rigorous and persuasive, it remains abstract, lacking the specificities required for smooth operationalisation in social research. Marcuse, in contrast, while providing more targeted engagements through his analysis of the technical *a priori* and repressive desublimation, does not make an explicit study into social pathology. As such, a Fromm-Marcuse synthesis offers an ideal avenue for a philosophically undergirded social research endeavour, as envisaged by first-generation Frankfurt School theorists.

Fromm provides us with a master framing of 'pathological normalcy', which offers a radical alternative to the norm-supporting scholarship of today's critical theory. Unpacking Fromm's meta-diagnosis in Chapter 6, I identified two primary social-theoretical framings, the notion of 'socially patterned defects' and 'consensual validation'. Both are, of course, thoroughly contextualised within his broader interdisciplinary diagnosis. While Fromm turns to literature to substantiate his abstract theoretical frameworks – for instance by turning to H. G. Wells's story of the village of blind – Marcuse offers an immediate sociological referent for critical social research. In this regard, one can read the 'technical *a priori*' as a textbook example of a 'socially patterned defect', a deformation of the subject which is produced by the irrational social order. The subject is victim to 'constitutive power' which serves to impede their optimal cognitive development so they are unable to appreciate the irrationality of their social world.

Likewise, one can see mass adherence to the 'instrumentalist horizon' of the technical *a priori* as inducing a form of 'consensual validation', widespread adoption of this worldview serves to nullify dissent, naturalising the distorted phenomenology. Similarly, where Fromm provides a philosophical and abstract discussion of pathological normalcy as a situation where the foundational needs of subjects are not met, Marcuse's account of repressive desublimation offers an operationalisable research direction for interdisciplinary critical study.

When taken together, Fromm and Marcuse provide the social-theoretical foundations for a disclosing and immanent-transcendent critique, capable of engaging in social-systemic and phenomenological analysis. United, Fromm and Marcuse offer a critical depth psychology with the benefits of the epistemic focus of left-Hegelian social research. Their fusion of depth psychology, Hegelian philosophy, and Marxian sociology offers the ideal grounding for a renewed critical theory. Such an account is an ideal antidote to the domesticated framing of social pathology which abounds today. While the recognition-cognitive orthodoxy is fundamentally neo-Idealist, viewing the subject as possessing cognitive capacities which are immune to social-structural power, Fromm and Marcuse are explicitly Marxian in their acknowledgement of the primacy of constitutive power on the subject. Both the technical *a priori* and repressive desublimation locate the subject as existing within a world of power relations, in which the subject's intersubjective capabilities are conditioned by broader social norms and compulsions.

Crucially, Marcuse and Fromm present an avenue for study which proclaims an objectivity. In contrast to the fashionable 'ethico-cultural relativism' (Ratner, 2017) which represses claims to ethical partisanship, both Fromm and Marcuse argued for the objective irrationality of the social world. In direct opposition to post-structural currents, they both argued that subjects have objective 'needs' for a good life, which are ascertainable and deliverable, and the extant social system fails to deliver them while distorting the subject's consciousness so as to obscure this reality. Returning to the discussion on the philosophical tenability of pathology diagnosing social research of Chapter 1, Fromm and Marcuse both offer explicit justifications for their ethical partisanship which I believe remain persuasive today. Marcuse's account remains strictly dialectical, analysing the contradictions extant within the manifest social world. Fromm's account, as discussed, focuses on the objective failure of the social system in light of the precipitant psycho-pathologies, principally alienation. Both point to an alternate social order, in which the systems of production and distribution are more rationally organised on the basis of there existing no contradiction between the subject's material labour and the subject's material self-interest. Such foundations for normative critique remain persuasive today.

Notes

1 This is not to say that Marcuse's ideas have not been productively developed. Consider the extensive work of Andrew Feenberg, for example.
2 For instance, he routinely refers to the study *Labour Looks at Labour*.

Conclusion: the Frankfurt School beyond recognition

The COVID-19 pandemic has highlighted and exacerbated the tragic inequalities and irrationalities of neoliberalism. But is has also emboldened activists and academics to return to the primary research questions which first inspired critical theory. How is this irrational and exploitative social formation maintained? Why has the pandemic not brought about a permanent qualitative social transformation? Where is the revolutionary agent who could make such a change happen? Writing outside the Frankfurt School register, Andreas Malm (2020a) in *Corona, Climate, Chronic Emergency: War Communism in the Twenty-First Century* presses these concerns expertly. Malm asks the crucial question: if global capitalism can temporarily be 'paused' when the world's most privileged feel vulnerable, what is stopping a radical social transformation in response to global warming the rest of the time? And, what can be done to make such permanent change come about? The obstacles to social transformation are increasingly the topic of scholarly discussion, with ever more radical possibilities being introduced (Malm, 2020b). Critical theory is arriving late to these discussions.

There is an increasing space and urgency for 'thicker' social critique and clear scope for an exploration of the 'pathological normalcy' of the current conjuncture. Today's world is crying out for a critical theory of society which points towards avenues for immanent-transcendence. Critical theory has so much to offer; however, third-generation Frankfurt School scholarship has severed all meaningful links with socialist politics, and has largely embraced the neoliberal status quo. As such, neo-Idealist critical theory is of little interest to today's activists and radical scholars. Honneth and Forst are largely ignored – categorised, along with Rawls, as an irrelevance, too distanced from critical sociological inquiry and urgent anti-capitalist politics. Few copies of *Freedom's Right* or *The Right to Justification* were being hastily packed into rucksacks by XR activists. In contrast, Marcuse had an enrapt activist following. Even though Adorno ultimately failed to captivate the activists of his day, they did initially turn to him for inspiration and political strategy. There was once a link between critical theory and radical activism. This needs to be rebuilt.

As I have presented throughout *Critical Theory and Social Pathology*, contemporary critical theory has lost relevance as it now fails to offer a meaningful confrontation with organised power. I have argued that this stems from the monistic 'recognition-cognitivist' understanding of social pathology which drew out of the 'intersubjective turn'. The foundations upon which the contemporary Frankfurt School research project are built need to be urgently re-examined. The understanding of social pathology which dominates today is problematic politically, philosophically, and social-theoretically.

Politically – contemporary critical theory, as epitomised by *Freedom's Right*, valorises the norms of neoliberal institutions as being 'freedom-guaranteeing'. Much contemporary critical theory is politically quiescent and unsuited to an academic-activist audience seeking rapid qualitative socio-economic change in light of pressing existential threats.

Philosophically – all forms of theory which accord an ontological and causal primacy to an intersubjective dyad are irretrievably 'neo-Idealist'. Contemporary critical theory fails to appreciate that the subject is shaped by forms of 'constitutive power' which impede their capacity for critical thought. Socially patterned defects are validated through mass consensus and a pathological form of social being emerges, which recognition theorists are unable to account for.

Social-Theoretically – 'recognition-cognitivist' framings of social pathology are unable to capture the full range of problems which exist within the social world. The Zurn-Honneth approach is irredeemably monistic and cognitivist. As such, the majority of social pathologies are left inaccessible.

Yet, despite these well-documented failings, the recognition paradigm retains its remarkable hold over a widespread group of nominal 'critical theorists'. Concurrently, and relatedly, the Frankfurt School moves ever more into the political centre and into the analytic philosophical mainstream. Michael J. Thompson (2016) is thus absolutely correct to challenge the 'domestication of critical theory' and to identify the loss of the tradition's radical diagnostic heritage. Indeed, one may reasonably question whether Honneth is actually a 'critical theorist' in his most recent work. Beyond his lack of sociological content, the lack of left-Hegelianism, and his embrace of the 'justice' register, his work is also marked by a fundamental lack of political *urgency*. As such, the third generation risks killing off Frankfurt School critical theory as a distinctive, anti-capitalist, interdisciplinary research endeavour.

As a result, activists and radical scholars increasingly return directly to Marx and to alternate sources of 'critical theory' beyond today's Frankfurt

School. For example, Oliva, Oliva, and Novara's (2020) edited volume, *Marx and Contemporary Critical Theory*, makes no engagement whatsoever with the work of Honneth or Forst, instead returning to Alfred Sohn-Rethel as a fulcrum around which to base critical social research. Other authors, such as Thomas Piketty (2013) and Wolfgang Streeck (2016), who pose some of the questions originally central to Frankfurt School scholarship, make little or no engagement with the work of Honneth and Forst. This is because the central questions driving original critical theory are no longer being addressed by its contemporary primary practitioners. As a result, activists and radical scholars have turned elsewhere, losing interest in today's Frankfurt School scholarship, and reasonably searching new territory in their quest for a critical theory of society. We can see radical students turning in droves to decolonial, post-colonial, post-structuralist, and queer theory, in addition to a return to explicitly Marxist scholarship.

I believe deserting Frankfurt School scholarship at its moment of crisis is the wrong course to adopt. In contrast, I argue that the original ideas of Frankfurt School critical theory continue to offer a remarkably potent fusion of traditions in a philosophically undergirded form of normative social research. The failure of *contemporary* Frankfurt School scholars requires not the abandoning of critical theory, rather the *displacement of its current account of social pathology*. What is required is a philosophically justifiable vehicle for normative social research, and the original Frankfurt School proponents continue to offer the most exciting and potent opportunity to commence upon such a project. I consider the challenge to be rebuilding the social-theoretical foundations provided by the first generation to produce a research programme apposite to today's social world.

In this endeavour, in Part II of this book, I reconstructed the original foundations of the Frankfurt School's approach to social pathology through a sympathetic re-reading of Rousseau and Hegelian-Marxism. I identified four key features of pathology diagnosing social research which I argued were crucial to the perspective's diagnostic potency: the focus on the deformation of the subject's viscerally felt 'needs', the presence of pathological circular logics, the erosion of the subject's cognitive capacities, and a sensitivity to the foundational insights of historical materialism. In Part III, I located such insights within Fromm's and Marcuse's work. I argued for the merits of combining Fromm and Marcuse's theoretical apparatus, utilising Marcuse's understanding of the technical *a priori* and repressive desublimation to give specificity to Fromm's understanding of pathological normalcy.

Instead of following Honneth, and embracing the norms of dominant institutions as providing the opportunities for healthy recognition relationships, Fromm enables the scholar to consider the entire social formation to be a manifestation of a 'pathological normalcy'. Rather than embracing the current neoliberal social order, Fromm's theoretical infrastructure enables the researcher to adopt a critical distantiation, conducive to genuinely immanent-transcendent analysis. Based upon the subject's anxiety response to an alienated social world, Fromm provides philosophically grounded foundations for a formally 'objective', normative critique.

Fromm's account is complemented by Marcuse's critical theory. Marcuse's work provides an operationalisable framing for social research with his analysis of the technical *a priori* (of the subject's impeded phenomenology) and his identification of logics of repressive desublimation. Together, Fromm and Marcuse offer the foundations for a renaissance in critical social research which seeks to understand the pathological nature of the neoliberal world, exploring the means of its perpetuation, and disclosing the possibilities for emancipation. In contrast to the bizarre abstraction of *Freedom's Right*, where Honneth determines the dominant norms of a 'Western' society unilaterally and transcendentally, Fromm and Marcuse offer the foundations for an interdisciplinary research programme which can be based on an empirical analysis of the social world itself, and of the subject's cognitive capacities.

Limitations and considerations for future scholarship

This book is offered as a potential foundation for a renewal of pathology diagnosing critical theory. My suggestion of a Fromm-Marcuse synthesis is just that, a 'suggestion' for a possible direction in which to explore. This is not presented as the sole route for a renaissance of critical social research inspired by the ideas of the original Frankfurt School. I consciously do not offer some completed cartography, but rather a sketch of one possible avenue for future development. In this regard, and in the spirit of productive self-criticism, and of collaborative socialist research, I identify three central areas in which any such diagnostic project can be continued and extended. I then discuss the potential merits of developing a 'positive' correlate of a more healthy society.

First, I have repeatedly invoked Nancy Fraser's work on the importance of developing a 'multilateral and polycentric' critical theory, rather than being seduced by a 'monist' approach to social critique. With this in mind, I stress the utility of drawing on a wider range of theorists and traditions to add further nuance to future pathology diagnosing social research. Fromm and Marcuse have much to offer, and I believe the potential synthesis I outlined can offer fruitful avenues for future research. However, this is by no means exhaustive. The social theories of countless other authors could potentially be incorporated and developed, and I plan to continue my own work in this endeavour. Good critical theory is always open to innovations. My rejection of the Honneth/Zurn recognition approach is *not* that it marks a 'deviation' from the orthodox, or some desecration of the critical theory 'canon'. Rather, the problem with third-generation critical theory is that it is simply inadequate in and of itself.

Second, a crucial component of original Frankfurt School research was psychoanalysis, enabling critical theorists to explore how the subject's libidinal drives and desires have been interpolated by capitalism. While I have worked to support a Fromm-Marcuse synthesis, I admit my own limitations – I am not a psychoanalyst, and my scholarship is not informed by analytic practice. The possibilities for a more nuanced psychoanalytic inflection in pathology diagnosing research most certainly exist, and I would be delighted to see this explored further. In this regard, I suggest the merits of turning to Amy Allen's (2020) *Critique on the Couch* as a useful guide here.

Third, there is a need for social-theoretical resources which can enable social researchers to focus in depth on the impact of bureaucratic-administrative systems of the subject. Weber's ideas were crucial to the original Frankfurt School, and his work most definitely inflected Marcuse's notion of the technical *a priori*. However, there is further scope for a Weberian analysis of the subject's own interpretation of their lifeworld with a focus on the mundane practices of neoliberal society. There are possibilities for productive syntheses of Weber and Arendt, for example. The 'banality of evil', which Arendt discusses, can be a productive framework through which to comprehend the behaviours and norms which perpetuate extractivist and ecocidal dynamics. From filling up a car with petrol, to employees compiling documents for neo-colonial multinational corporations, the basis of much pathological social behaviour is mundane, tedious, and shrouded in the monotony of administrative rationality. As such, a Fromm-Weber-Arendt synthesis offers productive potential lines for future development. The bureaucratic banality of authoritarian neoliberalism offers a possible future entry point for research exploring the reproduction of the pathological normalcy.

Theorising healthy societies

There is most definitely merit in 'negative' philosophy and in 'negative' social critique. This is a crucial lesson to take from Adorno. When teaching my students, I present the example of a flight inspector who is trained to identify problems with critical flight components without being trained in how to fix them. It would be absurd to deny that knowing that a helicopter has developed a serious flaw is crucial information in and of itself. The inspector can correctly deem the aircraft to be unairworthy, and 'ground' it, potentially saving lives. The technician need not be skilled in 'repair' to be of tremendous social utility; the insight that something is fundamentally wrong is, in itself, of life-saving importance. Likewise, with critical theory. The diagnosis of the social pathologies of the present has merit in and of itself: one does not need to have knowledge of what a 'healthy society' looks like, or how to get there, in order to provide a valuable critique of the existing social order. Simply by disclosing how the present conjuncture is irrational, critical theorists can induce a desire for social change.

Social pathology 'diagnosis' can undoubtedly be of merit without an accompanying 'prescription' for social change. Yet while such information is not *necessary* for social critique, it can most definitely provide a valuable complement to it. It is often easier to explain a problem if one can also provide a solution. For a patient to meaningfully comprehend the nature of, for example, a kidney disorder, it is useful that they understand the 'healthy' functioning of a kidney. Likewise, with reference to the broken helicopter example above, if you want to persuade the helicopter's owner they need to spend lots of money replacing parts, they will want to know what they do and why. Thus, providing a positive referent can be of merit, both in terms of enabling political change, but also with regard to disclosing the nature of the pathology itself.

In this regard, Honneth, whose substantive philosophy I have remorselessly critiqued through this book, is to be praised. Unlike Adorno, Honneth submits an extensive understanding of a healthy society as one in which all subjects are able to attain healthy recognition relationships. An optimal society is held to be one in which social institutions are organised so as to enable subjects to achieve recognition. As demonstrated, such an account is unviable as a basis for social research and has contributed to the 'domestication' of the Frankfurt School project more broadly. However, the presence of a positive referent is something to be encouraged, and it certainly contributes to the appeal of Honneth's work. Honneth is not new in this regard: Rousseau's *Social Contract* and Hegel's *Philosophy of Right* both provide descriptions of healthy societies. Amongst first-generation Frankfurt School scholars, Fromm comes closest to undertaking such a project; however. he never made any serious advances upon his proposed 'Science of Man'.

I suggest that an important avenue for future pathology diagnosing research is the construction of a complementary theory of a 'healthy society' as a possible positive referent.[1] In no way do I seek to dispute the merit of negative philosophy in and of itself. Simply, an accompany positive referent can serve as an important tool for critical theory, providing extra political and diagnostic potency.

Beyond recognition

The Frankfurt School is in crisis. Like any crisis point, stasis is untenable: critical theorists must eventually make a choice. One possibility, which looks most likely, is that they continue fully down the road towards liberalism and analytic philosophy. I hope this does not happen, as it would forever sever the relationship between critical theory and radical political praxis. Third-generation critical theory has already extinguished all but a residual activist interest in the Frankfurt School's output. Yet, what many third-generation Frankfurt School scholars do not appreciate in their all-too-quiescent embrace of the current academy is the perilous situation of the humanities and social sciences within academia today. Critical social theory, already pilloried and distrusted, is anathema to neoliberal rationality. As neoliberal imperatives increase and the space for dissent lessens, studying the Frankfurt School may be seen as a renaissance indulgence, worthy of suspicion and decidedly unworthy of research funding. In keeping with the academic world of many South Asian countries, education will likely be increasingly centred around vocations rather than ideas. There will be schools of law, schools of engineering, institutes of management. As the 2020 Jawaharlal Nehru University attack demonstrated, such an ecology provides no safe harbour for the dialectical imagination (Ayyub, 2020).

The alternative is for critical theorists to return to an explicit confrontation with structural power. For critical theory to be relevant today, it must regain political urgency and challenge neoliberalism head-on. Activist students need to be demanding that critical theory is taught. This will ironically keep critical theory alive within the juddering contradiction that is the 'University Industry'. The funding of dialectical minds by such neoliberal institutions encapsulates the possibilities for immanent transcendence which remain. Critical theory continues to hold the tools to enable progressive actors to destabilise from within the system, to lean upon the contradictions within the social world. For such critical social research to be of use, however, it must be built upon reliable social theoretical foundations. As such, I urge critical theorists to think *beyond recognition*.

Note

1 Hartmut Rosa's *Resonance* (2016) may begin to offer some possibilities here.

References

Abad-Santos, Alex (2018), 'How LGBTQ Pride Month Became a Branded Holiday', *Vox*, 26 June, available at www.vox.com/2018/6/25/17476850/pride-month-lgbtq-corporate-explained (accessed 15 January 2021).
Adorno, Theodor W. (2004 [1970]), *Aesthetic Theory*, translated by Robert Hullot-Kentor (New York: Continuum).
Adorno, Theodor W. (2005 [1951]), *Minima Moralia: Reflections from Damaged Life*, translated by E. F. N. Jephcott (London: Verso).
Adorno, Theodor W. (2007 [1966]), *Negative Dialectics*, translated by E. B. Ashton (London: Bloomsbury Academic).
Adorno, Theodor W. (2018 [1946]), 'Social Science and Sociological Tendencies in Psychoanalysis', in Wolfgang Bock (ed.), *Dialektische Psychologie* (Weisbaden: Springer Fachmedein), pp. 623–642.
Adorno, Theodor W., and Horkheimer, Max (1997 [1944]), *Dialectic of Enlightenment*, translated by John Cumming (London: Verso).
Adorno, Theodor W., and Marcuse, Herbert (1999), 'Correspondence on the German Student Movement', *New Left Review*, 233: 123–136.
Affeldt, Steven (1999), 'The Force of Freedom: Rousseau on Forcing to be Free', *Political Theory*, 27.3: 299–333.
Ahmed, Nafeez (2010), *A User's Guide to the Crisis of Civilisation: And How to Save It* (London: Pluto).
Alberg, Jeremiah (2001), 'Rousseau and the Original Sin', *Revisita Portuguesa de Filosofia*, 57.4: 773–790.
Alexander, Jeffrey C. (1985), 'Habermas's New Critical Theory: Its Promise and Problems', *American Journal of Sociology*, 91.2: 400–424.
Alexander, Jeffrey C., and Lara, Maria (1995), 'Honneth New Critical Theory of Recognition', *New Left Review*, 220, 126–136.
Allen, Amy (2016), *The End of Progress: Decolonizing the Normative Foundations of Critical Theory* (New York: Columbia University Press).
Allen, Amy (2020), *Critique on the Couch: Why Critical Theory Needs Psychoanalysis* (New York: Columbia University Press).
Anderson, Joel (1995 [1992]), 'Translator's Introduction', in Axel Honneth (ed.), *The Struggle for Recognition: The Moral Grammar of Social Conflicts*, translated by J. Anderson (Cambridge: Polity Press), pp. x–xxi.

References

Antonio, Robert J. (1981), 'Immanent Critique as the Core of Critical Theory: Its Origins and Developments in Hegel, Marx and Contemporary Thought', *The British Journal of Sociology*, 32.3: 330–345.

Arnade, Chris (2020), 'Riding the Protest Wave: How Elites Will Co-opt BLM', *The Commons*, 21 June, available online at https://americancompass.org/the-commons/respect-the-rage/ (accessed 10 June 2021).

Aronowitz, Stanley (2002), 'Introduction', in Max Horkheimer (ed.), *Critical Theory: Selected Essays* (New York: Continuum), pp. xi–xxi.

Arthur, Chris (1983), 'Hegel's Master/Slave Dialectic and a Myth of Marxology', *New Left Review*, 142: 67–75.

Ash, Konstantin, and Obradovich, Nick (2019), 'Climactic Stress, Internal Migration, and Syrian Civil War Onset', *Journal of Conflict Resolution*, 64.1: 3–31.

Ayyub, Rana (2020), 'I Saw Police Stand By as Masked Men Attacked Students at a Top Delhi University. It Was Yet Another Assault on India's Intellectuals', *Time*, 8 January, available at https://time.com/5760597/what-happened-during-jnu-attack-india/ (accessed 30 January 2022).

Banaji, Jairus, 'Allen Ginsberg', *Historical Materialism* (blogpost), available at www.historicalmaterialism.org/node/1722 (accessed 23 February 2020).

Bartonek, Anders, and Burman, Anders, eds (2018), *Hegelian Marxism: The Uses of Hegel's Philosophy in Marxist Theory from Georg Lukács to Slavoj Zizek* (Södertörn: Södertörn Academic Studies).

Benjamin, Walter (1968 [1955]), 'Theses on the Philosophy of History', in Walter Benjamin (ed.), *Illuminations*, translated by Hannah Arendt (San Diego, CA: Harcourt Brace Jovanovich), pp. 255–266.

Benjamin, Walter (1982), *The Arcades Project* (Frankfurt: Suhrkamp).

Berlant, Lauren (2000), 'The Subject of True Feeling', in Sara Ahmed, Jane Kilby, Celia Lury, Maureen McNeil, and Beverley Skeggs (eds), *Transformations: Thinking Through Feminism* (London: Routledge), pp. 33–47.

Berlin, Isaiah (1969), *Four Essays on Liberty* (Oxford: Oxford University Press).

Berry, David (2014), *Critical Theory and the Digital* (London: Bloomsbury).

Bhambra, Gurminder K., Gebrial, Dalia, and Nişancıoğlu, Kerem (2018), *Decolonising the University* (London: Pluto).

Biddiss, Michael (1997), 'Disease and Dictatorship: The Case of Hitler's Reich', *Journal of the Royal Society of Medicine*, 90.6: 342–346.

Bowring, Finn (2012), 'Repressive Desublimation and Consumer Culture: Re-Evaluating Herbert Marcuse', *New Formations*, 75: 8–24.

Brandom, Robert, B. (2019), *A Spirit of Trust: A Reading of Hegel's Phenomenology* (Cambridge, MA: Harvard University Press).

Braune, Joan (2014), *Erich Fromm's Revolutionary Hope: Prophetic Messianism as a Critical Theory of the Future* (Leiden: Brill).

Braune, Joan (2020), 'Conclusion: Why Anti-Fascism Needs Erich Fromm's Critical Theory Today', in Kieran Durkin and Joan Braune (eds), *Erich Fromm's Critical Theory: Hope, Humanism, and the Future* (London: Bloomsbury), pp. 216–226.

Bronner, Stephen Eric (2011), *Critical Theory: A Very Short Introduction* (Oxford: Oxford University Press).

Bucher, Geoff (2012), *Understanding Marxism* (Durham, NC: Acumen).
Buchwalter, Andrew (2016), 'The Concept of Normative Reconstruction: Honneth, Hegel, and the Aims of Critical Social Theory', in Harry F. Dahms and Eric R. Lybeck (eds), *Reconstructing Social Theory, History and Practice* (Bingley: Emerald), pp. 57–88.
Bulaitis, Zoe Hope (2020), *Value and the Humanities: The Neoliberal University and Our Victorian Inheritance* (London and New York: Palgrave Macmillan).
Bunyard, Tom, and Bosseau, Denis C., eds (2022), *Critical Theory in (A Time of) Crisis* (New York: Palgrave Macmillan).
Burleigh, Michael, and Wippermann, Wolfgang (1991), *The Racial State: Germany 1933–1945* (Cambridge: Cambridge University Press).
Burston, Daniel (1991), *The Legacy of Erich Fromm* (Cambridge, MA: Harvard University Press).
Burston, Daniel, and Olfman, Sharna (1996), 'Freud, Fromm and the Pathology of Normalcy', in Mauricio Cortina and Michael Maccoby (eds), *A Prophetic Analyst: Erich Fromm's Contributions to Psychoanalysis* (Northvale, NJ: Jason Aronson), pp. 301–324.
Butler, Judith (2008), 'Taking Another's View: Ambivalent Implications', in Axel Honneth (ed.), *Reification: A New Look at an Old Idea* (Oxford: Oxford University Press), pp. 97–119.
Canguilhem, Georges (1991 [1966]), *The Normal and the Pathological*, translated by Carolyn R. Fawcett and Robert S. Cohen (New York: Zone Books).
Casillo, Robert (1992), 'Lewis Mumford and the Organicist Concept in Social Thought', *Journal of the History of Ideas*, 53.1: 91–116.
Chancer, Lynn (2020), 'Feminism, Humanism, and Erich Fromm', in Kieran Durkin and Joan Braune (eds), *Erich Fromm's Critical Theory: Hope, Humanism, and the Future* (London: Bloomsbury), pp. 96–107.
Colletti, Lucio (1973), *From Rousseau to Lenin: Studies in Ideology and Society* (New York: Monthly Review Press).
Cooper, David (2015), *The Dialectics of Liberation* (London: Verso).
Corradetti, Claudio (2021), 'The Frankfurt School and Critical Theory', *Internet Encyclopaedia of Philosophy*, available at https://iep.utm.edu/critical-theory-frankfurt-school/ (accessed 12 February 2022).
Cullen, Daniel E. (1993), *Freedom in Rousseau's Political Philosophy* (DeKalb, IL: Northern Illinois University Press).
Damrosch, Leo (2005), *Jean-Jacques Rousseau: Restless Genius* (Boston, MA: Mariner Books).
Darling, John, E. (1994), *Child Centred Education and its Critics* (London: Paul Chapman Publishing).
Delaney, James (2009), *Starting with Rousseau* (London: Continuum).
Delanty, Gerard (2011), 'Varieties of Critique in Sociological Theory and Their Methodological Implications for Social Research', *Irish Journal of Sociology*, 19.1: 68–92.
Delanty, Gerard (2020), *Critical Theory and Social Transformation* (Abingdon: Routledge).

Delanty, Gerard, and Harris, Neal (2021), 'Critical Theory Today: Legacies and New Directions', in Gerard Delanty and Stephen Turner (eds), *Routledge International Handbook of Contemporary Social and Political Theory* (Abingdon: Routledge), pp. 119–130.

Della Volpe, Galvano (1979), *Rousseau and Marx*, translated by John Fraser (Atlantic Highlands, NJ: Humanities Press).

Deranty, Jean-Phillipe (2009), *Beyond Communication: A Critical Study of Axel Honneth's Social Philosophy* (Leiden: Brill).

Derrida, Jacques (2006), *Spectres of Marx: The State of the Debt, the Work of Mourning and the New International*, translated by Peggy Kamuf (London: Routledge).

Dey, Abhishek (2019), 'JNU "Sedition" Case: Unanswered Questions in the Chargesheet [sic] against Kanhaiya Kumar and others', *Scroll.In*, 15 January, available at https://scroll.in/article/909518/jnu-sedition-case-unansweredquestions-in-the-chargesheet-against-kanhaiya-kumar-and-others (accessed 10 January 2022).

Douglass, Robin (2015), *Rousseau and Hobbes: Nature, Free Will, and the Passions* (Oxford: Oxford University Press).

Dreyfus, Hubert, and Rabinow, Paul (1982), *Beyond Structuralism and Hermeneutics* (Brighton: Harvester).

Dupré, Louis (1998), 'Kant's Theory of History and Progress', *The Review of Metaphysics*, 51.4: 813–828.

Durant, Will, and Durant, Ariel (1967), *Rousseau and Revolution: A History of Civilization in France, England, and Germany from 1756, and in the Remainder of Europe from 1715 to 1789* (New York: Simon and Schuster).

Durkheim, Émile (1960), *Montesquieu and Rousseau: Forerunners of Sociology*, translated by R. Manheim (Ann Arbor, MI: University of Michigan Press).

Durkin, Kieran (2014), *The Radical Humanism of Erich Fromm* (New York: Palgrave Macmillan).

Elmgren, Heidi (2021), 'Hindrances to Recognition in Finnish Music Schools', *International Journal of Music Education*, 39.2: 202–217.

Fanon, Franz (1967 [1952]), *Black Faces, White Masks*, translated by C. Markmann (London: Pluto).

Feenberg, Andrew (1996), 'Marcuse or Habermas: Two Critiques of Technology', *Inquiry: An Interdisciplinary Journal of Philosophy*, 39.1: 45–70.

Feenberg, Andrew (2005), *Heidegger and Marcuse: The Catastrophe and Redemption of History* (New York and London: Routledge).

Feenberg, Andrew (2013a), 'Heidegger and Marcuse: On Reification and Concrete Philosophy', in François Raffoul and Eric S. Nelson (eds), *The Bloomsbury Companion to Heidegger* (London: Bloomsbury Press) pp. 171–176.

Feenberg, Andrew (2013b), 'Marcuse's Phenomenology: Reading Chapter Six of One-Dimensional Man', *Constellations*, 20.4: 604–614.

Ferrara, Alessandro (2017), *Rousseau and Critical Theory* (Leiden: Brill).

Flick, Sabine (2016), 'Treating Social Suffering? Work-Related Suffering and Its Psychotherapeutic Re/interpretation', *Distinktion: Journal of Social Theory*, 17.2: 149–173.

Foster, Mark F., Hristeva, Galina, and Giefer, Michael (2016), 'Georg Groddeck: The "Pinch of Pepper" of Psychoanalysis', *American Journal of Psychoanalysis*, 76.2: 161–182.
Foucault, Michel (2003 [1963]), *The Birth of the Clinic: An Archaeology of Medical Perception*, translated by A. Sheridan (London: Routledge).
Fraser, Nancy (1995), 'Recognition or Redistribution? A Critical Reading of Iris Young's Justice and the Politics of Difference', *Journal of Political Philosophy*, 3.2: 166–180.
Fraser, Nancy (1997), 'A Rejoinder to Iris Marion Young', *New Left Review*, 223: 126–129.
Fraser, Nancy (2008), 'From Redistribution to Recognition? Dilemmas of Justice in a "Post-Socialist" Age', in Kevin Olson (ed.), *Adding Insult to Injury: Nancy Fraser Debates Her Critics* (London: Verso), pp. 68–93.
Fraser, Nancy, and Honneth, Axel (2001), *Redistribution or Recognition? A Political-Philosophical Exchange* (London, Verso).
Freud, Sigmund (1930), *Civilisation and Its Discontents*, translated by J. Riviere (London: Hogarth Press).
Freud, Sigmund (1959), *Civilized Sexual Morality and Modern Nervous Illness*, translated by J. Strachey, A. Freud, A. Strachey, and A. Tyson (London: Read Books).
Freyenhagen, Fabian (2013), *Adorno's Practical Philosophy: Living Less Wrongly* (Cambridge: Cambridge University Press).
Freyenhagen, Fabian (2015), 'Honneth on Social Pathologies: A Critique', *Critical Horizons*, 16.2: 131–152.
Friedman, Lawrence J., and Schreiber, Anke M. (2013), *The Lives of Erich Fromm: Love's Prophet* (New York: Columbia University Press).
Fromm, Erich (1941), *Escape from Freedom* (New York: Farrar and Rinehart).
Fromm, Erich (1944), 'Individual and Social Origins of Neurosis', *American Sociology Review*, 9.4: 380–384.
Fromm (1947), *Man For Himself: An Inquiry into the Psychology of Ethics* (New York: Rinehart).
Fromm (1961), *Marx's Concept of Man* (New York: Frederick Ungar).
Fromm, Erich (1963 [1955]), *The Sane Society*, translated by E. Rotten (New York: Rinehart and Winston).
Fromm, Erich (1973), *The Anatomy of Human Destructiveness* (New York: Holt, Rinehart and Winston).
Fromm, Erich (1979 [1976]), *To Have Or to Be?* (London: Abacus).
Fromm, Erich (1983 [1962]), *Beyond the Chains of Illusion: My Encounter with Marx and Freud* (London: Abacus).
Fromm, Erich (2008 [1956]), *The Art of Loving* (New York: Continuum).
Fromm, Erich (2010 [1991]), *The Pathology of Normalcy* (Riverdale, NY: AMHF).
Fuchs, Christian (2016), *Critical Theory of Communication: New Readings of Lukacs, Adorno, Marcuse, Honneth and Habermas in the Age of the Internet* (London: University of Westminster Press).
Fuchs, Christian (2020), 'Erich Fromm and the Critical Theory of Communication', *Humanity and Society*, 44.3: 298–325.

Fultner, Barbara (2011), 'Introduction', in Barbara Fultner (ed.), *Jürgen Habermas Key Concepts* (Abingdon: Routledge), pp. 1–12.
Funk, Rainer (2000), *Erich Fromm: His Life and Ideas* (New York: Continuum).
Gay, Peter (2009 [1959]) *Voltaire's Politics: The Poet as Realist* (Princeton, NJ: Princeton University Press).
Ginsberg, Allen (2009 [1956]), *Howl, Kaddish and Other Poems* (London: Penguin).
Groddeck, G. (1929). Psychical treatment of organic disease. *British Journal of Medical Psychology*, 9.2: 179–186.
Groddeck, Georg (1977), *The Meaning of Illness*, translated by L. Schacht (Madison, CT: International Universities Press).
Groddeck, Georg (2012 [1913]), *Der gesunde und kranke Mensch* (Mannheim: Outlook Verlag).
Gunderson, Ryan (2021), 'Things Are the Way They Are: A Typology of Reification', *Sociological Perspectives*, 64.1: 127–150.
Gutman, Brandon (2012), 'American Express Proves that Diversity Drives the Bottom Line and Provides 5 Step Process', *Forbes*, 8 August, available at www.forbes.com/sites/marketshare/2012/08/08/american-express-proves-that-diversity-drives-the-bottom-line-and-provides-5-step-process/?sh=658abcf97558 (accessed 8 January 2022).
Habermas, Jürgen (1971 [1967]), *Towards a Rational Society*, translated by Jeremy J. Shapiro (London: Heinemann).
Habermas, Jürgen (1977), *Mit Heidegger gegen Heidegger denken. Zur Veröffentlichung von Vorlesungen aus dem Jahre 1935*, Frankfurter Allgemeine Zeitung, 25 July 1953 [English].
Habermas, Jürgen (1984 [1981]), *Theory of Communicative Action, Volume One: Reason and the Rationalization of Society*, translated by Thomas A. McCarthy (Boston, MA: Beacon Press).
Habermas, Jürgen (1987 [1981]), *Theory of Communicative Action Volume Two: Lifeworld and System: A Critique of Functionalist Reason*, 3rd edn, translated by Thomas A. McCarthy (Boston, MA: Beacon Press).
Habermas, Jürgen (1990), *Postmetaphysical Thinking: Philosophical Essays*, translated by William M. Hohengarten (Cambridge, MA: MIT Press).
Habermas, Jürgen (2017), *Postmetaphysical Thinking II*, translated by Ciaran Cronin (Cambridge: Polity).
Hardimon, Michael (1992), 'The Project of Reconciliation: Hegel's Social Philosophy', *Philosophy and Public Affairs*, 21.2: 165–195.
Harnecker, Marta (1976), *Elementary Concepts of Historical Materialism* (Sydney: University of Sydney Press).
Harris, H. S. (1958), 'Hegelianism of the "Right" and "Left"', *The Review of Metaphysics*, 11.4: 603–609.
Harris, Neal (2018), 'Review of *Critical Theory in Critical Times*, ed by Penelope Deutscher and Christina Lafont', *European Journal of Social Theory*, 21.4: 569–573.
Harris, Neal (2019a), 'Pathologies of Recognition: An Introduction', *European Journal of Social Theory*, 22.1: 3–9.

Harris, Neal (2019b), 'Reconstructing Erich Fromm's "Pathology of Normalcy": Transcending the Recognition-Cognitive Paradigm in the Diagnosis of Social Pathologies', *Social Science Information*, 58.4: 714–733.

Harris, Neal (2019c), 'Recovering the Critical Potential of Social Pathology Diagnosis', *European Journal of Social Theory*, 22.1: 45–62.

Harris, Neal (2021), 'Social Pathology and Social Research', in Neal Harris (ed.), *Pathology Diagnosis and Social Research: New Applications and Explorations* (New York: Palgrave Macmillan), pp. 1–19.

Heath, Joseph (2010), 'System and Lifeworld', in Barbara Fultner (ed.), *Jürgen Habermas: Key Concepts* (Durham, NC: Acumen Press), pp. 74–90.

Hegel, Georg Wilhelm Friedrich (1953 [1822]), *Reason in History: General Introduction to the Philosophy of History*, translated by R. Hartman (Indianapolis, IN: Bobbs-Merrill).

Hegel, Georg Wilhelm Friedrich (1977 [1807]), *Phenomenology of Spirit*, translated by A. V. Miller (Oxford: Clarendon Press).

Hegel, Georg Wilhelm Friedrich (1991 [1820]), *Philosophy of Right*, translated by H. B. Nesbitt (Cambridge: Cambridge University Press).

Held, David (1980), *Introduction to Critical Theory* (Cambridge: Polity Press).

Heywood, Andrew (2007), *Political Ideologies: An Introduction* (Basingstoke: Palgrave Macmillan).

Hirvonen, Onni (2015), 'Pathologies of Collective Recognition', *Studies in Social and Political Thought*, 25.1: 209–226.

Hirvonen, Onni, and Pennanen, Joonas (2019), 'Populism as a Pathological Form of Recognition', *European Journal of Social Theory*, 22.2: 27–44.

Holton, R. (1987), 'The Idea of Crisis in Modern Society', *The British Journal of Sociology*, 38.4: 502–520.

Honneth, Axel (1995 [1992]), *The Struggle for Recognition: The Moral Grammar of Social Conflicts*, translated by J. Anderson (Cambridge: Polity Press).

Honneth, Axel (2000), 'The Possibility of a Disclosing Critique of Society: The *Dialectic of Enlightenment* in Light of Current Debates in Social Criticism', *Constellations*, 7.1: 116–127.

Honneth, Axel (2004), 'A Social Pathology of Reason: On the Intellectual Legacy of Critical Theory', in Fred Rush (ed.), *The Cambridge Companion to Critical Theory* (Cambridge: Cambridge University Press), pp. 19–42.

Honneth, Axel (2007), *Disrespect: The Normative Foundations of Critical Theory* (Cambridge: Polity Press).

Honneth, Axel (2008), *Reification: A New Look at an Old Idea* (Oxford: Oxford University Press).

Honneth, Axel (2009), *Pathologies of Reason: On the Legacy of Critical Theory*, translated by J. Ingram (New York: Columbia University Press).

Honneth, Axel (2014), 'The Diseases of Society: Approaching a Nearly Impossible Concept', *Social Research*, 81.3: 683–703.

Honneth, Axel (2014 [2011]), *Freedom's Right: The Social Foundations of Democratic Life*, translated by Joseph Ganahl (Cambridge: Polity).

Honneth, Axel (2016), *The Idea of Socialism: Towards a Renewal*, translated by Joseph Ganahl (Cambridge: Polity Press).

Horkheimer, Max (1972), 'Postscript', in *Critical Theory: Selected Essays* (New York: Seabury Press), pp. 244–252.
Horkheimer, Max (1973), 'Foreword', in Martin Jay (ed.), *The Dialectical Imagination: A History of the Frankfurt School and the Institute for Social Research, 1923-1950* (Berkeley, CA: University of California Press), pp. xxv–xxvi.
Horkheimer, Max (1993 [1931]), *Between Philosophy and Social Science. Selected Early Writings*, translated by John Torpey (Cambridge, MA: MIT Press).
Horkheimer, Max (1993), 'Reason Against Itself: Some Remarks on Enlightenment', *Theory, Culture and Society*, 10: 79–88.
Horkheimer, Max (2002 [1937]), 'Traditional and Critical Theory', in Max Horkheimer (ed.), *Critical Theory: Selected Essays*, translated by Matthew J. O'Connell (New York: Continuum), pp. 188–244.
Horkheimer, Max (2018), 'The State of Contemporary Social Philosophy and the Tasks of an Institute for Social Research (1931)', *Journal for Cultural Research*, 22.2: 113–121.
Houlgate, Stephen (2012), *Hegel's Phenomenology of Spirit: A Reader's Guide* (London: Bloomsbury).
Houston, Stan (2009), 'Communication, Recognition and Social Work: Aligning the Ethical Theories of Habermas and Honneth', *The British Journal of Social Work*, 39.7: 1274–1290.
Houston, Stan, and Montgomery, Lorna (2017), 'Reflecting Critically on Contemporary Social Pathologies: Social Work and "The Good Life"', *Critical and Radical Social Work*, 5.2: 181–196.
Hulliung, Mark L. (1994), *The Autocritique of Enlightenment: Rousseau and the Philosophes* (Cambridge, MA: Harvard University Press).
Hyppolite, Jean (1973 [1955]), *Studies on Marx and Hegel*, translated by John O'Neill (New York: Harper Torch Books).
Ikäheimo, Heikki (2007), 'Recognizing Persons', *Journal of Consciousness Studies*, 14.5/6: 224–247.
Ivković, Marjan (2017), 'The Habermasian Foundations and Aims of Axel Honneth's Theory of Recognition', *Ideias*, 7.2: 99–122.
Jaeggi, Rahel (2018), *Critique of Forms of Life* (Cambridge, MA: Harvard University Press).
Jarvis, Simon (1998), *Adorno: A Critical Introduction* (Cambridge: Polity Press).
Jay, Martin (1984), *Marxism and Totality: The Adventures of a Concept from Lukacs to Habermas* (Berkeley, CA: University of California Press).
Jay, Martin (2008), 'Introduction', in Axel Honneth (ed.), *Reification: A New Look at an Old Idea* (Oxford: Oxford University Press), pp. 3–16.
Jeffries, Stuart (2017), *Grand Hotel Abyss: The Lives of the Frankfurt School* (London: Verso).
Kant, Immanuel (1997 [1788]), *Critique of Practical Reason* (Cambridge: Cambridge University Press).
Kant, Immanuel (2007 [1787]), *Critique of Pure Reason* (Basingstoke: Palgrave Macmillan).

Kant, Immanuel (2007 [1790]), *Critique of Judgement* (Oxford: Oxford University Press).
Keucheyan, Razmig (2013), *The Left Hemisphere: Mapping Critical Theory Today* (London: Verso).
Kelly, George (1966), 'Notes on Hegel's "Lordship and Bondage"', *The Review of Metaphysics* 19.4: 780–802.
Knox, T. M. (1940), 'Hegel and Prussianism', *Philosophy*, 15.57: 51–63.
Kojève, Alexandre (1980 [1947]), *Introduction to the Reading of Hegel* (Ithaca, NY: Cornell University Press).
Kok, Arthur, and Van Houdt, John, eds (2014), *Reconsidering the Origins of Recognition: New Perspectives on German Idealism* (Newcastle-upon-Tyne: Cambridge Scholars).
Kouvelakis, S. (2019), *La Critique Défaite. Emergence et domestication de la Théorie Critique* (Paris: Éditions Amsterdam).
Krishnamurti, Jiddu (2008 [1962]), *Krishnamurti's Notebook* (Ojal, CA: K Publications).
Kunneman, Harry (1990), 'Some Critical Remarks on Habermas's Analysis of Science and Technology', *Theory, Culture, and Society*, 7.4: 117–125.
Lafont, Cristina (2020), 'Heidegger and the Frankfurt School', in Peter E. Gordon, Espen Hammer, and Axel Honneth (eds), *The Routledge Companion to the Frankfurt School* (Abingdon: Routledge), pp. 282–294.
Laitinen, Arto and Särkelä, Arvi (2019), 'Four Conceptions of Social Pathology', *European Journal of Social Theory*, 22.1: 80–102.
Laitinen, Arto, Särkelä, Arvi, and Ikäheimo, Heikki (2015), 'Pathologies of Recognition: An Introduction', *Studies in Social and Political Thought*, 25.1: 1–24.
Lamas, Andrew T., Wolfson, Todd, and Funke, Peter, N., eds (2017), *The Great Refusal: Herbert Marcuse and Contemporary Social Movements* (Philadelphia, PA: Temple University Press).
Lawrence, Charles R. III (2015), 'The Fire This Time: Black Lives Matter, Abolitionist Pedagogy and the Law', *Journal of Legal Education*, 65.2: 381–404.
Lemmey, Huw (2020), 'Party and Protest: The Radical History of Gay Liberation Stonewall and Pride', *Guardian*, 25 June, available at www.theguardian.com/world/2020/jun/25/party-and-protest-lgbtq-radical-history-gay-liberation-stonewall-pride (accessed 13 February 2022).
Lenin, Vladimir (1977), *Collected Works*, translated by G. Hanna (Moscow: Progress Publishers).
Lukács, György (1971 [1920]), *The Theory of the Novel: A Historico-Philosophical Essay on the Forms of Great Epic Literature*, translated by Anna Bostock (Cambridge, MA: MIT Press).
Lukács, György (1972 [1923]), *History and Class Consciousness: Studies in Marxist Dialectics*, translated by R. Livingston (Cambridge, MA: MIT Press).
MacLay, G. R. (1990), *The Social Organism: A Short History of the Idea That a Human Society May Be Regarded as a Gigantic Living Creature* (Great Barrington, MA: North River Press).

Madhok, Sumi (2013), *Rethinking Agency: Developmentalism, Gender and Rights* (London: Routledge).
Malm, Andreas (2020a), *Corona, Climate, Chronic Emergency: War Communism in the Twenty-First Century* (London: Verso).
Malm, Andreas (2020b), *How to Blow Up a Pipeline: Learning to Fight in a World on Fire* (London, Verso).
Maqbool, Aleem (2020), 'Black Lives Matter: From Social Media Post to Global Movement', BBC, 10 July, available at www.bbc.co.uk/news/world-us-canada-53273381 (accessed 3 February 2022).
Marcuse, Herbert (1969a), *An Essay on Liberation* (Boston, MA: Beacon Press).
Marcuse, Herbert (1969b), *Reason and Revolution: Hegel and the Rise of Social Theory* (London: Routledge and Kegan Paul).
Marcuse (1969c), 'Revolution aus Ekel. Spiegel-Gespräch mit dem Philosophen Herbert Marcuse', *Der Spiegel*, 31/1969.
Marcuse, Herbert (1998 [1956]), *Eros and Civilisation: A Philosophical Inquiry into Freud* (London: Routledge).
Marcuse, Herbert (2005), *Heideggerian Marxism*, eds Richard Wolin and John Abromeit (Lincoln, NE: University of Nebraska Press).
Marcuse, Herbert (2007 [1964]), *One Dimensional Man: Studies in the Ideology of Advanced Industrial Society*, 2nd edn (London and New York: Routledge).
Margolies, Richard (1996), 'Self Development and Psychotherapy in a Period of Rapid Social Change', in Mauricio Cortina and Michael Maccoby (eds), *A Prophetic Analyst: Erich Fromm's Contributions to Psychoanalysis* (Northvale, NJ: Jason Aronson), pp. 361–401.
Martineau, Wendy, Meer, Nasar, and Thompson, Simon (2012), 'Theory and Practice in the Politics of Recognition and Misrecognition', *Res Publica*, 18.1: 1–9.
Mau, Søren (2019), 'Mute Compulsion: A Theory of the Economic Power of Capital' (PhD Thesis, University of Southern Denmark).
Marx, Karl (1975 [1844]), *Early Writings* (London: Penguin).
Marx, Karl (1976 [1867]), *Capital: Volume 1: A Critique of Political Economy*, translated by Ben Fowkes. London: Penguin.
Marx, Karl (1998 [1932]), *The German Ideology: Including Theses on Feuerbach and Introduction to The Critique of Political Economy* (Amherst, NY: Prometheus Books).
Marx, Karl (2010 [1859]), 'Foreword to A Contribution to the Critique of Political Economy', in J. F. Sitton (ed.), *Marx Today* (New York: Palgrave Macmillan), 91–94.
McCarthy, Thomas A. (1978), *The Critical Theory of Jürgen Habermas* (Cambridge, MA: MIT Press).
McInnes, Paul (2021), 'Premier League Drops Black Lives Matter Badge from Shirts for Own Campaign', *Guardian*, 10 September, available at www.theguardian.com/football/2020/sep/10/premier-league-drop-black-lives-matter-badge-from-shirts-for-own-campaign (accessed 17 January 2022).
McLaughlin, Neil (2021), *Erich Fromm and Global Public Sociology* (Bristol: Bristol University Press).

McLellan, David (1969), *The Young Hegelians and Karl Marx* (London and Basingstoke: MacMillan).
McLellan, David (1985), *Karl Marx: His Life and Thought* (London and Basingstoke: MacMillan).
McNay, Lois (2008), *Against Recognition* (Cambridge: Polity Press).
Mehrotra, Santosh (1991), 'On the Social Specifications of Use Value in Marx's Capital', *Social Scientist*, 19.8/9: 72–77.
Metropolis (1927), dir. by Fritz Lang (UFA).
Mudde, Cas (2010), 'The Populist Radical Right: A Pathological Normalcy', *West European Politics*, 33.6: 1167–1186.
Müller-Doohm, Stefan (2005), *Adorno: A Biography*, translated by Rodney Livingstone (Cambridge: Polity Press).
Murphy, Mark (2016), 'Introduction: Putting Habermas to Work in Social Research', in Mark Murphy (ed.), *Habermas and Social Research* (Abingdon: Routledge), pp. 15–32.
Nájera, Rafael (2017), 'Scholastic Philosophers on the Role of the Body in Knowledge', in Justin E. H. Smith (ed.), *Embodiment: A History* (Oxford: Oxford University Press), pp. 143–170.
Neuhouser, Frederick (1993), 'Freedom, Dependence and the General Will', *The Philosophical Review*, 102.3: 363–395.
Neuhouser, Frederick (2008), *Rousseau's Theodicy of Self-Love: Evil, Rationality, and the Drive for Recognition* (Oxford: Oxford University Press).
Neuhouser, Frederick (2012), 'Rousseau und die Idee einer pathologischen Gesellschaft', *Politische Vierteljahresschrift*, 53.4: 628–745.
Niemi, Petteri (2015), 'The Professional Form of Recognition in Social Work', *Studies in Social and Political Thought*, 25.1: 174–190 (182–185).
Noone, John, B. (1980) *Rousseau's Social Contract* (Athens, GA: University of Georgia Press).
Oliva, Antonio, Oliva, Angel, and Novara, Ivan, eds (2020), *Marx and Contemporary Critical Theory: The Philosophy of Real Abstraction* (New York: Palgrave Macmillan).
Olson, Kevin (2010), 'Deliberative Democracy', in Barbara Fultner (ed.), *Jürgen Habermas: Key Concepts* (Durham, NC: Acumen Press), pp. 74–90.
O'Neill, Shane, and Smith, Nicholas H. (2012), *Recognition Theory as Social Research* (Basingstoke: Palgrave Macmillan).
Oppenheim, Maya (2018), 'Hungarian Prime Minister Viktor Orban Bans Gender Studies Programmes', *Independent*, 25 October.
Osborne, Peter (2020), 'Adorno and Marx', in P. E. Gordon, E. Hammer, and M. Pensky (eds), *A Companion to Adorno* (Oxford: Blackwell), pp. 303–319.
Pal, Maïa (2020), *Jurisdictional Accumulation: An Early Modern History of Law, Empires, and Capital* (Cambridge: Cambridge University Press).
Parini, Jay, and Miller, Brett (1994), *The Columbia History of American Poetry* (New York: Columbia University Press).
Petherbridge, Danielle (2013), *The Critical Theory of Axel Honneth* (Washington, DC: Lexington Books).

Petrovic, Gajo (1983), 'Reification', in Tom Bottomore (ed.), *A Dictionary of Marxist Thought* (Cambridge, MA: Harvard University Press), pp. 411–413.
Piketty, Thomas (2013), *Capital in the Twenty-First Century* (Cambridge, MA: Belknap Press).
Pippin, Robert (1981), 'Hegel's Political Argument and the Problem of Verwirklichung', *Political Theory*, 9.4: 509–532.
Piroddi, Corrado (2021), 'Pathologies of Society and Social Philosophy: New Perspectives from Finland', *Distinktion*, 22.1: 60–82.
Plattner, Marc F. (1979), *Rousseau's State of Nature: An Interpretation of the Discourse on Inequality* (DeKalb, IL: Northern Illinois University Press).
Popper, Karl (1994 [1945]), *The Open Society and Its Enemies* (Princeton, NJ: Princeton University Press).
Ratner, Carl (2014), 'Pathological Normalcy: A Construct for Comprehending and Overcoming Psychological Aspects of Alienation', *The Humanistic Psychologist*, 42: 298–303.
Ratner, Carl (2017), 'The Generalized Pathology of Our Era: Comparing the Biomedical Explanation, the Cultural-Political Explanation and a Liberal-Humanistic-Postmodernist Perspective', *International Critical Thought*, 7.1: 72–92.
Rawls, John (1971), *A Theory of Justice* (Cambridge, MA: Harvard University Press).
Rayson, Steven (2020), *The Fall of the Red Wall: 'The Labour Party No Longer Represents People Like Us'* (Independent Publisher).
Richter, Gerhard, and Adorno, Theodor W. (2002), 'Who's Afraid of the Ivory Tower? A Conversation with Theodor W. Adorno', *Monatshefte*, 94.1: 10–23.
Rickert, John (1986), 'The Fromm-Marcuse Debate Revisited', *Theory and Society*, 15.3: 351–400.
Ricoeur, Paul (2005), *The Course of Recognition* (Cambridge, MA: Harvard University Press).
Roberts, Julian (2004), 'The Dialectic of Enlightenment', in Fred Rush (ed.), *The Cambridge Companion to Critical Theory* (Cambridge: Cambridge University Press), pp. 57–73.
Roberts, William (2013), 'Feuerbach and the Left and Right Hegelians', in Alan D. Schrift, *The History of Continental Philosophy* (Chicago, IL: University of Chicago Press), pp. 377–394.
Robinson, Peter (2008), 'Jean-Jacques Rousseau and History: Moral Truth at the Expense of Facticity', *Rethinking History*, 12.3: 417–431.
Rorty, Richard (1990), *Objectivity, Realism and Truth* (Cambridge: Cambridge University Press).
Rosa, Hartmut (2019 [2016]), *Resonance: A Sociology of Our Relationship to the World*, translated by James Wagner (Cambridge: Polity).
Rousseau, Jean-Jacques (1911 [1762]), *Émile, or On Education*, translated by B. Foxley (London: Everyman's Library).
Rousseau, Jean-Jacques (1953 [1752]), *The Confessions*, translated by J. M. Cohen (London: Penguin).

Rousseau, Jean-Jacques (1968 [1758]), *Letter to d'Alembert*, translated by A. Bloom (Ithaca, NY: Cornell University Press).
Rousseau, Jean-Jacques (1968 [1762]), *The Social Contract*, translated by Maurice Cranston (London: Penguin).
Rousseau, Jean-Jacques (1979 [1782]), *Reveries of the Solitary Walker*, translated by P. France (London: Penguin).
Rousseau, Jean-Jacques (1984 [1762]), *Discourse on the Origins of Inequality*, translated by Maurice Cranston (London: Penguin), pp. 77–78.
Rousseau, Jean-Jacques (1990 [1761]), 'The State of War', translated by Grace Roosevelt, in Grace Roosevelt (ed.), *Reading Rousseau in the Nuclear Age* (Philadelphia, PA: Temple University Press), pp. 14–22.
Rousseau, Jean-Jacques (1993 [1750]), 'A Discourse on the Arts and Sciences', translated by G. D. H. Cole, in Jean-Jacques Rousseau (ed.), *The Social Contract and Discourses* (London: Everyman), pp. 1–29.
Rousseau, Jean-Jacques (1995 [1753]), 'Letter on French Music', in B. Gagnebin, M. Raymond et al. (eds), *Rousseau's Oeuvres Complètes* (Gallimard: Bibliothèque de la Pléiade), vol. 12–13.
Rousseau, Jean-Jacques (1997 [1761]), *Julie, or the New Heloise: Letters of Two Lovers Who Live in a Small Town at the Foot of the Alps*, translated by J. Vaché and P. Stewart (Hanover, NH, and London: University Press of New England).
Rush, Fred (2004a), 'Conceptual Foundations of Frankfurt School Critical Theory', in Fred Rush (ed.), *The Cambridge Companion to Critical Theory* (Cambridge: Cambridge University Press), pp. 6–39.
Rush, Fred (2004b), 'Introduction', in Fred Rush (ed.), *The Cambridge Companion to Critical Theory* (Cambridge: Cambridge University Press), pp. 1–5.
Saini, Rima (2020), 'From Management Meetings to Meaningful Change: Risks of Institutional Capture in the Decolonisation of UK Higher Education and Recommendations for Delivering Structural Change', *LSE Impact Blog*, 11 August, available at https://blogs.lse.ac.uk/impactofsocialsciences/2020/08/11/from-management-meetings-to-meaningful-change-risks-of-institutional-capture-in-the-decolonisation-of-uk-higher-education-and-recommendations-for-delivering-structural-change/ (accessed 12 March 2022).
Schaub, Jörg (2015), 'Misdevelopments, Pathologies, and Normative Revolutions: Normative Reconstruction as Method of Critical Theory', *Critical Horizons*, 16.2: 107–130.
Schaub, Jörg and Odigbo, Ikechukwu M. (2019), 'Expanding the Taxonomy of (Mis-)Recognition in the Economic Sphere', *European Journal of Social Theory*, 22.1: 103–122.
Schecter, Darrow (2010), *The Critique of Instrumental Reason from Weber to Habermas* (London: Continuum).
Schecter, Darrow (2019), *Critical Theory and Sociological Theory* (Manchester: Manchester University Press).
Schwartz, Laura (2017), 'LSE Cleaners' Strike: Don't Let Women's History Month Become Groundhog Day', *Red Pepper*, 15 March, available at www.redpepper.org.uk/lse-cleaners-strike-dont-let-womens-history-month-become-groundhog-day/ (accessed 12 March 2022).

Smith, Robert C. (2017), *Society and Social Pathology: A Framework for Progress* (London: Palgrave Macmillan).
Spengler, Oswald (1991 [1918]), *The Decline of the West*, edited and abridged by Helmut Werner. English edn edited by Arthur Helps, translated by Charles Francis Atkinson (New York: Oxford University Press).
Stahl, Titus (2013), 'Habermas and the Project of Immanent Critique', *Constellations*, 20.4: 533–552.
Stoner, Alexander, M. (2020), 'Things Are Getting Worse on our Way to Catastrophe: Neoliberal Environmentalism, Repressive Desublimation, and the Autonomous Ecoconsumer', *Critical Sociology*, 47.3: 491–506.
Streeck, Wolfgang (2016), *How Will Capitalism End?* (London: Verso).
Strong, Tracy (1994), *Jean-Jacques Rousseau: The Politics of the Ordinary* (London: Sage).
Strydom, Piet (2008), 'Immanent Transcendence: Critical Theory's Left-Hegelian Heritage', Conference Paper Presented for the *European Journal of Social Theory*'s Tenth Anniversary at the University of Sussex, 'Europe since 1989'. Presented 19–21 June.
Strydom, Piet (2011), *Contemporary Critical Theory and Methodology* (Abingdon: Routledge).
Strydom, Piet (2020), 'On the Origin of the Left-Hegelian Concept of Immanent-Transcendence: Reflections on the Background of Classical Sociology', *Journal of Classical Sociology*, 20.1: 3–21.
Sutherland, Edwin, H. (1945), 'Social Pathology', *American Journal of Sociology*, 50.6: 429–435.
Taylor, Charles (1992), *Multiculturalism and The Politics of Recognition* (Princeton, MA: Princeton University Press).
Thompson, Annette (2009), *Erich Fromm: Shaper of the Human Condition* (Basingstoke: Palgrave Macmillan).
Thompson, Michael J. (2016), *The Domestication of Critical Theory* (London: Rowman and Littlefield).
Thompson, Michael J. (2017a), 'Normative Humanism as Redemptive Critique', in Seyed Javad Miri, Robert Lake, and Tricia M. Kress (eds), *Reclaiming the Sane Society* (Boston: Sense), pp. 37–58.
Thompson, Michael J. (2017b), 'Review of *Critical Theory in Critical Times*, ed. by Deutscher, Penelope and Lafont, Christina', *Contemporary Political Theory*, 18.4: 284–289.
Thompson, M. J. (2020), *The Spectre of Babel: A Reconstruction of Political Judgement* (New York: SUNY Press).
Tracy, Theodore James (1969), *Physiological Theory and the Doctrine of the Mean in Plato and Aristotle* (Chicago, IL: Loyola University Press).
Tucker, R. C. (1964), *Philosophy and Myth in Karl Marx* (Cambridge: Cambridge University Press).
Van den Brink, B. and Owen, D. (2007), *Recognition and Power: Axel Honneth and the Tradition of Critical Social Theory* (Cambridge: Cambridge University Press).
Varga, Somogny, and Gallagher, Shaun (2012), 'Critical Social Theory, Honneth and the Role of Primary Intersubjectivity', *European Journal of Social Theory*, 15.2: 243–260.

Veita, Marcelo (2016), 'Marcuse's "Transcendent Project" at 50: "Post-Technological Rationality" for Our Times', *Radical Philosophy Review*, 19.1: 143–172.
Višić, Maroje (2020), 'Ivory Tower and Barricades: Marcuse and Adorno on the Separation of Theory and Praxis', *Philosophy and Society*, 31.2: 220–241.
Wark, McKenzie (2021), *Capital is Dead: Is This Something Worse?* (London: Verso).
Wearden, Graeme (2011), 'JD Sports Mulls Multimillion-Pound Riot Claim against Police', *Guardian*, 21 September, available at www.theguardian.com/business/2011/sep/21/jd-sports-riot-claim-police (accessed 12 March 2022).
Weber, Max (1947), *The Theory of Social and Economic Organisation*, translated by A. M. Henderson and Talcott Parsons (New York: Oxford University Press).
Weber, Max (1992 [1905]), *The Protestant Ethic and the Spirit of Capitalism*, translated by Talcott Parsons (London: Routledge).
Westerman, Richard (2019), *Lukács' Phenomenology of Capitalism: Reification Revalued* (New York: Palgrave Macmillan).
Wheen, Francis (2004), *How Mumbo-Jumbo Conquered the World* (London: Harper Perennial).
White, Stephen K. (1983), 'The Normative Basis For Critical Theory', *Polity*, 16.1: 150–164.
Whitehead, Alfred N. (1979), *Process and Reality* (New York: Free Press).
Will, Herbert (1984), *Die Geburt der Psychosomatik. Georg Groddeck, der Mensch und Wissenchaftler* (Munich: Urban and Schwarzenberg).
Witenberg, Earl G. (1997), 'Erich Fromm, as Seen by Analysts of the 1990s', *Contemporary Psychoanalysis*, 33.2: 334–339.
Wokler, Robert (2001), *Rousseau: A Very Short Introduction* (Oxford: Oxford University Press,).
Wolin, Richard, ed. (1991a), *The Heidegger Controversy: A Critical Reader* (New York: Columbia University Press).
Wolin, Richard (1991b), 'Introduction to Herbert Marcuse and Martin Heidegger: An Exchange of Letters', *New German Critique*, 53: 19–27.
Wood, Allen W. (2007), *Kantian Ethics* (Cambridge: Cambridge University Press).
Woodward, Alex (2020), '"We Are the Ones who Keep Us Safe": How Abolitionists See an America without Police and Prisons', *Independent*, 19 June, available at www.independent.co.uk/news/world/americas/abolish-police-us-prison-reform-defund-13th-amendment-a9571816.html (accessed 14 January 2022).
Yates, Richard (1961), *Revolutionary Road* (Boston, MA: Little, Brown and Company).
Žižek, Slavoj (2010), 'How to Begin from the Beginning', in Costas Douzinas and Slavoj Žižek (eds), *The Idea of Communism* (London: Verso), pp. 209–226.
Zurn, Christopher (2011), 'Social Pathologies as Second-Order Disorders', in Danielle Petherbridge (ed.), *Axel Honneth: Critical Essays* (Leiden: Brill), pp. 345–370.
Zurn, Christopher (2015), *Axel Honneth: A Critical Theory of the Social* (Cambridge: Polity Press).

Index

Adorno, T. W. 6–7, 26–27, 60–61, 81, 104, 111–117, 125, 127, 136, 143, 146, 148, 170–171
Ahmed, N. 79
alienation 21, 25, 91, 100, 111, 129–133, 137, 138, 142, 151, 161, 164
Allen, A. 61
Althusser, L. 28
anxiety 21, 25–26, 28, 50
Aristotle 23

Beckett, S. 29
Benjamin, W. 16, 60, 104, 135
Berlant, L. 52–53
Berlin, I. 71
Bhambra, G. 55
Black Lives Matter (BLM) 54
Braune, J. 128
Butler, J. 8, 39

Canguilhem, G. 28
capitalism 44, 54–57, 60, 76, 78, 81, 108, 110–112, 115–117, 126–129, 135–136, 146, 153, 166, 170
climate crisis 79, 151, 166
coloniality 51
consciousness 51, 53, 56, 70, 78, 81, 104, 107–112, 114, 116–117, 146, 151–156, 163–164
consensual validation 5, 13, 27, 30, 37, 97, 133–137, 140, 155, 163–164
constitutive power 9, 13, 49, 50, 56, 61, 95–96, 116, 119, 162–164
co-option 54–56
COVID-19 33, 166

critique
  disclosing 6, 13–14, 26, 29–30, 97, 146, 151, 164
  immanent 39, 59, 73, 77, 146, 164, 166, 169, 172

decoloniality 14, 55, 61, 168
Delanty, G. 2, 9, 160
Derrida, J. 67
dialectics
  immanent-transcendence 3–5, 9–10, 12, 36, 37, 59, 73, 77, 146, 150, 164, 166
  as method 11, 24, 34, 36, 73, 77, 110, 113, 152, 172
  negative 61, 111, 157
  sublation 5, 25, 59, 60, 73, 107, 110, 113–114, 146
Dissent debate 38, 127, 146
domestication of critical theory 1, 9–12, 19, 20, 39, 56, 57, 118, 149, 160, 167, 171

ethical life 44, 46
Eurocentrism 79
Extinction Rebellion (XR) 166

Fanon, F. 51
Feenberg, A. 143, 146, 148, 155, 159
Finnish School 63–67
Fitzgerald, F. Scott 29
food banks 58, 66–67
form of life 23, 27, 32, 36, 60, 72, 80, 89, 96, 111, 133, 153
Forst, R. 8, 166, 168
Foucault, M. 8, 29, 32–33
Fraser, N. 50–56, 61, 63–67, 87, 101, 117, 145, 169

Index

Freud, S. 25, 27–31, 114–116, 120, 126–133, 146–147, 156
Freyenhagen, F. 10, 68–70, 72, 74–76
Fromm, E. 2, 3, 5, 6, 12–13, 21, 26, 27, 29, 31, 37, 78, 81–82, 97, 104, 114, 120, 125–165
Fuchs, C. 7, 8
Funk, R. 127, 132

Geist 5, 25, 106–110, 113–114, 118, 121, 152, 162
Ginsberg, A. 29–30, 38
Groddeck, G. 38, 128, 143, 146

Habermas, J. 6–8, 11, 14, 39, 42–43, 118, 125–126, 128, 136, 142–143, 147–149
Harris, N. 1, 2, 9, 11, 63, 70, 108, 131
Hegel, G. W. F. 4–12, 24–28, 40–45, 59–60, 66, 70–71, 78–80, 87–88, 104–121, 130, 152–153, 155, 163–164, 167, 171
Hegelian-Marxism 1, 10, 27, 37, 87, 104–121, 131, 137, 168
Hirvonen, O. 2, 40, 63–65
Horkheimer, M. 1–6, 14, 24, 26–27, 36, 53, 60, 104–105, 112, 114, 115, 141, 157

Ideal theory 21, 46
Ikäheimo, I. 40, 43, 64, 66
inclusion vs. transformation 53–55, 61

Jaeggi, R. 8
Jay, M. 6, 14, 38–39
Jeffries, S. 127–128, 146
justice 1, 20–21, 23, 36, 37, 39, 45, 47, 52, 60–62, 72, 80, 83, 89, 167

Kant, I. 10, 24, 40–41, 80, 105–110, 117–118, 121, 152
Keucheyan, R. 8
Kojève, A. 42, 62
Kouvelakis, S. 1, 19, 39, 65
Krishnamurti, J. 29, 38

Laitinen, A. 64, 66, 70, 128, 150
Lang, F. 30
Lasègue-Falret syndrome 78, 83, 134
left-Hegelianism 3, 6, 9, 11–12, 108, 118, 120, 153, 155, 164, 167

legal freedom 71, 73
legitimacy 20–23, 36
London riots 159
Lukács, G. 56–57, 60, 89, 96, 99, 101, 104–105, 110–112, 114–117, 120, 125

McNay, L. 7, 9, 39, 44, 47–53, 60–61, 65–66, 117
Marcuse, H. 2, 6, 12–13, 21, 26–30, 38, 63–65, 79, 81–83, 104, 108, 114, 125–127, 145–164
Marx, K. 1–8, 10–12, 14, 25, 29, 30, 38, 41, 53, 56, 61–62, 67, 79–82, 100, 104–123, 129–139, 143, 146, 152, 167
Mau, S. 155
moral freedom 72–75
Mudde, C. 29

needs 78–79, 88, 97, 158
neo-Idealism 8, 9, 48–49, 53, 61, 87, 117–120, 164, 166, 167
neoliberalism 11, 56–57, 60, 145, 159, 166
Neuhouser, F. 35–36, 38, 90, 95, 97–98, 103, 141, 161
neurosis 27, 115, 128, 132, 135–136
Noone, J. B. 87, 89, 97, 99
normativity 36–40, 45–46, 51–53, 140–142

one-dimensionality 2, 6, 30, 146, 148–150, 153, 159, 176, 182
Otto-Apel, K. 7

pathological normalcy 3, 13, 27, 29, 37, 78, 97, 125–165
pathologies of recognition 2, 19, 63–85
perspectival monism/dualism 47, 60, 62–64, 87–88, 94, 101, 113
phenomenology 41, 107, 112, 130, 146, 153, 164
Piketty, T. 168
Piroddi, C. 64
Plato 22–23
Popper, K. 78
positivism 4, 36, 113, 141
post-metaphysics 34, 119, 142
precariat 55, 159

rationality 1–2, 5, 9, 21, 24–27, 33, 45, 49, 54, 56, 61–62, 68, 76, 80, 110, 112–117, 129, 134–135, 138, 146, 148, 150–156, 163–164, 170, 172
Ratner, C. 31, 34, 129, 133, 140–141, 143, 150, 164
Rawls, J. 20, 46, 80, 166
recognition-cognitivism 12, 30, 60–68
reification 3, 68, 99, 110–112, 114–115, 117, 121, 154
repressive desublimation 13, 28, 37, 126, 145, 147, 150–152, 156–169
resilience 116
Ricoeur, P. 40
Rorty, R. 34
Rosa, H. 8, 172
Rousseau, J.-J. 23–26, 28, 31, 38, 64, 71, 80, 87–102, 104, 120, 136, 137, 161, 171

Särkelä, A. 40, 43, 64, 66, 128
Schaub, J. 58–59, 66–68, 70, 72, 75, 77
Schecter, D. 109, 114–116
Smith, R. C. 79, 81
socialism 62, 70
socially patterned defects 68, 131, 133, 135–140, 163, 167
social organicism 32

Socrates 22, 30
Spengler, O. 29
Streeck, W. 168
struggle for recognition 1, 41, 43–45, 63, 70, 142
Strydom, P. 5, 10, 32, 36, 59, 78, 108, 134
Sutherland, E. H. 29

Taylor, C. 42–43, 62
technical *a priori* 145–147, 150–156, 159, 160, 162–164, 168
Thompson, A. 138
Thompson, M. J. 1, 3, 7–11, 14, 19, 39, 42, 44, 47–50, 53, 56–57, 60–61, 65–66, 82, 87, 96, 116–120, 126–128, 149, 167

universalism 50, 140

vicious circles 12, 28, 88, 94, 96–101, 137, 157, 161–162

Weber, M. 105, 113–114, 116, 120, 155, 170

Yates, R. 29

Zurn, C. 2, 39, 63, 68–70, 132, 167, 170

Lightning Source UK Ltd.
Milton Keynes UK
UKHW050716041222
413082UK00014BA/370